T0353348

Ubiquitous Machine Learning and Its Applications

Pradeep Kumar
Maulana Azad National Urdu University, India

Arvind Tiwari
DIT University, India

A volume in the Advances in
Computational Intelligence and
Robotics (ACIR) Book Series

www.igi-global.com

Published in the United States of America by
    IGI Global
    Information Science Reference (an imprint of IGI Global)
    701 E. Chocolate Avenue
    Hershey PA, USA 17033
    Tel: 717-533-8845
    Fax: 717-533-8661
    E-mail: cust@igi-global.com
    Web site: http://www.igi-global.com

Library of Congress Cataloging-in-Publication Data

Names: Kumar, Pradeep, 1977- editor. | Tiwari, Arvind, 1980- editor.
Title: Ubiquitous Machine Learning and Its Applications / Pradeep Kumar and Arvind Tiwari, editors.
Description: Hershey, PA : Information Science Reference, [2017]
Identifiers: LCCN 2017005142 | ISBN 9781522525455 (hardcover) | ISBN 9781522525462 (ebook)
Subjects: LCSH: Ubiquitous computing. Machine learning. Application software.
Classification: LCC QA76.5915 .U267 2017 | DDC 004--dc23 LC record available at https://lccn.loc.gov/2017005142

This book is published in the IGI Global book series Advances in Computational Intelligence and Robotics (ACIR) (ISSN: 2327-0411; eISSN: 2327-042X)

British Cataloguing in Publication Data
A Cataloguing in Publication record for this book is available from the British Library.

All work contributed to this book is new, previously-unpublished material.
The views expressed in this book are those of the authors, but not necessarily of the publisher.

For electronic access to this publication, please contact: eresources@igi-global.com.

Advances in Computational Intelligence and Robotics (ACIR) Book Series

ISSN:2327-0411
EISSN:2327-042X

Editor-in-Chief: Ivan Giannoccaro, University of Salento, Italy

MISSION

While intelligence is traditionally a term applied to humans and human cognition, technology has progressed in such a way to allow for the development of intelligent systems able to simulate many human traits. With this new era of simulated and artificial intelligence, much research is needed in order to continue to advance the field and also to evaluate the ethical and societal concerns of the existence of artificial life and machine learning.

The **Advances in Computational Intelligence and Robotics (ACIR) Book Series** encourages scholarly discourse on all topics pertaining to evolutionary computing, artificial life, computational intelligence, machine learning, and robotics. ACIR presents the latest research being conducted on diverse topics in intelligence technologies with the goal of advancing knowledge and applications in this rapidly evolving field.

COVERAGE

- Cyborgs
- Computer Vision
- Adaptive and Complex Systems
- Brain Simulation
- Artificial Intelligence
- Algorithmic Learning
- Neural Networks
- Artificial Life
- Natural language processing
- Computational Logic

IGI Global is currently accepting manuscripts for publication within this series. To submit a proposal for a volume in this series, please contact our Acquisition Editors at Acquisitions@igi-global.com or visit: http://www.igi-global.com/publish/.

Titles in this Series

www.igi-global.com

701 East Chocolate Avenue, Hershey, PA 17033, USA
Tel: 717-533-8845 x100 • Fax: 717-533-8661
E-Mail: cust@igi-global.com • www.igi-global.com

Table of Contents

Detailed Table of Contents

Chapter 1

Arvind Kumar Tiwari, DIT University, India

Machine learning refers to the changes in systems that perform tasks associated with artificial intelligence. This chapter presents introduction types and application of machine learning. This chapter also presents the basic concepts related to feature selection techniques such as filter, wrapper and hybrid methods and various machine learning techniques such as artificial neural network, Naive Bayes classifier, support vector machine, k-nearest-neighbor, decision trees, bagging, boosting, random subspace method, random forests, k-means clustering and deep learning. In the last the performance measure of the classifier is presented.

Chapter 2

Shitala Prasad, GREYC – Imaging Lab, CNRS, France

In human's life plant plays an important part to balance the nature and supply food-&-medicine. The traditional manual plant species identification method is tedious and time-consuming process and requires expert knowledge. The rapid developments of mobile and ubiquitous computing make automated plant biometric system really feasible and accessible for anyone-anywhere-anytime. More and more research are ongoing to make it a more realistic tool for common man to access the agro-information by just a click. Based on this, the chapter highlights the significant growth of plant identification and leaf disease recognition over past few years. A wide range of research analysis is shown in this chapter in this context. Finally, the chapter showed the future scope and applications of AaaS and similar systems in agro-field.

Deep Learning (DL) took Artificial Intelligence (AI) by storm and has infiltrated into business at an unprecedented rate. Access to vast amounts of data extensive computational power and a new wave of efficient learning algorithms, helped Artificial Neural Networks to achieve state-of-the-art results in almost all AI challenges. DL is the cornerstone technology behind products for image recognition and video annotation, voice recognition, personal assistants, automated translation and autonomous vehicles. DL works similarly to the brain by extracting high-level, complex abstractions from data in a hierarchical and discriminative or generative way. The implications of DL supported AI in business is tremendous, shaking to the foundations many industries. In this chapter, I present the most significant algorithms and applications, including Natural Language Processing (NLP), image and video processing and finance.

Chapter 4

An urban system is a complex system. There are many factors which significantly influences the different aspects of it. The influencing factors possess different characteristics as they may be environmental, economical, socio-political or cognitive factors. It is not feasible to characterize an urban system with deterministic approach. Therefore there is a need of study on computational frameworks that can investigate cities from a system's perspective. This kind of study may help in devising different ways that can handle uncertainty and randomness of an urban system efficiently and effectively. Therefore the primary objective of this work is to highlight the significance of affective sciences in urban studies. In addition, how machine intelligence techniques can enable a system to control and monitor the randomness of a city is explained. Finally the utility of machine intelligence technique in deciphering the complexity of way finding is conceptually demonstrated.

Chapter 5

Angela Pimentel, FCT-UNL, Portugal
Hugo Gamboa, FCT-UNL, Portugal
Isa Maria Almeida, APDP-ERC, Portugal
Pedro Matos, APDP-ERC, Portugal
Rogério T. Ribeiro, APDP-ERC, Portugal
João Raposo, APDP-ERC, Portugal

Heart diseases and stroke are the number one cause of death and disability among people with type 2 diabetes (T2D). Clinicians and health authorities for many years have expressed interest in identifying individuals at increased risk of coronary heart disease (CHD). Our main objective is to develop a prognostic workflow of CHD in T2D patients using a Holter dataset. This workflow development will be based on machine learning techniques by testing a variety of classifiers and subsequent selection of the best performing system. It will also assess the impact of feature selection and bootstrapping techniques over these systems. Among a variety of classifiers such as Naive Bayes (NB), Random Forest (RF), Support Vector Machine (SVM), Alternating Decision Tree (ADT), Random Tree (RT) and K-Nearest Neighbour (KNN), the best performing classifier is NB. We achieved an area under receiver operating characteristics curve (AUC) of 68,06% and 74,33% for a prognosis of 3 and 4 years, respectively.

Chapter 6

Pradeep Kumar, Maulana Azad National Urdu University, India

Software reliability is a statistical measure of how well software operates with respect to its requirements. There are two related software engineering research issues about reliability requirements. The first issue is achieving the necessary reliability, i.e., choosing and employing appropriate software engineering techniques in system design and implementation. The second issue is the assessment of reliability as a method of assurance that precedes system deployment. In past few years, various software reliability models have been introduced. These models have been developed in response to the need of software engineers, system engineers and managers to quantify the concept of software reliability. This chapter on software reliability prediction using ANNs addresses three main issues: (1) analyze, manage, and improve the reliability of software products; (2) satisfy the customer needs for competitive price, on time delivery, and reliable software product; (3) determine the software release instance that is, when the software is good enough to release to the customer.

Chapter 7

Feature selection is an important topic in data mining, especially for high dimensional dataset. Feature selection is a process commonly used in machine learning, wherein subsets of the features available from the data are selected for application of learning algorithm. The best subset contains the least number of dimensions that most contribute to accuracy. Feature selection methods can be decomposed into three main classes, one is filter method, another one is wrapper method and third one is embedded method. This chapter presents an empirical comparison of feature selection methods and its algorithm. In view of the substantial number of existing feature selection algorithms, the need arises to count on criteria that enable to adequately decide which algorithm to use in certain situation. This chapter reviews several fundamental algorithms found in the literature and assess their performance in a controlled scenario.

The feature selection from gene expression data is the NP hard problem, few of evolutionary techniques give optimal solutions to find feature subsets. In this chapter, authors introduce some evolutionary optimization techniques and proposed a Binary Particle Swarm Optimization (BPSO) based algorithm for feature subset selection. The Feature selection is one of the important and challenging tasks for gene expression data where many traditional methods failed and evolutionary based methods were succeeded. In this study, the initial datasets are preprocessed using a quartile based fast heuristic technique to reduce the crude domain features which are less relevant in categorizing the samples of either group. The experimental results on three bench-mark datasets vis-a-vis colon cancer, defused B-cell lymphoma and leukemia data are evaluated by means of classification accuracies. Detailed comparative studies with some of popular existing algorithms like Genetic Algorithm (GA), Multi Objective GA are also made to show the superiority and effectiveness of the proposed method.

Chapter 9

Face recognition has been one of the most interesting and important research areas for real time applications. There is a need and necessity to design efficient machine leaning based approach for automatic recognitions and surveillance systems. Face recognition also used the knowledge from other disciplines such as neuroscience, psychology, computer vision, pattern recognition, image processing, and machine learning, etc. This chapter provides a review of machine learning based techniques for the face recognition. First, it presents an overview of face recognition and its challenges then, a literature review of machine learning based approaches for face detection and recognition is presented.

Chapter 10

Many people as they age face a greater challenge of muscular dexterity around their facial muscles. This results in difficulty producing certain sounds, and sometimes the problem is so severe that they are unintelligible. People who could benefit from the methods in this chapter are those who are hard of hearing and do not have feedback readily accessible and people with ALS. This chapter describes a method that uses a computer learning algorithm that predicts what people are about to say based on earlier content and learns what the natural sound of their voice sounds like. This chapter illustrates speech trajectory and voice shaping. Clear Audio is a biologically inspired framework for studying natural language. Like the story behind Jurassic Park, Clear Audio attempts to make predictions about data from existing data, inspired by biological processes. Its main goal is to give feedback for speech pathology purposes.

Chapter 11

This chapter summarize and concludes the issues and challenges elaborated in different chapters using machine learning approaches presented by various authors. It identifies the importance of supervised and unsupervised learning algorithms establishing classification, prediction, clustering, security policies along with object recognition and pattern matching structures. A systematic position for future research and practice is also described in detail. This book presents the capabilities of machine learning methods and ideas on how these methods could be used to solve real-world problems related to health, social and engineering applications.

Foreword

In recent years machine learning has made its way from artificial intelligence into areas of medical science, data mining, object recognition, administration, commerce, and industry. Data mining is particularly the most widely known demonstration of this migration, complemented by less publicized applications of machine learning like adaptive systems in industry, financial prediction, medical diagnosis and the construction of user profiles for Web browsers.

This book presents the capabilities of machine learning methods and ideas on how these methods could be used to solve real-world problems related to health, social and engineering applications.

With the ever increasing amounts of data becoming available there is enough reason to believe that smart data analysis will become even more pervasive as a necessary ingredient for technological progress. Over the past two decades Machine Learning has become one of the main-stays of information technology rather part of our life.

The purpose of this book is to provide the reader with some specific applications of machine learning over the vast range of applications which have at their heart a machine learning problem. After that, we will discuss some basic tools from statistics and probability theory, since they form the language in which many machine learning problems must be phrased to become amenable to solving. Machine learning can appear in many ways i.e., the types of data they deal with, and finally, we formalize the problems in a somewhat more stylized fashion. We can use examples of translations to learn how to translate. This machine learning approach proved quite successful.

This book composed of eleven chapters assess the current state of the art of machine learning, from symbolic concept learning and conceptual clustering to case-based reasoning, neural networks, deep learning, and genetic algorithms. Edited chapters introduces the reader to innovative applications of machine learning techniques in the fields of biometric system, urban sciences, heart disease prognosis, software reliability prediction, data mining, knowledge discovery, computational intelligence, human language technology, user modeling data analysis and discovery sciences.

Many other security applications like access control using face recognition as one of its components. That is, given the photo (or video recording) of a person, recognize who this person is. In other words, the system needs to classify the faces into one of many categories (Alan, Alice, Bob, Charlie, David, Maria, and so on) or decide that it is an unknown face. A similar, yet conceptually quite different problem may be of verification. Here the goal is to verify whether the person in question is who he claims to be. Note this is now a yes/no question. To deal with different lighting conditions, facial expressions, whether a person is wearing sun glasses, hairstyle, etc., it is desirable to have a system which learns which features are relevant for identifying a particular person.

Since this is an edited book we may be biased in our selection of references towards easily accessible work rather than the original references. While this may not be in the interest of the inventors of these concepts, it greatly simplifies access to all such topics. Hence we encourage the readers to follow references in the cited works should they be interested in finding out who may claim intellectual ownership of certain key ideas throughout this book.

Over the past few years machine learning has made its way into various areas of administration, commerce, and industry, in an impressive way. Data mining is the most popular widely known demonstration of this phenomenon, complemented by less publicized applications of machine learning, such as adaptive systems in various industrial settings, financial prediction, medical diagnosis, and the construction of user profiles for WWW-browsers. This transfer of machine learning approach from the research labs to the "real world" has caused increased interest in learning techniques, dictating further effort in informing people from other disciplines about the state of the art in machine learning and its uses. The objective of this book is to provide the reader with sufficient information about the research oriented capabilities of machine learning methods, as well as ideas about how the user could make use of these methods to solve real-world problems.

The book is structured in a way that reflects its objective of educating the reader on how machine learning can be applied in real life problems. The book chapters are focused on some specific field of machine learning ranging from business application of deep learning, Significance of affective sciences and machine intelligence to decipher complexity rooting in urban sciences and conceptual clustering to case-based reasoning, neural networks, and genetic algorithms. The research issues addressed in book chapters include the relationship of machine learning to knowledge discovery in databases, software reliability prediction, the handling of noisy data, and the modification of the learning problem through feature selection algorithms for classification and clustering.

The first chapter of the book introduces the reader to innovative applications of machine learning and explore a range of applications, from data mining in finance, marketing, and economics to learning in human language technology and user modeling. The last chapter focused on how games improve language in people with language dysfunctions exposing Jurassic park style extrapolation increases speech to speech engine accuracy's.

Most of these chapters are based on the research work presented in various conferences, workshops and seminars. Each such chapter describes the types of problem that have been approached with the use of machine learning in a particular domain and gives an overview of the work in this area, as presented at the relevant workshop/seminar or conferences.

We hope that the combination of theoretical and empirical knowledge in this book will be of necessary help to the reader who is interested in entering this exciting research field and using mature machine learning techniques to solve real-world problems. The editors of the book would like to thank the distinguished authors for their willingness and cooperation in making this volume a reality.

Pradeep Kumar
Maulana Azad National Urdu University, India

Arvind Kumar Tiwari
DIT University, India

Preface

In the '90s and 2000s, software and the internet transformed the way that companies do the business. Similarly, in the 2010s and 2020s, powerful analytics and machine learning are transforming industries again, just as software transformed the world over the past 30 years. There are numerous applications of machine learning in the field of medical sciences, marketing, and finance particularly for making predictions. It's actually hard to realize how much machine learning has achieved in real world applications. Machine learning is generally just a way of fine tuning a system with tuneable parameters. It is a way of making a system better with examples, usually in a supervised or unsupervised manner. Machine learning algorithms are being used in lots of places in interesting ways. It's becoming increasingly ubiquitous with more and more applications in places where we cannot even think of. ML can be applied to problems like predicting hospital readmissions, predicting strokes, heart failure, wait time, etc.

Machine learning makes it relatively easier to develop sophisticated software systems without much effort on the human side. Instead of spending years handcrafting features or fine tuning a system with a lot of parameters, machine learning does it easily and quickly. ML requires training data only to learn better features or parameters needed to improve a given system. The only drawback is that machine learning doesn't work well for non-convex problems or problems with discrete parameters that are not differentiable.

The term *machine learning* refers to a set of topics dealing with the creation and evaluation of algorithms that facilitate pattern recognition, classification, and prediction, based on models derived from existing data. There are two facets of mechanization that should be acknowledged when considering machine learning in broad terms. First, it is intended that classification and prediction tasks can be accomplished by a suitably programmed computing machine. Second, it is intended that the creation of the classifier should itself be highly mechanized, and should not involve too much human input. The basic objective is that the use of automatic algorithm construction methods can minimize the possibility that human biases could affect the selection and performance of the algorithm. Both the creation of the algorithm and its operation to classify objects or predict events are to be based on concrete, observable data.

The history of relations between biology and the field of machine learning is long and complex. An early technique for machine learning called the multilayer perceptron constituted an attempt to model actual neuronal behaviour, and the field of artificial neural network (ANN) design emerged from this attempt. In the intervening years, the flexibility of machine learning techniques has grown along with mathematical frameworks for measuring their reliability, and it is natural to hope that machine learning methods will improve the efficiency of discovery and understanding in the mounting volume and complexity of biological data.

Two main paradigms in the field of machine learning may be described as namely *supervised* and *unsupervised* learning. In supervised learning, objects in a given collection are classified using a set of attributes, or features. The result of the classification process is a set of rules that prescribe assignments of objects to classes based solely on values of features. In a biological context, examples of *object*-to-*class* mappings are tissue gene expression profiles to disease group, and protein sequences to their secondary structures. The features in these examples are the expression levels of individual genes measured in the tissue samples and the presence/absence of a given amino acid symbol at a given position in the protein sequence, respectively. The goal in supervised learning is to design a system able to accurately predict the class membership of new objects based on the available features. Besides predicting a categorical characteristic such as class label, (similar to classical *discriminant analysis*), supervised techniques can be applied as well to predict a continuous characteristic of the objects (similar to *regression analysis*).

In any application of supervised learning, it would be useful for the classification algorithm to return a value of indicating that it is not clear which one of several possible classes the object should be assigned to or indicating that the object is so unlike any previously observed object that the suitability of any decision on class membership is questionable. In contrast to the supervised framework, in unsupervised learning, no predefined class labels are available for the objects under study. In this case, the goal is to explore the data and discover similarities between objects. Similarities are used to define groups of objects, referred to as *clusters*. In other words, unsupervised learning is intended to unveil natural groupings in the data.

The two paradigms may informally be contrasted as (a) in supervised learning, the data come with class labels, and we basically learn how to associate labeled data with classes and (b) in unsupervised learning, all the data are unlabeled, and the learning procedure consists of both defining the labels and associating objects with them. Life science applications of unsupervised and/or supervised machine learning techniques abound in the literature. For instance, gene expression data was successfully used to classify patients in different clinical groups and to identify new disease groups, while genetic code allowed prediction of the protein secondary structure.

ORGANIZATION OF THE BOOK

This book is organized into 11 chapters. A brief description of each of the chapters follows:

Chapter 1 identifies the fundamental issues and challenges in machine learning approaches in the new millennium. The chapter sets the scene for discussions presented by various authors. This chapter also presents the basic concepts related to feature selection techniques such as filter, wrapper and hybrid methods and various machine learning techniques such as artificial neural network, Naive Bayes classifier, support vector machine, k-nearest-neighbor, decision trees, bagging, boosting, random subspace method, random forests, k-means clustering and deep learning. In the last the performance measure of the classifier is presented.

Chapter 2 contends that by investing in the development of a mobile vision for plant biometric system. Author of this chapter investigates the human's behaviour where plant plays an important part to balance the nature and supply food and medicine. The traditional manual plant species identification method is tedious and time-consuming process and requires expert knowledge. The rapid developments of mobile and ubiquitous computing make automated plant biometric system really feasible and accessible for anyone-anywhere-anytime. More and more research are ongoing to make it a more realistic tool for common man to access the agro-information by just a click. Based on this, the chapter highlights the significant growth of plant identification and leaf disease recognition over past few years. A wide range of research analysis is shown in this chapter in this context. Finally, the chapter showed the future scope and applications of AaaS and similar systems in agro-field.

Chapter 3 takes philosophical orientation and debates about the applications of Deep learning. The author examines some challenges in ethical management of information technology resources. The overall aim of the chapter is to consider moral issues pertaining to machine learning and articulate methods of thinking through various concerns. DL is the cornerstone technology behind products for image recognition and video annotation, voice recognition, personal assistants, automated translation and autonomous vehicles. DNN works similarly to the brain by extracting high-level, complex abstractions from data in a hierarchical and discriminative or generative way. A key feature of DL algorithms is their capability to learn from large amounts of data with minimal supervision – contrary to shallow models that normally require less data, but with labels and easily reach an accuracy plateau. DL however, comes with a cost: there is no theory to guide the learning algorithms and architecture optimization and hyper-parameters selection rely on complex and time-consuming heuristics – training a single model can take weeks on well-equipped PCs.

Chapter 4 aims to explain the significance of affective sciences in deciphering the complexity of an urban system. In addition, the pivotal role which machine intelligence techniques are capable of in characterizing an urban system is described. The proposed chapter begins with a note on urban system outlining its various facets. Then "affective science" is explained in detail, and how the idea of affective science is relevant in functioning of an urban system is outlined. Later, the proposed chapter details the applicability of machine intelligence techniques in studying an urban system under the realm of affective sciences. Having provided a detailed description on the significance of machine intelligence techniques, and their utility in understanding a complex system; a research problem on way finding using a machine intelligent technique and decision tree is demonstrated. This chapter ends with concluding remarks, and suggestions that can be incorporated to strengthen the present study.

Chapter 5 describes the issues related to healthcare industry which generate large amounts of data, driven by record keeping, compliance and regulatory requirements, and patient care. With the potential to improve the quality of healthcare delivery, while reducing costs, these massive quantities of data (known as 'big data') supports a wide range of medical and healthcare functions, which includes clinical decision support, disease surveillance, and population health management. Machine learning enables the extraction of implicit, previous unknown and potentially useful information from data. With machine learning techniques, supervised or unsupervised methods are applied in order to extract and evaluate data patterns which can be used to take better decisions and to present the knowledge extracted in a better way. This chapter proposes a new prognostic approach of CHD for T2D patients based on a Holter dataset. This approach, based on machine learning methods, supports the applicability of using the Holter dataset, to efficiently predict T2D patients that are likely to develop CHD.

Chapter 6 reviews the machine learning techniques applied for predicting software reliability. This chapter focus and investigate three main issues: (1) How accurately and precisely the machine learning based models predict the reliability of software at any point of time during testing phase? (2) Is the performance of machine learning methods such as RBFN, GRNN, SVM, FIS, ANFIS, GEP, GMDH and MARS better than classical method (LR)? (3) Correlate between machine learning methods and statistical approach for software reliability prediction since their performance varies when applied to different past failure data in a realistic environment. The contribution of our chapter is summarized as follows: First, applied liner regression method and analysed the correlation metrics. Second, applied modern machine learning methods (RBFN, GRNN, SVM, FIS, ANFIS, GEP, GMDH and MARS) to study the impact of statistical failure data while making future predictions.

Chapter 7 presents an analysis of issues and concerns in feature selection algorithms for classification and clustering. The feature selection problem is inescapable in inductive machine learning or data mining setting and its significance is beyond doubt. The main benefit of a correct selection is the terms of learning speed, speculation capacity or simplicity of the induced model. On the other hand there are the straight benefits related with a smaller number of features: a reduced measurement cost and hopefully a better understanding of the domain. A feature selection algorithm (FSA) is a computational solution that should be guided by a certain definition of subset relevance although in many cases this definition is implicit or followed in a loose sense. The feature selection algorithm can be classified according to the kind of output one are giving a (weighed) linear order of features and second are giving a subset of the original features. In this chapter several fundamental algorithms found in the literature are studied to assess their performance in a controlled scenario

Chapter 8 deals with the application of Optimization techniques for Gene Expression data analysis. In this chapter, authors introduce some evolutionary optimization techniques and proposed a Binary Particle Swarm Optimization (BPSO) based algorithm for feature subset selection. The Feature selection is one of the important and challenging tasks for gene expression data where many traditional methods failed and evolutionary based methods were succeeded. In this study, the initial datasets are pre-processed using a quartile based fast heuristic technique to reduce the crude domain features which are less relevant in categorizing the samples of either group. The experimental results on three bench-mark datasets vis-a-vis colon cancer, defused B-cell lymphoma and leukemia data are evaluated by means of classification accuracies. Detailed comparative studies with some of popular existing algorithms like Genetic Algorithm (GA), Multi Objective GA are also made to show the superiority and effectiveness of the proposed method.

Chapter 9 applies the machine learning based approach for face recognition. Face recognition has been one of the most interesting and important research areas for real time applications. There is a need and necessity to design efficient machine leaning based approach for automatic recognitions and surveillance systems. Face recognition also used the knowledge from other disciplines such as neuroscience, psychology, computer vision, pattern recognition, image processing, and machine learning, etc. This chapter provides a review of machine learning based techniques for the face recognition. First, it presents an overview of face recognition and its challenges followed by the detailed literature review of machine learning based approaches for face detection and recognition is presented.

Chapter 10 describes and analyses how games improve language in people with language dysfunctions. Since, many people as they age face a greater challenge of muscular dexterity around their facial muscles. This results in difficulty producing certain sounds, and sometimes the problem is so severe that they are unintelligible. People who could benefit from the methods in this chapter are those who are hard of hearing and do not have feedback readily accessible and people with ALS. This chapter describes a method that uses a computer learning algorithm that predicts what people are about to say based on earlier content and learns what the natural sound of their voice sounds like. This paper illustrates speech trajectory and voice shaping. Clear Audio is a biologically inspired framework for studying natural language. Like the story behind Jurassic Park, Clear Audio attempts to make predictions about data from existing data, inspired by biological processes. Its main goal is to give feedback for speech pathology purposes.

Chapter 11 concludes the issues and challenges in machine learning approaches presented by the authors in different chapters. This chapter summarize the global orientation of businesses and the related problems with application of machine learning techniques and best practices. It also identifies the importance of supervised and unsupervised learning algorithms establishing classification, prediction, clustering, security policies along with object recognition and pattern matching structures. A systematic position for future research and practice is also elaborated.

Acknowledgment

The editors would like to acknowledge the help of all the people involved in this project and, more specifically, to the authors and reviewers who took part in the review process. Without their support, this book would not have become a reality to shape in the present format.

First, the editors would like to thank each one of the authors for their constructive contributions. Our sincere gratitude goes to the chapter's authors who contributed their time, effort and expertise to this book.

Second, the editors wish to acknowledge the valuable contributions of the reviewers regarding the improvement of quality, coherence, and content presentation of chapters. We are highly grateful and appreciate their timely concern and efforts put all together to complete this project in time.

Pradeep Kumar
Maulana Azad National Urdu University, India

Arvind Kumar Tiwari
DIT University, India

Chapter 1
Introduction to Machine Learning

Arvind Kumar Tiwari
DIT University, India

ABSTRACT

Machine learning refers to the changes in systems that perform tasks associated with artificial intelligence. This chapter presents introduction types and application of machine learning. This chapter also presents the basic concepts related to feature selection techniques such as filter, wrapper and hybrid methods and various machine learning techniques such as artificial neural network, Naive Bayes classifier, support vector machine, k-nearest-neighbor, decision trees, bagging, boosting, random subspace method, random forests, k-means clustering and deep learning. In the last the performance measure of the classifier is presented.

1. INTRODUCTION

Learning means to gain knowledge, or understanding of, or skill in, by study, instruction, or experience, and modification of a behavioral tendency by experience. Machine learning refers to the changes in systems that perform tasks associated with artificial intelligence. These tasks involve recognition, diagnosis, planning, robot control, prediction, etc. Machine Learning is coming into its own, with a growing recognition that machine learning plays a key role in a wide range of critical applications, such as data mining, natural language processing, image recognition, and expert systems. Machine learning provides potential solutions in all these domains. We need machine learning in the following reasons.

DOI: 10.4018/978-1-5225-2545-5.ch001

1. Some tasks cannot be defined well except by example; that is, we might be able to specify input/output pairs but not a concise relationship between inputs and desired outputs. We would like machines to be able to adjust their internal structure to produce correct outputs for a large number of sample inputs and thus suitably constrain their input/output function to approximate the relationship implicit in the examples.
2. It is possible that hidden among large piles of data are important relationships and correlations. Machine learning methods can often be used to extract these relationships.
3. Human designers often produce machines that do not work as well as desired in the environments in which they are used. In fact, certain characteristics of the working environment might not be completely known at design time. Machine learning methods can be used for on-the-job improvement of existing machine designs.
4. The amount of knowledge available about certain tasks might be too large for explicit encoding by humans. Machines that learn this knowledge gradually might be able to capture more of it than humans would want to write down.
5. Environments change over time. Machines that can adapt to a changing environment would reduce the need for constant redesign.
6. New knowledge about tasks is constantly being discovered by humans.

2. TYPES OF MACHINE LEARNING

Machine learning algorithms are based on the desired outcome of the algorithm. Common algorithm types include:

- **Supervised Learning:** Where the algorithm generates a function that maps inputs to desired outputs. One standard formulation of the supervised learning task is the classification problem: the learner is required to learn (to approximate the behavior of a function which maps a vector into one of several classes by looking at several input-output examples of the function.
- **Unsupervised Learning:** Which models a set of inputs labeled examples are not available.
- **Semi-Supervised Learning:** Which combines both labeled and unlabeled examples to generate an appropriate function or classifier.

- **Reinforcement Learning:** Where the algorithm learns a policy of how to act given an observation of the world. Every action has some impact in the environment, and the environment provides feedback that guides the learning algorithm.
- **Transduction:** Similar to supervised learning, but does not explicitly construct a function, instead, tries to predict new outputs based on training inputs, training outputs, and new inputs.
- **Learning to Learn:** Where the algorithm learns its own inductive bias based on previous experience.

The performance and computational analysis of machine learning algorithms is a branch of statistics known as computational learning theory. Machine learning is about designing algorithms that allow a computer to learn. Learning is not necessarily involves consciousness but learning is a matter of finding statistical regularities or other patterns in the data. Thus, many machine learning algorithms will barely resemble how human might approach a learning task. However, learning algorithms can give insight into the relative difficulty of learning in different environments.

Table 1. Types of machine learning

Learning Types	Data Processing Tasks	Distinction Norm	Learning Algorithms
Supervised learning	Classification/Regression/Estimation	Computational classifiers	Support vector machine
		Statistical classifiers	Naïve Bayes
			Hidden Markov model
			Bayesian networks
		Connectionist classifiers	Neural networks
Unsupervised learning	Clustering/Prediction	Parametric	K-means
			Gaussian mixture model
		Nonparametric	Dirichlet process mixture model
			X-means
Reinforcement learning	Decision-making	Model-free	Q-learning
			R-learning
		Model-based	TD learning
			Sarsa learning

3. APPLICATION OF MACHINE LEARNING

There are numerous applications of machine learning. It's actually hard to realize how much machine learning has achieved in real world applications.

Machine learning is generally just a way of fine tuning a system with tunable parameters. It is a way of making a system better with examples, usually in a supervised or unsupervised manner.

Machine learning is normally applied in the offline training phase. Thus machine learning is used to improve the following applications.

1. **Face Detection:** The face detection feature in mobile cameras is an example of what machine learning can do. Cameras can automatically snap a photo when someone smiles more accurately now than ever before because of advances in machine learning algorithms.

2. **Face Recognition:** This is where a computer program can identify an individual from a photo. You can find this feature on Facebook for automatically tagging people in photos where they appear. Advances in machine learning means more accurate auto-face tagging software.

3. **Image Classification:** A good example is the application of deep learning to improve image classification or image categorization in apps such as Google photos. Google photos would not be possible without advances in deep learning.

4. **Speech Recognition:** Another good example is Google now. Improvements in speech recognition systems has been made possible by, you guessed right, machine learning specifically deep learning.

5. **Google:** Google defines itself as a machine learning company now. It is also a leader in this area because machine learning is a very important component to it's core advertising and search businesses. It applies machine learning to improve search results and search suggestions.

6. **Anti-Virus:** Machine learning is used in Anti-virus software to improve detection of malicious software on computer devices.

7. **Anti-Spam:** machine learning is also used to train better anti-spam software systems.

8. **Genetics:** Classical data mining or clustering algorithms in machine learning such as agglomerative clustering algorithms are used in genetics to help find genes associated with a particular disease.

9. **Signal Denoising:** Machine learning algorithms such as the K-SVD which is just a generalization of k-means clustering are used to find a dictionary of vectors that can be sparsely linearly combined to approximate any given input signal. Thus such a technique is used in video compression and denoising.

10. **Weather Forecasting:** Machine learning is applied in weather forecasting software to improve the quality of the forecast.
11. **Anomaly Detection:** Machine Learning (ML) are at play to flag any malpractice in very high volume high frequency data transactions / communications. ML powered systems can now detect a possible insider trading in a stock market, also ML can flag a rogue customer transaction as a fraudulent transaction in high volume business doing market place websites also.
12. **Classification:** The classification (or topic modelling) algorithms are behind how news articles from thousands of sources gets neatly segregated under topics in Google News or any major news aggregating portals.

4. MACHINE LEARNING TECHNIQUES

4.1. Feature Selection Techniques

Feature selection is the process of selecting a best subset of features, among all the features that are useful for the learning algorithms. The goals of feature selection are:

- To provide faster and more cost effective models by reducing the size of the problem and hence reducing computational time and space required to run classifiers.
- To improve the performance of the classifiers, firstly by removing noisy or irrelevant features secondly by reducing the likelihood of overfitting to noisy data. So the basic objective of feature selection algorithms to improve the performance of the classifier, i.e. prediction performance in the case of classification and better cluster detection in the case of clustering.

4.1.1. Filter Method

Filter methods assess the relevance of features by looking only at the intrinsic properties of the data. Filter method calculates the relevance score of the features by using the essential properties of the data and low scoring features are removed. It evaluates features in isolation so not consider the correlation between features. Afterwards, this subset of features is presented as input to the classification algorithm. Advantages of filter techniques are that they easily scale to very high-dimensional datasets, they are computationally simple and fast and they are independent of the classification algorithm. As a result, feature selection needs to be performed only once and then different classifiers can be evaluated.

A common disadvantage of filter methods is that they ignore the interaction with the classifier and that most proposed techniques are univariate. This means that each feature is considered separately thereby ignoring feature dependencies which may lead to worse classification performance when compared to other types of feature selection techniques. In order to overcome the problem of ignoring feature dependencies, a number of multivariate filter techniques were introduced, aiming at the incorporation of feature dependencies to some degree.

4.1.2. Wrapper Method

The wrapper method uses the classifier for searching the subset of features. It uses the backward elimination process to remove the irrelevant features from the subset of features. In wrapper method the rank of the features is calculated recursively and low rank features are removed from the result. Advantages of wrapper approaches include the interaction between feature subset search and model selection, and the ability to take into account feature dependencies. A common drawback of these techniques is that they have a higher risk of over-fitting than filter techniques and are very computationally intensive, especially if building the classifier has a high computational cost.

4.1.3. Hybrid Method

In the hybrid feature selection the search for an optimal subset of features is built into the classifier construction and can be seen as a search in the combined space of feature subsets and hypotheses. Just like wrapper approaches, hybrid methods are thus specific to a given learning algorithm. Hybrid methods have the advantage that they include the interaction with the classification model, while at the same time being far less computationally intensive than wrapper methods. So Instead of choosing one particular feature selection method, and accepting its outcome as the final subset, different feature selection methods can be combined using ensemble feature selection approaches.

4.2. Machine Learning Techniques

This section presents an overview of various machine learning techniques used in protein function prediction such as artificial neural network, Naive Bayes classifier, support vector machine, k-nearest-neighbor, decision trees, bagging, boosting, random subspace method and random forests.

4.2.1. Artificial Neural Network (ANN)

An artificial neural networks Hagan *et al.* (1996), Schalkoff (1997) is inspired by the concept of biological nervous system. ANNs are the collection of computing elements (neurons) that may be connected in various ways. In ANNs the effect of the synapses is represented by the connection weight, which modulates the input signal. The architecture of artificial neural networks is a fully connected, three layered (input layer, hidden layer and output layer) structure of nodes in which information flows from the input layer to the output layer through the hidden layer. ANNs are capable of linear and nonlinear classification. An ANN learns by adjusting the weights in accordance with the learning algorithms. It is capable to process and analyze large complex datasets, containing non-linear relationships. There are various types of artificial neural network architecture that are used in protein function prediction such as perceptron, multi-layer perceptron (MLP), radial basis function networks and kohonen self-organizing maps.

4.2.2. Naive Bayes Classifier

Naive Bayes classifier Keller (2002) is a statistical method based on Bayes theorem. It calculates the probability of each training data for each class. The class of test data assigns by using the inverse probability. It assumes the entire variables are independent, so only mean and variance are required to predict the class. So the main advantage of the naive Bayes classifier is that it requires a small amount of training data to estimate the mean and variances that are used to predict the class.

4.2.3. Support Vector Machine (SVM)

Support vector machine Cortes and Vapnik (1995) is based on the statistical learning theory. The SVM is capable of resolving linear and non-linear classification problems. The principal idea of classification by support vector is to separate examples with a linear decision surface and maximize the margin of separation between the classes to be classified. SVM works by mapping data with a high-dimensional feature space so that data points can be categorized, even when the data are not otherwise linearly separable. A separator between the categories is found, and then the data are transformed in such a way that the separator could be drawn as a hyperplane. Following this, characteristics of new data can be used to predict the group to which a new record should belong. After the transformation, the boundary between the two categories can be defined by a hyperplane. The mathematical function used for the transformation is known as the kernel function. SVM supports the linear, polynomial, radial basis function (RBF) and sigmoid kernel types. When there is a straightforward linear separation then linear function is used otherwise we used polynomial, radial basis function (RBF) and sigmoid kernel function. Besides the separating line between the categories, a SVM also finds marginal lines that define the space between the two categories. The data points that lie on the margins are known as the support vectors.

4.2.4. K-Nearest Neighbor (k-NN)

The k-Nearest Neighbors algorithm Cover and Hart (1967) is a non-parametric method used for classification and regression. In both cases, the input consists of the k closest training examples in the feature space. The output depends on whether k-NN is used for classification or regression. In k-NN classification, the output is a class membership. The k-NN classifiers are based on finding the k nearest neighbor and taking a majority vote among the classes of these k neighbors to assign a class for the given query. The k-NN is a type of instance based learning, or lazy learning where the function is only approximated locally and all computation is deferred until classification. The k-NN is more efficient for large datasets and robustness when processing noisy data but high computation cost reduces its speed.

4.2.5. Decision Trees

The decision trees are a branch test-based classifiers such as such as ID3 (Iterative Dichotomiser 3) Quinlan (1996), C 5.0 (See5) Quinlan (2004), Classification And Regression Tree (CART) Breiman *et al.* (1984) and CHi-squared Automatic Interaction Detector (CHAID) Kass (1980) etc. These classifiers use the knowledge of training data it creates a decision trees that is used to classify test data. In the decision tree every branch represents a set of classes and a leaf represent a particular class. A decision node identifies a test on a single attribute value with one branch and its subsequent classes represent as class outcomes. To maximize interpretability these classifiers are expressed as decision trees or rule sets (IF-THEN), forms that are generally easier to understand than neural networks. Decision tree based classifiers are easy to use and does not presume any special knowledge of statistics or machine learning.

4.2.6. Bagging

Bagging Breiman (1996) is ensemble classifiers. In bagging '*n*' random instances are selected using a uniform distribution (with replacement) from a training dataset of size '*n*'. The learning process starts using these '*n*' randomly selected instances and this process can be repeated several times. Since the selection is with replacement, usually the selected instances will contain some duplicates and some omissions as compared to the original training dataset. Each cycle through the process results in one classifier. After the construction of several classifiers, taking a vote of the predictions of each classifier performs the final prediction.

4.2.7. Boosting

Boosting Freund and Schapire (1996) is similar to bagging except that one keeps track of the performance of the learning algorithm and forces it to concentrate its efforts on instances that have not been correctly learned. Instead of selecting the '*n*' training instances randomly using a uniform distribution, one chooses the training instances in such a manner as to favors the instances that have not been accurately learned. After several cycles the prediction is performed by taking a weighted vote of the predictions of each classifier with the weights being proportional to each classifier's accuracy on its training set.

4.2.8. Random Subspace Method

Random subspace Ho (1998) method or attribute bagging Bryll (2003) is an ensemble classifier that consists of several classifiers and outputs the class based on the outputs of these individual classifiers. Random subspace method has been used for linear classifiers, support vector machines, nearest neighbors and other types of classifiers. This method is also applicable to one-class classifiers. It is an attractive choice for classification problems where the number of features is much larger than the number of training objects. The ensemble classifier is constructed using the following algorithm:

- Let the number of training objects be N and the number of features in the training data be D.
- Choose L to be the number of individual classifiers in the ensemble.
- For each individual classifier C, choose d_c ($d_c < D$) to be the number of input variables for C. It is common to have only one value of d_c for all the individual classifiers.
- For each individual classifier C, create a training set by choosing d_c features from D without replacement and train the classifier.
- For classifying a new object, combine the outputs of the L individual classifiers by majority voting or by combining the posterior probabilities.

4.2.9. Random Forests

Random forest classifier Breiman (2001) used an ensemble of random trees. Each of the random trees is generated by using a bootstrap sample data. At each node of the tree a subset of feature with highest information gain is selected from a random subset of entire features. Thus random forest used bagging as well as feature selection to generate the trees. Once a forest is generated every tree participates in classification by voting to a class. The final classification is based on the majority voting of a particular class. It performs better in comparison with single tree classifiers such as CART and C 5.0 etc.

4.2.10. K-Means Clustering

k-means clustering Hartigan, J. A., & Wong, M. A. (1979) aims to partition n observations into k clusters in which each observation belongs to the cluster with the nearest mean, serving as a prototype of the cluster. Given a set of observations $(x_1, x_2, ..., x_n)$, where each observation is a d-dimensional real vector, k-means clustering aims to partition the n observations into k $(\leq n)$ sets $S = \{S_1, S_2, ..., S_k\}$ so as to minimize the within-cluster sum of squares i.e. sum of distance functions of each point in the cluster to the K center.

4.2.11. Deep Learning

Deep learning Yu, D. *et.al.* (2014) is use a cascade of many layers of nonlinear processing units for feature extraction and transformation. Each successive layer uses the output from the previous layer as input. The algorithms may be supervised or unsupervised and applications include pattern analysis and classification. It is based on the learning of multiple levels of features or representations of the data. Higher level features are derived from lower level features to form a hierarchical representation. It is a part of the broader machine learning field of learning representations of data. It learns multiple levels of representations that correspond to different levels of abstraction; the levels form a hierarchy of concepts. The composition of a layer of nonlinear processing units used in a deep learning algorithm depends on the problem to be solved. Layers that have been used in deep learning include hidden layers of an artificial neural network and sets of complicated propositional formulas. It may also include latent variables organized layer-wise in deep generative models such as the nodes in Deep Belief Networks and Deep Boltzmann Machines. Deep learning algorithms are based on distributed representations. The underlying assumption behind distributed representations is that observed data are generated by the interactions of factors organized in layers. Deep learning adds the assumption that these layers of factors correspond to levels of abstraction or composition. Varying numbers of layers and layer sizes can be used to provide different amounts of abstraction. Deep learning exploits this idea of hierarchical explanatory factors where higher level, more abstract concepts are learned from the lower level ones. These architectures are often constructed with a greedy layer-by-layer method. Deep learning helps to disentangle these abstractions and pick out which features are useful for learning. For supervised learning tasks, deep learning methods obviate feature engineering, by translating the data into compact intermediate representations akin to principal components, and derive layered structures which remove redundancy in representation. Many deep learning algorithms are applied to unsupervised learning tasks. This is an important benefit because unlabeled data are usually more abundant than labeled data. Examples of deep structures that can be trained in an unsupervised manner are neural history compressors and deep belief networks.

5. PERFORMANCE MEASURES

The performance of the classifiers is measured by using 10-fold cross validation. In *K*-fold cross validation the dataset of all proteins is partitioned into *K* subsets where one subset is used for validation and remaining *K-1* subsets is used for training. This process is repeated for *K* times so that every subset is used once as a test data. In this thesis, accuracy (*ACC*), receiver operating characteristics (ROC), precision, sensitivity, specificity and Matthew's correlation coefficient (*MCC*) are used to measure the performance.

The performance of the classifiers is measured by the quantity of True positive (TP), True Negative (TN), False Positive (FP), False Negative (FN). Where TP (True Positive) is the number of positive instances that are classified as positive, FP (False Positive) is the number of negative instances that are classified as positive, TN (True Negative) is the number of negative instances that are classified as negative and FN (False Negative) is the number of positive instances that are classified as negative. By using these quantities standard accuracy, sensitivity, specificity, precision, MCC and ROC area performance measures are defined as:

Table 2. Confusion matrix to measure the performance of the classifiers

	Predicted Class		
	Positive	Negative	Total
Positive	TP	FN	P
Negative	FP	TN	N

Accuracy: Accuracy is defined as the proportion of instances that are correctly classified.

$$Accuracy = \frac{(TP + TN)}{(P + N)}$$

Sensitivity: Sensitivity is defined as the proportion of positive instances that are correctly classified as positive.

$$Senstivity = \frac{(TP)}{(P)}$$

Specificity: Specificity is defined as the the proportion of negative instances that are correctly classified as negative.

$$Specificity = \frac{(TN)}{(N)}$$

Precision: Precision is defined as the proportion of instances classified as positive that are really positive.

$$Pr\,ecision = \frac{(TP)}{(TP + FP)}$$

Matthew's Correlation Coefficient (MCC): The MCC is a balanced measure that considers both true and false positives and negatives. The MCC can be obtained as

$$MCC = \frac{(TP)(TN) - (FP)(FN)}{\sqrt{(TP + FP)(TP + FN)(TN + FP)(TN + FN)}}$$

Receiver Operating Characteristics (ROC): The ROC Hanley and McNeil (1982); Worster *et al.* (2006) is a graph that shows the performance of a classifier by plotting TP rate versus FP rate at various threshold settings. Area under ROC curve (AUC) of a classifier is the probability that the classifier ranks a randomly chosen positive instance higher than a randomly chosen negative instance.

6. CONCLUSION

Machine learning refers to the changes in systems that perform tasks associated with artificial intelligence. This chapter presented introduction types and application of machine learning. In this chapter the basic concepts related to feature selection techniques such as filter, wrapper and hybrid methods and various machine learning techniques such as artificial neural network, Naive Bayes classifier, support vector machine, k-nearest-neighbor, decision trees, bagging, boosting, random subspace method, random forests, k-means clustering and deep learning also presented. In the last the performance measure of the classifier was presented.

REFERENCES

Bradley, A. P. (1997). The use of the area under the ROC curve in the evaluation of machine learning algorithms. *Pattern Recognition, 30*(7), 1145–1159. doi:10.1016/S0031-3203(96)00142-2

Breiman, L. (1996). Bagging predictors. *Machine Learning, 24*(2), 123–140. doi:10.1007/BF00058655

Breiman, L. (2001). Random forests. *Machine Learning, 45*(1), 5–32. doi:10.1023/A:1010933404324

Breiman, L., Friedman, J., Stone, C. J., & Olshen, R. A. (1984). *Classification and regression trees*. CRC Press.

Bryll, R., Gutierrez-Osuna, R., & Quek, F. (2003). Attribute bagging: Improving accuracy of classifier ensembles by using random feature subsets. *Pattern Recognition, 36*(6), 1291–1302. doi:10.1016/S0031-3203(02)00121-8

Cortes, C., & Vapnik, V. (1995). Support-vector networks. *Machine Learning, 20*(3), 273–297. doi:10.1007/BF00994018

Cover, T., & Hart, P. (1967). Nearest neighbor pattern classification, Information Theory. *IEEE Transactions on, 13*(1), 21–27.

Deng, L., & Yu, D. (2014). Deep Learning. *Signal Processing, 7*, 3–4.

Hagan, M. T., Demuth, H. B., & Beale, M. H. (1996). *Neural network design*. Boston: Pws Pub.

Hartigan, J. A., & Wong, M. A. (1979). Algorithm AS 136: A k-means clustering algorithm. *Journal of the Royal Statistical Society. Series C, Applied Statistics, 28*(1), 100–108.

Ho, T. K. (1998). The random subspace method for constructing decision forests, Pattern Analysis and Machine Intelligence. *IEEE Transactions on, 20*(8), 832–844.

Kass, G. V. (1980). An exploratory technique for investigating large quantities of categorical data. *Applied Statistics, 29*(2), 119–127. doi:10.2307/2986296

Keller, F. (2002). *Naive Bayes Classifiers*. Connectionist and Statistical Language Processing, Course at Universität des Saarlandes.

LeCun, Y., Bengio, Y., & Hinton, G. (2015). Deep learning. *Nature, 521*(7553), 436–444. doi:10.1038/nature14539 PMID:26017442

Quinlan, J. R. (1996). Learning decision tree classifiers. *ACM Computing Surveys, 28*(1), 71–72. doi:10.1145/234313.234346

Quinlan, J. R. (2014). *C4. 5: programs for machine learning*. Elsevier.

Quinlan, J. R. (1996). Bagging, boosting, and C4. 5. AAAI/IAAI, 1, 725-730.

Quinlan, R. (2004). *Data mining tools See5 and C5*. Academic Press.

Saeys, Y., Inza, I., & Larrañaga, P. (2007). A review of feature selection techniques in bioinformatics. *Bioinformatics, 23*(19), 2507-2517.

Schalkoff, R. J. (1997). *Artificial neural networks*. New York: McGraw-Hill.

Worster, A., Fan, J., & Upadhye, S. (2006). Understanding receiver operating characteristic (ROC) curves. *Canadian Journal of Emergency Medical Care, 8*(1), 19–20. doi:10.1017/S1481803500013336 PMID:17175625

Yu, D., Deng, L., & Yu, D. (2014). *Deep Learning Methods and Applications*. Foundations and Trends in Signal Processing.

Chapter 2

Mobile Vision for Plant Biometric System

Shitala Prasad
GREYC – Imaging Lab, CNRS, France

ABSTRACT

In human's life plant plays an important part to balance the nature and supply food-&-medicine. The traditional manual plant species identification method is tedious and time-consuming process and requires expert knowledge. The rapid developments of mobile and ubiquitous computing make automated plant biometric system really feasible and accessible for anyone-anywhere-anytime. More and more research are ongoing to make it a more realistic tool for common man to access the agro-information by just a click. Based on this, the chapter highlights the significant growth of plant identification and leaf disease recognition over past few years. A wide range of research analysis is shown in this chapter in this context. Finally, the chapter showed the future scope and applications of AaaS and similar systems in agro-field.

INTRODUCTION[1]

At the beginning of this century, there was a tremendous technological revolution in the field of wireless communication and mobile technology. Mobile and ubiquitous computers are increasing their magnitude in every small, portable, wireless computing and communication fields. The technological omnipresence of ubiquitous devices invisibly activates the world by providing accessibility *anywhere-anytime* computing. However, this revolution is still slow in the agricultural sphere, despite the advancements in technologies making it possible to build and deploy

DOI: 10.4018/978-1-5225-2545-5.ch002

wireless sensor networks (WSN) in fields that would radically improves the farming efficiencies. This is because the current wireless technologies are too expensive and complicated for farmers to use especially in the developing countries like India. Two-way radios have long been used by farmers in many such developed countries with large farmlands to contact their employees, farm suppliers, equipment dealers, agents, buyers and farm awareness. Today, world-wide availability of smartphones and cellular networks, the use of mobile phones in agricultural sector is popularly, replacing the use of two-way radios (Wang, Li, Zhu, & Xu, 2016). The advantage of using two-way radios and mobile phones is that these wireless tools are relatively cheap and very simple to use. Additionally, smartphones have several important advantages such as all the brands of mobile phones are generally compatible for running various types of application software, and are equipped with Wi-Fi, Bluetooth, camera(s) and GPS capabilities.

In Asia-Pacific region, India has outscored the other nations in terms of the number of mobile users. With such rapidly increasing tele-density, mobile penetration in rural areas is also growing strongly. These days, mobile phones are available to people even in rural India, especially among the agrarian community. Motivated by the advancement in mobile technology and the wide-spread use of phones in India, as discussed above, researchers are aiming to help the illiterate agrarian community to improve their agricultural activities through the use of mobile phones. Thus, a new agro-information technology needs to be introduced in order to bridge the gaps between the real and digital objects via mobile computing (MC) and augmented reality (AR).

Agricultural Scenario

In developing countries, agriculture accounts the major role of rural employment and holds the promise for socio-economic growth. In fact, agro-community is roughly five-times more effective in raising the income of poor farmers compared to any other sector. Agricultural improvement also directly impacts on the hunger and malnutrition and thus plays a significant role in decreasing the occurrences of famine. However, the growing global population has heightened the demand for foods. Due to the lack of infrastructure in rural areas, raising the food prices and the climatic change and the real effective and "smart" agriculture is essential. Together with geographic information systems (GIS) and virtual reality (VR) smartphones can play an important role in precision agriculture environment (Bakhsh, Colvin, Jaynes, Kanwar, & Tim, 2000; Jain, Tim, & Jolly, 1995; Tim, 1995). Some of the uses of on-farm wireless network technologies in improving the agricultural productions are discussed in (Vellidis et al. 2007; Izzat, Ismail, Mehat, & Haroon, 2009; Revenaz, Ruggeri, & Martelli, 2010).

Mobile-Based Agriculture

Information and Communication Technology (ICT), particularly mobile technologies, are often seen as the 'game changer' in agro-community. The already existing *m*-Agricultural information system provides a giant leap in agriculture that offers a plethora of services, serving as a tool for information dissemination (Brugger, 2011). Various mobile-based services such as Internet-based, SMS-based information services (Gore, Lobo, & Doke, 2012), voice-based agro-advisory services like mKRISHI -(Shinde et al. 2014), and videos over mobile networks (Pande, Jagyasi, & Choudhuri, 2009) are utilized for transferring general knowledge about the farming techniques and trends, information of the plants and their varieties regarding how to keep them disease free. The general awareness in India by using *m*-Agriculture techniques since last decade are listed in Figure 1. But due to the limited and disconnected services they did not server the real needy.

Specifically, *m*-Agriculture refers to the delivery of agriculture-related services via mobile communication technology (Brugger, 2011). In order to make decisions on agricultural measures, it provides an individual decision support systems and services. These decision are based on the local contextual information, *i.e.*, delivering location-specific information like climatic patterns, soil and water conditions. Here, *m*-Agricultural termed to involve gathering of related information through mobile technologies like automated weather stations or sensors used in mobile. Thus, *m*-Agriculture involves a two-way advisory systems that provides individual

Figure 1. Mobile-based ICT agro-services launched in India

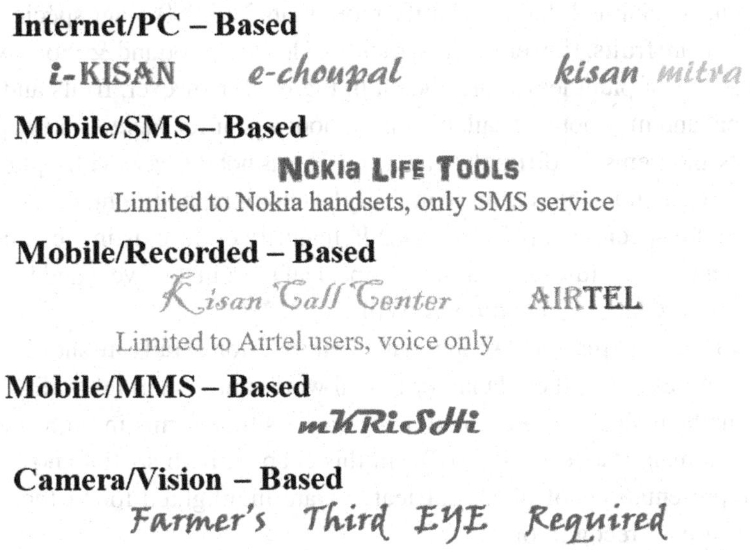

Internet/PC – Based
   i-KISAN   *e-choupal*   *kisan mitra*

Mobile/SMS – Based
              NOKIa LIFE TOOLS
        Limited to Nokia handsets, only SMS service

Mobile/Recorded – Based
        Kisan Call Center   AIRTEL
        Limited to Airtel users, voice only

Mobile/MMS – Based
              mKRiSHi

Camera/Vision – Based
           Farmer's Third EYE Required

feedbacks and advices like remote diagnosis of diseases by experts using some fertilizers/chemicals. These advisory systems typically include smartphones and intermediaries for wireless communication with the farmers and require remote sensing instruments like GIS.

m-Agriculture projects are built on the opportunities to increase the use of mobile/ubiquitous devices by farmers in the developing countries. Therefore, the primary objective of this chapter is to project such mobile-based vision systems for plant species identification and disease diagnosis using plant leaf imaging. Why an agro-vision system? Because famers or the other illiterate (non-botanical) person may not be able to explain the exact visual symptoms occurred on the crop to the expert to get a proper solution for the problem(s).

Motivation

The biodiversity is rapidly disappearing and we are losing the opportunities to know and understand the complexity of our mother-nature. Smart technologies are indispensable in order to rapidly identify the species and access the biodiversity information. If possible, it also develops the eco-informatics expert systems. Thus, mobile-based automated plant biometric system to automatically segment leaf from a complex background, followed by leaf analysis to identify the plant species, and diagnose the diseases on the leaf, is a need.

Currently, there are several plant classification methods such as plant genetics method, cytotaxonomy method and chemotaxonomy method. Plant species classification is not only botanic, but also is the foundation of ecology, medicine and life science (Wang, Li, Zhu, & Xu, 2016). According to a survey conducted in 2003, botanists claimed that to identify more than 3,15,000 plant species the key features used are fruits, flowers, stems, roots and leaves (Scotland & Wortley, 2003). Different types of plant leaves are shown in Figure 2. However, fruits and flowers are seasonal and may not be available throughout a year for identification purpose, while roots and stems are difficult to analyze. This is not the case with a plant leaf. It is available throughout the year and can easily be photographed; containing sufficient information for species analysis. As a result, majority of the existing techniques are based on plant leaf features such as leaf shape, leaf margin, leaf vein and leaf texture (Cope, Corney, Clark, Remagnino, & Wilkin, 2012).

Some of the basic plant leaf shapes with their venation details are shown in Figure 2. These features are well explanatory in real world but for virtual or digital world they are mathematically represented using various transforms in both spatial and frequency domain (Cope et al., 2012). In this chapter, both spatial and frequency domain representations of plant leaf features are highlighted for further analysis (specie or disease recognition).

Figure 2. The common shapes of simple leaves (Plant Glossary, 2009)

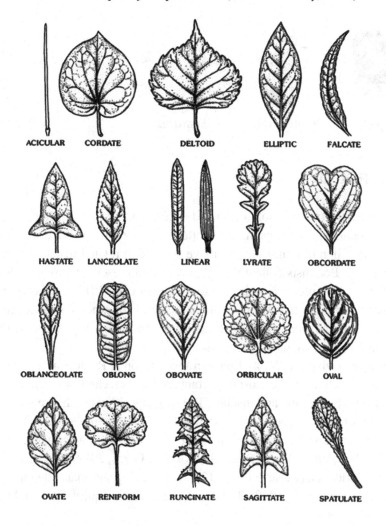

The chapter, especially focus on the novel techniques used for plant identification and disease diagnosis. The graphical abstract of the proposed system is shown in Figure 3 where the crop leaf (object) is photographed via mobile/ubiquitous device, and subsequently represented mathematically in feature space which is then projected for classification using an optimal classifier.

The next few sections describe the existing automated plant biometric systems and their limits with their comparison and results.

Figure 3. The graphical abstract of the proposed system

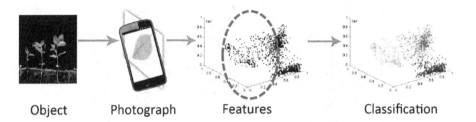

Object   Photograph   Features   Classification

BACKGROUND

As discussed, the manual monitoring and experimenting involves human expertise which is a tedious, time consuming, brittle and frustrating practice. Users need to traverse a decision tree manually to make a decision related to species, as shown in Figure 4(a). Botanists collect the specimens and preserve them in herbaria like Royal Botanical Gardens, Kew in London[2] (Kumar et al. 2012), as shown in Figure 4(b). The herbarium can be seen as a major collection of experts' knowledge in form of a structured repository and thus, to facilitate the access they are being digitized with images of species, dates, locations and so on.

In computer vision (CV) and pattern recognition (PR), feature representation and feature selection are the most important aspect of research since many decades. Various image processing and machine learning algorithms such as neural network (NN), support vector machine (SVM), and k-nearest neighbor (k-NN) are used in different domains like medical imaging (Orr, Peersson, Marquand, Sartori, & Mechelli, 2012), surveillance (Pogorelc, Bosni, & Gams, 2012), object recognition, species identification (Kumar et al. 2012) and designing automated defence systems (Heinze, Goss, & Pearce, 1999). The development and ubiquity of technologies like

Figure 4. (a) Hierarchy of biodiversity classification and (b) bio-specimens herbaria

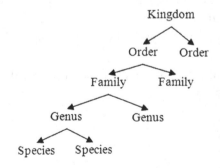

mobile cameras and mobile processors in related fields have brought such ideas close to the reality (MacLeod, Benfield, & Culverhouse, 2010). Therefore, various CV systems have been proposed for plant identification using their fruits, flowers or leaves[3], especially morphological studies, e.g., Tilia (Schneider, 1912), Ulmus (Melville, 1937), Betula (Natho, 1959) and many more.

There are many aspects of plants that are used by botanists in identification such as the 2-dimensional outlines of leaf, veins of leaf, margin of leaf and texture of leaf. Among these, leaf shape information is the mostly exposed and popular method among CV researchers. The two well know mobile applications launched in market for species identification are *LeafSnap* and *Leafview*. Both uses the leaf shape information for plant leaf identification via iPhone, as shown in Figure 5(a-b). *LeafZone*[4] (Figure 5c) is another app that not only identifies the plant species but also provides information about the effect of ozone on them making it more exciting for people to know their nature.

Leaf-Shape-Based Identification

Leaf shape has the maximum discriminative power among all the other parts of a plant. At the same time, leaves of the same plant may have different shapes and size. Over it, leaves of different species may have similar characteristic shape. As discussed above, the existing algorithms used to extract shape information in the frequency domain from a leaf I^3_{leaf} are Fourier analysis (McLellan & Endler, 1998), elliptic Fourier descriptors (EFDs) (Neto, Meyer, Jones, & Samal, 2006) and Fourier harmonics (Hearn, 2009). Following this, Principal Component Analysis (PCA)

Figure 5. (a) LeafSnap, (b) LeafView, and (c) Leafzone are the popular electronic plant information systems

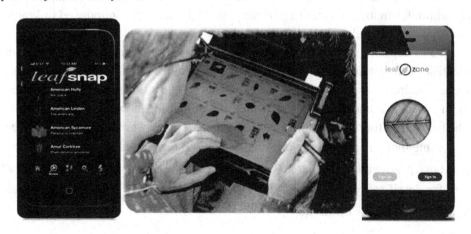

was also applied to reduce the dimensionality of the feature-space for efficient classification. The advantage of using such methods is that the shape can be reconstructed from its descriptors and are rotation invariant. Recently, EFDs was also used by different authors for leaf shape analysis (Andrade, Mayo, Kirkup, & Van-Den-Berg, 2008; Lexer et al. 2009; Neto et al. 2006). Next, a number of approach uses contour signatures for leaf shape classification such as the morphological description (Cope et al. 2012) and the centroid-contour distance (CCD) (Wang, Chi, & Feng, 2003). CCD is a sequence of distances between the center pixel to the contour of the object and hence, suffers from orientation problem. The other signatures include centroid-angle and tangents of the leaf outline. Meade and Parnell (2003) and Wang, Chi, and Feng (2003) attempted to increase the CCD accuracy when applied on leaf shape identification. A new time-series shapelets approach to calculate local features was proposed by Ye and Keogh (2009) and Prasad, Kumar, and Ghosh (2016). But a major difficulty with these contour based signatures is that they are sensitive to self-intersection which occurs quite often with multiple lobe leaves and in compound leaves. Prasad, Kumar, and Ghosh (2016) overcomes with this limitation to some extent. Another common approach for shape extraction is the use of movement invariant (MI) features (Zulkifli, Saad, & Mohtar, 2011), region-based features (Lee & Chen, 2006), and others. Warren (1997) proposed an automated system to recognize plant genus "Chrysanthemum" with thirty species. In Warren (1997), three basic mathematical descriptors such as the shape, color and size of leaf, flower and petal were used to identify the species. Similarly, authors (White, Marino, & Feiner, 2006 & 2007; White, Feiner, & Kopylec, 2007), used a morphological descriptor for shape information extraction from a complete leaf image. They designed a mobile vision Tablet-PC-based electronic field guide to identify plant leaves for the use of botanists and others to make their work much easier. Since *LeafSnap* is designed for iOS, Zhao et al. (2015), proposed *ApLeaf*, an Android based replica of *LeafSnap* with few pros-and-cons. Thus, Multiscale-ARCH-height (MARCH) a shape-based algorithm for mobile devices to retrieve plant leaf image was introduced in Wang, Brown, Gao, and Salle (2015).

In Prasad, Kumar, and Ghosh (2013b), the authors proposed a mobile plant identification system with a statistical leaf shape information. Here, they used the reduced shape and color mean information where the leaf image was down sampled to an acceptable and feasible limit which is optimal for mobile-level computing. The first step in this was to capture an isolated constant background plant leaf image I^3_{leaf} using mobile camera. The pre-processing step is minimal or negligible due to the above pre-segmented input leaf. The shape and color features are extracted and used for classification after limiting I^3_{leaf} to a fixed window size to make the approach translation and scale invariant.

Since shape or color cannot be used individually for a reliable leaf classification, as they may vary with different conditions and locations, researchers applied a decision level fusion to avoid such problem(s). The first level decision is based on shape information which is subsequently verified in the second level using color features (Prasad, Kumar, & Ghosh, 2013b). For the purpose of shape feature extraction, geometric features (elongation, roundness, circularity and porosity) and polar Fourier transform features were used. On the other hand, for color features, the mean, standard deviation, skewness and kurtosis were derived (Prasad, Kumar, & Ghosh, 2013b). To test the functionality two different datasets were used: Flavia dataset[5] and a set of hundred plant species dataset (Wu et al. 2007) with an accuracy of 91.34% and 76.21%, respectively. Other than this, few other authors have used some very specific leaf features to identify plant species, such as the leaf lobedness (Pauwels, Zeeuw, & Ranguelova, 2009) and fractal combined with Linear Discriminant Analysis (LDA) (Bruno, deOliveira Plotze, Falvo, & deCastro, 2008). It is found that fractal features are significant only if used with the combination of other features. In 2006, Du, Huang, Wang, and Gu proposed a polygonal representation of plant leaves for comparison limiting the method to a more generic tasks.

Leaf Veins and Margin-Based Identification

The second commonly used leaf information is its vein pattern. The common leaf vein structure are shown in Figure 2. The veins provides structure to a leaf and thus, the vein pattern of a leaf can serve as a measure for its identification. The algorithms proposed in these are Independent Component Analysis (ICA) (Li, Chi, & Feng, 2006) and Artificial Ant Swarm Intelligence (AASI) (Mullen, Monekosso, Barman, Remagnino, & Wilkin, 2008) to extract leaf edge and leaf vein patterns for species recognition. Cope, Remagnino, Barman, and Wilkin (2010) used Genetic Algorithm (GA) to identify vein pixels and non-vein pixels. Whereas, vein extraction is best achieved by using threshold and neural network approach, as claimed by Fu and Chi (2006). Some other similar methods are discussed by Nam, Hwang, and Kim (2008) and Park, Hwang, and Nam (2008).

The third information used to classify a plant species is by its leaf margin. However, it is not a perfect feature and, therefore, generally used only in combination with other features. The leaf margin often consists of teeth pattern, as shown in Figure 1, which offers a small contribution in automated plant species recognition. Clark (2004) used multi-layer perceptron for identifying species and in Clark (2009), he used a hair descriptor as one of the features in self-organizing map (SOM) for Tilia classification. Rumpunen and Bartish (2002) used a manual measure to calculate the angle and length of the leaf tooth. If undamaged leaves are available, then leaf margin may be a good option for the purpose. On the other hand, leaf vein combined with leaf margin may perform well in damaged leaf cases. But for taxa that do not have teeth, it may fail.

Leaf-Texture-Based Identification

Last but the most important information of a plant leaf is its texture and so many novel techniques have been proposed using it. The size and color of plant leaf varies arbitrarily and even in a single plant two leaves may have different sizes. Thus, the algorithm needs to be translation, scale and rotational invariant, as in case of Curvelet transform (CT) (Prasad, Kumar, & Tripathi, 2011). Image texture quantifies the perceived texture of an image and can be calculated using either structural approach or statistical approach. Backes, Gonalves, Martinez, and Bruno (2010) proposed multi-scale fractal approach to represent the texture of leaf and used neural network for classification. Other methods based on Gabor transform (GT) (Casanova, de Mesquita, & Brun, 2009; Cope et al. 2010, 2012), wavelet transform (Liu et al., 2009) and Relative sub-Image Coefficient (RSC) feature (Prasad, Kundiri, & Tripathi, 2011a) were proposed to extract leaf texture for species recognition.

In 2014, Yanikoglu, Aptoula, and Tirkaz used shape-texture-color features to identify plant species from photographed images with a maximum accuracy of 81% in various lighting, poses, and orientation conditions. Finally, each method has its own pros and cons. It is conjectured that texture combined with contour-based shape analysis may be the best solution in the present context.

The plant biometric also entered into the deep learning and come up with several convolutional approaches for plant leaf species classification (Lee, Chan, Wilkin, & Remagnino, 2015; Sünderhauf, McCool, Upcroft, & Perez, 2014; Reyes, Caicedo, & Camargo, 2015; Jassmann, 2015).

Based on Flowers and Other Parts of Plants

In the literature, there is a dearth of research done on leaf lamina feature extraction using wavelet and Gaussian interpolation (Gu, Du, & Wang, 2005). To other extent, 3D image processing has also been proposed for leaf feature extraction (Ma et al. 2008). They combined 2D leaf images to extract 3D leaf structure and together with 2D and 3D information, leaf boundary segmentation is achieved by applying normalized-cuts. They applied CCD for classifying leaf into palmate and cordate. Similarly, Teng, Kuo, and Chen (2009) used stereo imaging and stereo matching for the same purpose.

A number of approaches have also been proposed that use flower as a key to identify plant[6]. In case of flower, color is the most common and significant feature.

Nilsback & Zisserman, (2010) combined petal shape and color information to design flower segmentation algorithm. Hong, Gang, Jun-li, Chi, and Zhang (2004) used the same color-histogram with CCD and angle-code histogram to classify a set of fourteen species. Yoshioka, Iwata, Ohsawa, and Ninomiya (2004) used Elliptic Fourier Analysis (EFA) for shape analysis of petals in case of Primula sieboldii while Gage and Wilkin (2008) used EFA for outline analysis of tepals (such as petals and sepals) of three species of Sternbergia to validate whether they actually have distinct morphology. Huang, Huang, Du, Quan, and Gua (2006) used Gabor transform (GT) and radial Probabilistic Neural Network (PNN) for bark texture analysis. Lastly, few of the researchers used digital imaging on plant root to analyze root shapes and structures via polynomial curve fitting (Huang, Jain, Stockman, & Smucker, 1992; Zeng, Birchfield, & Wells, 2010). Recently, Mzoughi, Yahiaoui, Boujemaa, and Zagrouba (2015) proposed a hybrid approach for plant species identification. They used leaf arrangement, leaf lobation and leaf partition information to form the feature space necessary for classification. But again, this novel retrieval strategy lacks proper feature representation and selection for ImageCLEF 2011 leaf dataset[7]. Majority of them are content-based image retrieval which needs to be replaced by semantic and cognition based resulting higher level of accuracy in very small time of response (Candan, Kim, Nagarkar, Nagendra, & Yu, 2011; Li et al., 1997, 1998).

Mobile-Based Plant Species Identification System

On the other side of the coin, MC can aid timely access to agriculture related information such as production monitoring, bank policies, *m*-agriculture commerce, and so on, as claimed by Prasad, Kumar, and Ghosh (2013a). Other than Kumar et al. (2012), White et al. (2006), Zhao et al. (2015), Prasad, Kumar, and Ghosh (2013b), Prasad, Kumar, and Ghosh (2015) presented an *Agriculture-as-a-Service* (*AaaS*) framework combining MC, AR and wireless communication technologies with cloud computing (CC) to better serve the agricultural community (agro-community). As the *third eye* of farmer, *AaaS* automatically assists in monitoring their crop fields by a smart remote expert's eye. As discussed above, majority of works were desktop driven and limited to laboratory only. Few approaches are executed on mobile device as an interface such as the *LeafSnap, Apleaf,* and *AgroMobile*. Nonetheless, the mobile applications are very popular among the mass communities compared to other desktop-based systems. In addition to this, Mobile Cloud Computing (MC2) manages the energy consumption of a mobile phone supporting an off-line accessibility of plant information and pathological data, as shown in Figure 6. Accordingly, Kim et al. (2013) proposed a self-growing agriculture knowledge using CC services assisting farmers to make smart decisions. The detailed MC2 in agriculture is discussed in Prasad, Kumar, and Ghosh (2013a, 2015).

Figure 6. AgroMobile framework (Prasad, Kumar, & Ghosh, 2013a)

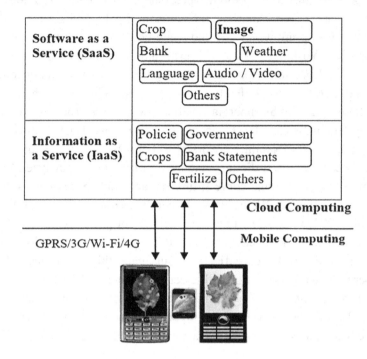

Disease

With recent advances in technology, Prasad, Kumar, and Ghosh (2016a) proposed a system that can recognize plant leaf disease using efficient CV algorithms. The author used Gabor Wavelet transform (GWT) over GLCM for disease patch pattern computation which is further used for classification using k-NN. The dataset used was a diseased leaf dataset with 5 different pathogen attacks on 4 different species. The system proposed is an Android-based mobile client-server architecture which even an illiterate farmer can operate. The server performs feature extraction followed by classification of the disease and inform the farmer in the field via a fax-back system. The accuracy reported by the author is 93% for diseased identification. In this paper, author have also mentioned an unsupervised leaf diseased patch segmentation in $L*a*b*$ color space which is quite acceptable (Prasad, Kumar, & Ghosh, 2016a). Such system in future may be used to monitor, control and manage the agricultural productions automatically without any manual expert via MC2 (Prasad, Kumar, & Ghosh, 2013a, 2015). The tremendous growth in MC2 and its rising popularity among people all over the globe have motivated researchers to develop ubiquitous plant disease diagnosis system.

DATASETS

For plant biometric system, several plant leaf datasets are introduces with different challenges like the first dataset which is mostly used by researchers is the Flavia Leaf dataset (Wu et al. 2007) having 32 different species and 1900+ high quality image samples. Secondly, ICL (Intelligent Computing Laboratory) Leaf dataset (ICL) with 220 species, third is 100 plant leaf dataset (Mallah, Cope, & Orwell, 2013), and fourth is Swedish leaf dataset 11 (Sderkvist, 2001). All these leaf datasets are semi-segmented and so pre-processing is reduced. While there is another big dataset called PlantCLEF 2015 dataset[8] which is composed of 113,205 plant images of 1000 different species (trees, herbs and ferns) in Western European regions (Goeau, 2015). A diseased leaf dataset collected from Indian Institute of Technology (IIT) Roorkee and Forest Research Institute (FIR) Dehradun campuses (Prasad, Kumar, & Ghosh, 2014, 2016a) is also available for plant leaf disease identification. More details related plant leaf datasets and research papers can be found on http://www.visionbib.com/bibliography/applicat84211.html.

COMPARISON EVALUATION

The contribution of automated plant biometric system since 2000 is shown using a graph (Figure 7), where y-axis shows the number of good related articles published in respective year on current topic (Wang et al., 2016). The increasing number shows the dedication of CV researchers in agriculture field. For comparison, several datasets are compared with different approaches proposed, as mentioned in this chapter, is shown in Table 1. The first column is for Flavia dataset and second for ICL leaf dataset. The third column is a mixed dataset highlighted only to compare the highest accuracy achieved by various researchers in recent years in plant species identification. From Table 1, it is seen that CNN is currently the best feature map

Figure 7. Distribution of standard publications in field of plant species identification

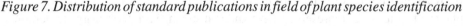
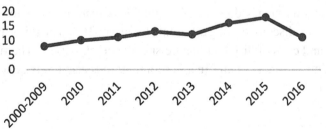

Table 1. State-of-the-art in plant biometric system

Flavia Dataset		ICL Dataset		Other Datasets	
Methods	**Accuracy (%)**	**Methods**	**Accuracy (%)**	**Methods**	**Accuracy (%)**
MCC (Adamek & Connor, 2004)	84.93	IDCS (Ling, Member, & Jacobs, 2007)	81.39	Wang et al., 2016	93.00
TAR (Alajlan, Kamel, & Freeman, 2007)	85.03	MCC (Adamek & Connor, 2004)	73.17	**Lee, Chan, Wilkin, & Remagnino, 2015**	**99.50**
IDSC (Ling, Member, & Jacobs, 2007)	88.11	TAR (Alajlan, Kamel, & Freeman, 2007)	78.25	Jassmann, 2015	81.60
TSLA (Mouine, Yahiaoui, & Verroust-Blondet, 2013)	93.53	Fourier (Wang et al. 2015)	60.08	Kruse et al., 2014	95.00
MARCH (Wang et al. 2015)	96.15	MARCH (Wang et al. 2015)	85.31	Arunpriya & Thanamani, 2014	88.60
Prasad, Kumar, & Ghosh, 2016	**97. 96**	**Prasad, Kumar, & Ghosh, 2016**	**96.50**	Priyankara & Withanage, 2015	96.48

to represent plant leaves for accurate classification. The problem with CNN is it needs a proper training with large datasets which requires huge number of resources.

AaaS framework in reality may server agro-community in all sectors with high accuracy assisting famers when, what and how to plant with what fertility rate and chemical/natural controls. It even aware one remote farmer working in other end of world with the situations of other farmer's failures while cultivation.

CONCLUSION

In this chapter, a brief survey of automated plant biometric systems since decades is presented highlighting the current state-of-the-art. According to several authors, plant leaf patterns are represented mathematically using various transforms including both spatial and frequency domain. More than fifty feature spaces for ten different plant datasets are discussed using different classifiers. Based on this survey, we find out the pros and cons of different feature spaces and classifiers. The future scopes and applications of such systems in agro-communities also motivate researchers to work in this field.

REFERENCES

Adamek, T., & Connor, N. E. O. (2004). A Multiscale Representation Method for Nonrigid Shapes with a Single Closed Contour. *IEEE Transactions on Circuits and Systems for Video Technology*, *14*(5), 742–753. doi:10.1109/TCSVT.2004.826776

Alajlan, N., El, I., Kamel, M. S., & Freeman, G. (2007). Shape retrieval using triangle-area representation and dynamic space warping. *Pattern Recognition*, *40*(7), 1911–1920. doi:10.1016/j.patcog.2006.12.005

Andrade, I. M., Mayo, S. J., Kirkup, D., & Van Den Berg, C. (2008). Comparative morphology of populations of Monstera Adans. (Araceae) from natural forest fragments in Northeast Brazil using elliptic Fourier analysis of leaf outlines. *Kew Bulletin*, *63*(2), 193–211. doi:10.1007/s12225-008-9032-z

Arunpriya, C., & Thanamani, A. S. (2014). A novel leaf recognition technique for plant classification. *Int J Comput Eng Appl*, *4*, 42–55.

Backes, A. R., Gonalves, W. N., Martinez, A. S., & Bruno, O. M. (2010). Texture analysis and classification using deterministic tourist walk. *Pattern Recognition*, *43*(3), 685–694. doi:10.1016/j.patcog.2009.07.017

Bakhsh, A., Colvin, T. S., Jaynes, D. B., Kanwar, R. S., & Tim, U. (2000). Using Soil Attributes and GIS for Interpretation of Spatial Variability in Yield. *Transactions of the ASAE. American Society of Agricultural Engineers*, *43*(3), 819–828. doi:10.13031/2013.2976

Brugger, F. (2011). *Mobile Applications in Agriculture*. Retrieved from http://www.gsma.com/mobilefordevelopment/wpcontent/uploads/2011/12/SyngentaReportonm-Agricultureabridgedwebversion.pdf

Bruno, O. M., deOliveira Plotze, R., Falvo, M., & deCastro, M. (2008). Fractal dimension applied to plant identification. *Inform. Sciences*, *178*(12), 2722–2733. doi:10.1016/j.ins.2008.01.023

Candan, K. S., Kim, J. W., Nagarkar, P., Nagendra, M., & Yu, R. (2011). RanKloud: Scalable multimedia data processing in server clusters. *IEEE MultiMedia*, *18*(1), 64–77. doi:10.1109/MMUL.2010.70

Casanova, D., de Mesquita Sa Junior, J. J., & Bruno, O. M. (2009). Plant leaf identification using Gabor wavelets. *International Journal of Imaging Systems and Technology*, *19*(3), 236–243. doi:10.1002/ima.20201

Clark, J. (2004). Identification of botanical specimens using artificial neural networks. *Proc. of the 2004 IEEE Symp. On Computational Intelligence in Bioinformatics and Computational Biology*, 87-94. Retrieved from http://ieeexplore.ieee.org/xpls/abs all.jsp?arnumber=1393938

Clark, J. Y. (2009). Neural networks and cluster analysis for unsupervised classification of cultivated species of Tilia (Malvaceae). *Botanical Journal of the Linnean Society*, *159*(2), 300–314. doi:10.1111/j.1095-8339.2008.00891.x

Cope, J. S., Remagnino, P., Barman, S., & Wilkin, P. (2010). The extraction of venation from leaf images by evolved vein classifiers and ant colony algorithms. In Advanced Concepts for Intelligent Vision Systems (Vol. 6474 LNCS, pp. 135-144). doi:10.1007/978-3-642-17688-3_14

Cope, J. S., Corney, D., Clark, J. Y., Remagnino, P., & Wilkin, P. (2012). Plant species identification using digital morphometrics: A review. *Expert Systems with Applications*, *39*(8), 7562–7573. doi:10.1016/j.eswa.2012.01.073

Du, J. X., Huang, D. S., Wang, X. F., & Gu, X. (2006). Computer-aided plant species identification (CAPSI) based on leaf shape matching technique. *Transactions of the Institute of Measurement and Control*, *28*(3), 275–285. doi:10.1191/0142331206tim176oa

Fu, H., & Chi, Z. (2006). Combined thresholding and neural network approach for vein pattern extraction from leaf images. *IEE Process-Vision, Image and Signal Process*, *153*(6), 881–892. doi:10.1049/ip-vis:20060061

Gage, E., & Wilkin, P. (2008). A morphometric study of species delimitation in Sternbergialutea (Alliaceae, Amaryllidoideae) and its allies S. sicula and S. greuteriana. *Botanical Journal of the Linnean Society*, *158*(3), 460–469. doi:10.1111/j.1095-8339.2008.00903.x

Goeau, H., Joly, A., & Bonnet, P. (2015). LifeClef plant identification task 2015. CLEF Working Notes 2015.

Gore, K., Lobo, S., & Doke, P. (2012). *GappaGoshti*: Digital inclusion for rural mass. In *2012 4th Int.Conf. on Communication Systems and Networks, COMSNETS 2012* (pp. 1-6). doi:10.1109/COMSNETS.2012.6151383

Gu, X., Du, J.-X., & Wang, X.-F. (2005). Leaf recognition based on the combination of wavelet transform and Gaussian interpolation. *Advances in Intelligent Computing*, 253-262. doi:2710.1007/11538059

Hearn, D. J. (2009). Shape analysis for the automated identification of plants from images of leaves. *Taxon*, *58*(3), 934–954.

Heinze, C., Goss, S., & Pearce, A. (1999). Plant recognition in military simulation: Incorporating machine learning with intelligent agents.*Proc. of IJCAI-99 Workshop on Team Behavior and Plan Recognition*, 53-64.

Hong, A., Gang, C., Jun-li, L., Chi, Z., & Zhang, D. (2004). A flower image retrieval method based on ROI feature. *Journal of Zhejiang University. Science*, *5*(7), 764–772. doi:10.1631/jzus.2004.0764 PMID:15495304

Huang, Q., Jain, A. K., Stockman, G. C., & Smucker, A. J. M. (1992). Automatic Image Analysis of Plant Root Structures. In *11th IEEE IAPR Int. Conf. on Pattern Recognition* (pp. 569-572). doi:10.1109/ICPR.1992.201842

Huang, Z., Huang, D.-S., Du, J.-X., Quan, Z., & Gua, S.-B. (2006). Bark Classification Based on Contourlet Filter Features. In Intelligent Computing (pp. 1121-1126). Springer Berlin Heidelberg.

Izzat Din Abdul Aziz, M. H. H., Ismail, M. J., Mehat, M., & Haroon, N. S. (2009). Remote monitoring in agricultural greenhouse using wireless. *Int. J. Engg. Techlon*, *9*(9), 35–43.

Jain, D. K., Tim, U., & Jolly, R. W. (1995). A spatial decision support system for livestock production planning and environmental management. *Applied Engineering in Agriculture*, *11*(5), 711–719. doi:10.13031/2013.25795

Jassmann, T. J. (2015). *Mobile Leaf Classification Application Utilizing a Convolutional Neural Network* (Doctoral dissertation). Appalachian State University.

Kim, T., Bae, N.-J., Shin, C.-S., Park, J. W., Park, D., & Cho, Y.-Y. (2013). An Approach for a Self-Growing Agricultural Knowledge Cloud in Smart Agriculture. In *Multimedia and Ubiquitous Eng* (pp. 699–706). Springer. doi:10.1007/978-94-007-6738-6_86

Kruse, O. M. O., Prats-Montalban, J. M., Indahl, U. G., Kvaal, K., Ferrer, A., & Futsaether, C. M. (2014). Pixel classification methods for identifying and quantifying leaf surface injury from digital images. *Computers and Electronics in Agriculture*, *108*, 155–165. doi:10.1016/j.compag.2014.07.010

Kumar, N., Belhumeur, P. N., Biswas, A., Jacobs, D. W., Kress, W. J., Lopez, I. C., & Soares, J. V. B. (2012). Leafsnap: A computer vision system for automatic plant species identification. In Comput. Vision - ECCV 2012 (Vol. 7573 LNCS, pp. 502-516). doi: 36 doi:10.1007/978-3-642-33709-3

Lee, C., & Chen, S. (2006). Classification of leaf images. *International Journal of Imaging Systems and Technology*, *16*(1), 15–23. doi:10.1002/ima.20063

Lee, S. H., Chan, C. S., Wilkin, P., & Remagnino, P. (2015, September). Deep-Plant: Plant Identification with convolutional neural networks. In *Image Processing (ICIP), 2015 IEEE International Conference on* (pp. 452-456). IEEE.

Lexer, C., Joseph, J., van Loo, M., Prenner, G., Heinze, B., Chase, M. W., & Kirkup, D. (2009). The use of digital image-based morphometrics to study the phenotypic mosaic in taxa with porous genomes. *Taxon*, 349–364.

Li, Y., Chi, Z., & Feng, D. D. (2006). Leaf vein extraction using independent component analysis. In *IEEE Int. Conf. on Systems, Man and Cybernetics*, (pp. 3890-3894). doi:10.1109/ICSMC.2006.384738

Li, W.-S., Candan, K. S., & Hirata, K. (1997). SEMCOG: An Integration of SEMantics and COGnition- based Approaches for Image Retrieval. In *12th Annual Symp. on Applied Computing (SAC-97)*, (pp. 36-43). doi:10.1145/331697.331727

Li, W.-S., Seluk Candan, K., Hirata, K., & Hara, Y. (1998). Hierarchical image modeling for object-based media retrieval. *Data & Knowledge Engineering*, *27*(2), 139–176. doi:10.1016/S0169-023X(97)00058-X

Ling, H., Member, S., & Jacobs, D. W. (2007). Shape Classification Using the Inner-Distance. *IEEE Transactions on Pattern Analysis and Machine Intelligence*, *29*(2), 286–299. doi:10.1109/TPAMI.2007.41 PMID:17170481

Liu, J., Zhang, S., & Deng, S. (2009). A method of plant classification based on wavelet transforms and support vector machines. In *Emerging Intelligent Computing Technology and Applicat* (pp. 253–260). Springer Berlin Heidelberg.

Ma, W. M. W., Zha, H. Z. H., Liu, J. L. J., Zhang, X. Z. X., & Xiang, B. X. B. (2008). Image-based plant modeling by knowing leaves from their apexes. In *2008 IEEE 19th Int. Conf. on Pattern Recognition*, (pp. 2-5). doi:10.1007/978-3-642-04070-2_29

Mallah, C., Cope, J., & Orwell, J. (2013). Plant leaf classification using probabilistic integration of shape, texture and margin features. Signal Processing. *Pattern Recognition and Applications*, *5*, 1.

MacLeod, N., Benfield, M., & Culverhouse, P. (2010). Time to automate identification. *Nature*, *467*(7312), 154–155. doi:10.1038/467154a PMID:20829777

McLellan, T., & Endler, J. A. (1998). The relative success of some methods for measuring and describing the shape of complex objects. *Systematic Biology*, *47*(2), 264–281. doi:10.1080/106351598260914

Meade, C., & Parnell, J. (2003). Multivariate analysis of leaf shape patterns in Asian species of the Uvaria group (Annonaceae). *Botanical Journal of the Linnean Society, 143*(3), 231–242. doi:10.1046/j.1095-8339.2003.00223.x

Melville, R. (1937). The accurate definition of leaf shapes by rectangular coordinates. *Annals of Botany, 1*, 673–679.

Mouine, S., Yahiaoui, I., & Verroust-Blondet, A. (2013). A Shape based Approach for Leaf Classification using Multiscale Triangular Representation. In *Process. of the 3rd ACM Conf. on Int. Conf. on multimedia retrieval*, (pp. 127134). ACM.

Mullen, R. J., Monekosso, D., Barman, S., Remagnino, P., & Wilkin, P. (2008). Artificial ants to extract leaf outlines and primary venation patterns. In Ant Colony Optimization and Swarm Intelligence, (Vol. 5217 LNCS, pp. 251-258). = doi:10.1007/978-3-540-87527-7_24

Mzoughi, O., Yahiaoui, I., Boujemaa, N., & Zagrouba, E. (2015). Semantic-based automatic structuring of leaf images for advanced plant species identification. *Multimedia Tools and Applicat.*, 1-32. doi:10.1007/s11042-015-2603-8

Nam, Y., Hwang, E., & Kim, D. (2008). A similarity-based leaf image retrieval scheme: Joining shape and venation features. *Computer Vision and Image Understanding, 110*(2), 245–259. doi:10.1016/j.cviu.2007.08.002

Natho, G. (1959). Variationsbreite und Bastardbildung bei mitteleuropischen Birkensippen. *Repertorium Novarum Specierum Regni Vegetabilis, 61*(3), 211–273. doi:10.1002/fedr.19590610304

Neto, J. C., Meyer, G. E., Jones, D. D., & Samal, A. K. (2006). Plant species identification using Elliptic Fourier leaf shape analysis. *Computers and Electronics in Agriculture, 50*(2), 121–134. doi:10.1016/j.compag.2005.09.004

Nilsback, M. E., & Zisserman, A. (2010). Delving deeper into the whorl of flower segmentation. *Image and Vision Computing, 28*(6), 10491062. doi:10.1016/j.imavis.2009.10.001

Orr, G., Pettersson-Yeo, W., Marquand, A. F., Sartori, G., & Mechelli, A. (2012). Using Support Vector Machine to identify imaging biomarkers of neurological and psychiatric disease: A critical review. *Neuroscience and Biobehavioral Reviews, 36*(4), 1140–1152. doi:10.1016/j.neubiorev.2012.01.004 PMID:22305994

Pande, A., Jagyasi, B. G., & Choudhuri, R. (2009). Late Blight Forecast Using Mobile Phone Based Agro Advisory System. In Pattern Recognition and Machine Intelligence, (pp. 609-614). Springer Berlin Heidelberg. doi:10.1007/978-3-642-11164-8_99

Park, J., Hwang, E., & Nam, Y. (2008). Utilizing venation features for efficient leaf image retrieval. *Journal of Systems and Software*, *81*(1), 71–82. doi:10.1016/j.jss.2007.05.001

Pauwels, E. J., de Zeeuw, P. M., & Ranguelova, E. B. (2009). Computer-assisted tree taxonomy by automated image recognition. Eng. *Applied Artificial Intelligence*, *22*(1), 26–31. doi:10.1016/j.engappai.2008.04.017

Plant Glossary. (2009). Retrieved April 12, 2015, from http://www.vplants.org/plants/glossary/index.html

Pogorelc, B., Bosni, Z., & Gams, M. (2012). Automatic recognition of gait-related health problems in the elderly using machine learning. *Multimedia Tools and Applications*, *58*(2), 333–354. doi:10.1007/s11042-011-0786-1

Prasad, S., Kudiri, K. M., & Tripathi, R. C. (2011). Relative sub-image based features for leaf recognition using support vector machine. In *Proceedings of the 2011 Int. Conf. on Commun., Computing & Security*, (pp. 343-346). Retrieved from doi:10.1145/1947940.1948012

Prasad, S., Kumar, P., & Tripathi, R. C. (2011). Plant leaf species identification using curvelet transform. In *2011 2nd Int. Conf. on Comput. and Communication Technology (ICCCT)*, (pp. 646-652). IEEE. doi:10.1109/ICCCT.2011.6075212

Prasad, S., Kumar, P. S., & Ghosh, D. (2013a). *AgroMobile*: A Cloud-Based Framework for Agriculturists on Mobile Platform. *Int. J. of Advanced Sci. and Technology*, *59*, 41–52. doi:10.14257/ijast.2013.59.04

Prasad, S., Kumar, P. S., & Ghosh, D. (2013b). Mobile Plant Species Classification: A Low Computational Approach. In *Process. of the 2013 IEEE Second Int. Conf. on Image Inform. Process.*, (pp. 405-409). doi:10.1109/ICIIP.2013.6707624

Prasad, S., Kumar, S. P., & Ghosh, D. (2014). Energy Efficient Mobile Vision System for Plant Leaf Disease Identification. In *IEEE Wireless Commun. and Networking Conf. (WCNC)*, (pp. 3356-3361). doi:10.1109/WCNC.2014.6953083

Prasad, S., Kumar, P. S., & Ghosh, D. (2015). Agriculture-as-a-Service. *IEEE Potentials*.

Prasad, S., Kumar, P. S., & Ghosh, D. (2016a). An efficient low vision plant leaf shape identification system for smart phones. *Multimedia Tools and Applications*, 1–25.

Prasad, S., Peddoju, S. K., & Ghosh, D. (2016b). Multi-resolution mobile vision system for plant leaf disease diagnosis. Signal. *Image and Video Processing*, *10*(2), 379–388. doi:10.1007/s11760-015-0751-y

Chathura, H. A., & Withanage, D. K. (2015) Computer assisted plant identification system for Android. Moratuwa engineering research conference, 148–153.

Revenaz, A., Ruggeri, M., & Martelli, M. (2010). Wireless communication protocol for agricultural machines synchronization and fleet management. In *IEEE Int. Symp. on Industrial Electron*, (pp. 3498-3504). doi:10.1109/ISIE.2010.5637476

Reyes, A. K., Caicedo, J. C., & Camargo, J. E. (2015). Fine-tuning deep convolutional networks for plant recognition. Working notes of CLEF 2015 conference.

Rumpunen, K., & Bartish, I. V. (2002). Comparison of differentiation estimates based on morphometric and molecular data, exemplified by various leaf shape descriptors and RAPDs in the genus Chaenomeles (Rosaceae). *Taxon*, *51*(1), 69–82. doi:10.2307/1554964

Schneider, C. K. (1912). *Illustriertes Handbuchder Laubholzkunde*. Ripol Klassik.

Scotland, R. W., & Wortley, A. H. (2003). How many species of seed plants are there? *Taxon*, *52*(1), 101–104. doi:10.2307/3647306

Sderkvist, O. J. O. (2001). *Computer Vision Classification of Leaves from Swedish Trees*. Academic Press.

Shinde, S., Piplani, D., Srinivasan, K., Singh, D., Sharma, R., & Mohnaty, P. (2014). *mKRISHI* Simplification Of IVR Based Services For Rural Community. In *Process. of the India HCI2014 Conf. on Human Comput. Interaction* (p. 154). ACM.

Sünderhauf, N., McCool, C., Upcroft, B., & Perez, T. (2014). Fine-Grained Plant Classification Using Convolutional Neural Networks for Feature Extraction. In CLEF (Working Notes) (pp. 756-762).

Teng, C. H., Kuo, Y. T., & Chen, Y. S. (2009). Leaf segmentation, its 3D position estimation and leaf classification from a few images with very close viewpoints. In *Image Analysis and Recognition* (pp. 937–946). Springer Berlin Heidelberg. doi:10.1007/978-3-642-02611-9_92

Tim, U. S. (1995). The application of GIS in environmental health sciences: Opportunities and limitations. *Environmental Research*, *71*(2), 75–88. doi:10.1006/enrs.1995.1069 PMID:8977616

Vellidis, G., Garrick, V., Pocknee, S., Perry, C., Kvien, C., & Tucker, M. (2007). How Wireless Will Change Agriculture. *Precision Agriculture*, *7*, 57–67.

Wang, Z., Chi, Z., & Feng, D. (2003). Shape based leaf image retrieval. IEE Process. -. *Vision, Image, and Signal Process.*, *150*(1), 34. doi:10.1049/ip-vis:20030160

Wang, B., Brown, D., Gao, Y., & La Salle, J. (2015). MARCH: Multiscale-arch-height description for mobile retrieval of leaf images. *Inform. Sciences*, *302*, 132–148. doi:10.1016/j.ins.2014.07.028

Wang, Z., Li, H., Zhu, Y., & Xu, T. (2016). Review of Plant Identification Based on Image Processing. *Archives of Computational Methods in Engineering*, 1–18.

Warren, D. (1997). Automated leaf shape description for variety testing in chrysanthemums. In *IET 6th Int. Conf. on Image Process. and its Applicat.* (pp. 497 - 501). doi:10.1049/cp:19970943

White, S., Feiner, S., & Kopylec, J. (2006). Virtual vouchers: Prototyping a mobile augmented reality user interface for botanical species identification. In *Process* (p. 133). IEEE Virtual Reality. doi:10.1109/VR.2006.145

White, S. M., Marino, D. M., & Feiner, S. (2006). *LeafView*: A User Interface for Automated Botanical Species Identification and Data Collection. In *ACM UIST 2006 Conf. Companion*, (pp. 1-2). Montreux, Switzerland: ACM.

White, S. M., Marino, D., & Feiner, S. (2007). Designing a mobile user interface for automated species identification. In Human Factors in Computing Systems, CHI'07, (pp. 291-294). doi:10.1145/1240624.1240672

Wu, S. G., Bao, F. S., Xu, E. Y., Wang, Y., Chang, Y., & Xiang, Q. (2007). A Leaf Recognition Algorithm for Plant Classification Using Probabilistic Neural Network. In *Int. Symp. on Signal Process. and Inform. Technology*, (pp. 11-16). doi:10.1109/ISSPIT.2007.4458016

Wu, S. G., Bao, F. S., Xu, E. Y., Wang, Y., Chang, Y., & Xiang, Q. (2007). A Leaf Recognition Algorithm for Plant Classification Using Probabilistic Neural Network. In *Int. Symp. on Signal Process. and Inform. Technology*, (pp. 11-16). doi:10.1109/ISSPIT.2007.4458016

Yanikoglu, B., Aptoula, E., & Tirkaz, C. (2014). Automatic plant identification from photographs. *Machine Vision and Applications*, *25*(6), 1369–1383. doi:10.1007/s00138-014-0612-7

Ye, L., & Keogh, E. (2009). Time series shapelets: a new primitive for data mining. *Process. of the 15th ACM SIGKDD Int.Conf. on Knowledge Discovery and Data Mining*, 947-956. doi:10.1145/1557019.1557122

Yoshioka, Y., Iwata, H., Ohsawa, R., & Ninomiya, S. (2004). Analysis of petal shape variation of Primula sieboldii by elliptic Fourier descriptors and principal component analysis. *Annals of Botany*, *94*(5), 657–664. doi:10.1093/aob/mch190 PMID:15374833

Zeng, G., Birchfield, S. T., & Wells, C. E. (2010). Rapid automated detection of roots in minirhizotron images. *Machine Vision and Applications*, *21*(3), 309–317. doi:10.1007/s00138-008-0179-2

Zhao, Z.-Q., Ma, L.-H., Cheung, Y., Wu, X., Tang, Y., & Chen, C. L. P. (2015). *ApLeaf*: An efficient android-based plant leaf identification system. *Neurocomputing*, *151*, 1112–1119. doi:10.1016/j.neucom.2014.02.077

Zulkifli, Z., Saad, P., & Mohtar, I. A. (2011). Plant leaf identification using moment invariants & General Regression Neural Network. In *2011 11th Int.Conf. on Hybrid Intelligent Systems (HIS)*, (pp. 430-435). doi:10.1109/HIS.2011.6122144

ENDNOTES

1   The author is currently in NTU, Singapore as Research Fellow.

2   http://apps.kew.org/herbcat/navigator.do_

3   Several research are going on Plants, Leaf Shapes, Leaf Analysis and Leaf Segmentation. http://www.visionbib.com/bibliography/applicat84211. html#Plants, Leaf Shapes, Leaf Analysis, Leaf Segmentation

4   http://leafzone.keydown.org/index.html_

5   http://flavia.sourceforge.net/

6   Several research going on Plants species, Flowers, Flower Shape and Flower Color. http://www.visionbib.com/bibliography/applicat842f1.html#Plants, Flowers, Flower Shape, Flower Color

7   http://www.imageclef.org/2011/Plants_

8   http://www.imageclef.org/_

Chapter 3
Business Applications
of Deep Learning

Armando Vieira
Redoctopus, UK

ABSTRACT

Deep Learning (DL) took Artificial Intelligence (AI) by storm and has infiltrated into business at an unprecedented rate. Access to vast amounts of data extensive computational power and a new wave of efficient learning algorithms, helped Artificial Neural Networks to achieve state-of-the-art results in almost all AI challenges. DL is the cornerstone technology behind products for image recognition and video annotation, voice recognition, personal assistants, automated translation and autonomous vehicles. DL works similarly to the brain by extracting high-level, complex abstractions from data in a hierarchical and discriminative or generative way. The implications of DL supported AI in business is tremendous, shaking to the foundations many industries. In this chapter, I present the most significant algorithms and applications, including Natural Language Processing (NLP), image and video processing and finance.

1. INTRODUCTION

Artificial Intelligence (AI) is a relatively new area of research – that started in the 50's – marked by some successes and many failures. The initial enthusiasm originated in the materialization of the first electronic computer, soon fade away with the realization that most problems that the brain do in a blink are in fact very hard to solve by machines. These problems include, locomotion in uncontrolled environments, language translation, or voice and image recognition. Despite many attempts, it also

DOI: 10.4018/978-1-5225-2545-5.ch003

become clear that the traditional approach to solve complex mathematical equations was insufficient to solve the most basic situations that a 2 years old toddler had no difficulty – like understand basic language concepts.

This lead to the so-called long "AI winter", where many researchers simply gave up of creating machines with human level cognitive capabilities – despite some successes in between, like the IBM machine Deep Blue that become the best Chess player in the world, or the application of neural networks for hand writing digits recognition in late 80's.

But AI is today one of the most exciting research fields with plenty of practical applications, from autonomous vehicles to drug discovery, robotics, language translation and games. Challenges that seemed insurmountable just a decade ago have been solved – sometimes with super-human accuracy - and are now present in products and ubiquitous applications, like voice recognition, navigation systems, facial emotion detection and even in art creation, like music and painting. For the first time, AI is leaving the research labs materializing in products that may seems to have emerged from Science Fiction movies.

How this revolution became possible in such a short period of time? What changed in recent years that puts us closer to the General AI dream? The answer is more a gradual improvement of algorithms and hardware than a single breakthrough. But certainly on the top of the list is Deep Neural Networks, or commonly referred Deep Learning (DL) (I. Goodfellow 2006).

Artificial Neural Networks is hardly a new field. They were around for about 50 years and got some practical recognition after mid 80's with the introduction of a method (Backpropagation) that allowed training of multiple layers neural networks. However the true birth on Deep Learning may be traced to the year of 2006, when Geoffrey Hinton (R. S. G. E. Hinton 2006) presented an algorithm to efficiently train deep neural networks in an unsupervised way – data without labels. They called them Deep Belief Networks, and consisting of staked Restrictive Boltzmann Machines. They differ from previous networks since they were generative models capable to learn the statistical properties of data being presented without any supervision.

Inspired by the depth structure of the brain, deep learning architectures have revolutionized the approach to data analysis (R. S. G. E. Hinton 2006) (I. Goodfellow 2006) (Schmidhuber 2015, Schmidhuber 2015). Deep Learning networks have won a paramount number of hard machine learning contests, from voice recognition, image classification, Natural Language Processing (NLP) to time-series prediction – sometimes by a large margin. Traditionally AI relied on heavily handcrafted features, for instance, to have decent results in image classification, several pre-processing techniques have to be applied, like filters, edge detection, etc. The beauty of DL is that most, if not all, features can be learned automatically from the data – provide enough (sometimes million) training data examples are available.

Figure 1. DL has a higher capacity to learn from large amounts of data

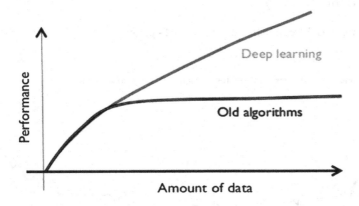

Being essentially non-supervised machines, deep neural architectures can be exponentially more efficient than shallow ones. The number of computational elements is only limited by the number of training samples – which can be of the order of billions. Deep models can be trained with hundreds of millions of weights and therefore tend to outperform shallow models such as SVMs. Moreover, theoretical results suggest that deep architectures are fundamental to learn the kind of complex functions that represent high-level abstractions (e.g. vision, language, semantics), characterized by many factors of variation that interact in non-linear ways, making the learning process difficult.

1.1. From a Long Winter to a Blossom Spring

Today it's difficult to find any AI based technology that do not rely on Deep Learning. The implications of DL in technological applications of AI will be so profound that we may be on the verge of the biggest technological revolution of all times.

One of the remarkable features of DL neural networks is their (almost) unlimited capacity to accommodate information from large quantities of data without overfitting – as long as strong regularizers are applied. DL is much of a science as of an Art and, while it's very common to train models with billions of parameters, on millions of training examples, that is only be possible with carefully selection and fine-tuning of the learning machine.

The main characteristics that make DNN unique can be summarized in the following points:

1. High learning capacity (since DNN have millions of parameters, they don't saturate easily - the more data you have the more they learn).

Figure 2. Evolution of interest on deep learning
Source: Google Trends

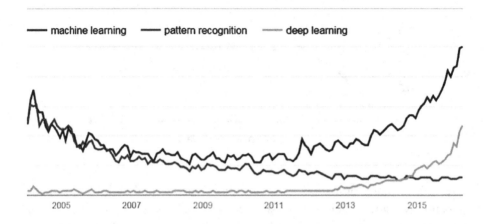

Interest over time. Web Search. Worldwide, 2004 - present.

2.   No feature engineering required (learning can be performed end-to-end – being robotic control, language translation or image recognition).
3.   Abstraction representation (DNN are capable of generating abstract concepts from data).
4.   High Generative capability (DNN are much more than simple discriminative machine – they can generate unseen - but plausible - data based on latent representations).
5.   Knowledge transfer (this is one of the most remarkable properties – we can teach a machine in one large set of data - images, music or biomedical data – and transfer the learning to a similar problem where less data is known. One of the most remarkable examples is DNN that capture and replicate artistic styles).
6.   Excellent unsupervised capabilities (as long as you have lots of data, DNN can learn hidden statistical representations without any labels required).
7.   Multimodal learning (DNN can integrate seamlessly disparate sources of high-dimensional data, like text, images, video and audio to solve hard problems like automatic video captions generation and visual questions and answers).
8.   They are relatively easy to compose and embed domain knowledge to handle uncertainty.

The less appealing aspects of DNN models are[1]:

1. They are hard to interpret - despite the ability to extract latent features from the data, DNN are black boxes that learn by associations and co-occurrences. They lack the transparency and interpretability of other methods, like decision trees.
2. They are only partially able to uncover complex causality relations or nested structural relationships, common in domains like biology.
3. They can be relatively complex and time consuming to train, with many hyper parameters that require careful fine-tuning.
4. They are sensitive to initialization and learning rate – its very easy the network to be unstable and not converge. This is particularly acute for recurrent neural networks.
5. A loss function has to be provided - sometimes is very hard to find a good one.
6. Knowledge is not incremental – each dataset has to be trained from scratch.
7. Knowledge transference is possible for certain models, but its specific for each problem.

1.2. Why DL Is Different?

Machine Learning (ML) is a vague but hardly new concept. It can be summarized in one simple sentence: finding patterns in data. These patterns can be anything from cycles in the stock market to distinguish images of cats from dogs. ML can also be described as the art of teaching machines how to make decisions. Yes, an art; perhaps more than a science.

ANNs started with a work by McCullogh and Pitts who showed that sets of simple units (artificial neurons) could perform all possible logic operations - thus capable of universal computation. This work was concomitant to Von Neumann and Turing who first dealt with statistical aspects of the information processing of the brain and how to build a machine capable of reproduce them. Frank Rosembalt invented the Perceptron machine to perform simple pattern classification. However, this new learning machine was incapable of solving simple problems, like the logic XOR. In 1969 Minsky and Papert showed that Perceptrons had intrinsic limitations that could not be transcended, thus leading to a fading enthusiasm for ANNs during the 70's.

1.3. The Multilayer Preceptron

The Multilayer Preceptron (MLP) was proposed to solve problems that were not linearly separable, i.e., categories that cannot be separate by a set of straight lines. An example of a multilayered perceptron MLP is shown in next Figure:

Figure 3. The multilayer preceptron

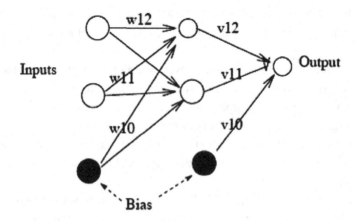

The ANN consists of a set of inputs, connected to a set of hidden unities through weights w. The hidden unities are connected to the output through weights v. Initially all the weights and the bias term are set to random numbers. The activity in the network is propagated forwards via weights from the input layer to the hidden layer where some function of the net activation is calculated, normally the transfer functions are sigmoid, *tanh* or, more recently, rectified linear unities (*ReLU*). Then the activity is propagated via more weights to the output neurons.

Two sets of weights must be updated: those between the hidden and output layers and those between the input and hidden layers. The error due to the first set of weights is calculable by Least Mean Square rule. To propagate backwards that part of the error due to the errors in the second set of weights (W) we used the backpropagation algorithm, that simply states that the errors should be proportional to the weight contribution. The algorithm has two main parameters: learning rate and momentum (to avoid traps in local minima). Also the number of unities in the hidden layer is an important input (more hidden unities will increase the computational power but it could also compromise the generalization capabilities).

The choice of the network parameters is normally performed by *n*fold cross validation: fixing *n*-1 parts of the training data for training and the remaining for testing, and then swapping these segments.

The key insight that makes this procedure relatively efficient for feedforward networks is that—simply by applying the chain rule from basic calculus—the derivatives of the error with respect to filter values in a given layer can be efficiently computed from those in the layer just above. Derivative computations thus start at the top layer and then propagate backwards through the network down to the first layers.

Another important technical innovation enabling large-scale backpropagation is stochastic gradient descent (SGD). SGD involves breaking training data into small, randomly chosen batches. Gradient descent is done on each batch in sequence until the training data are exhausted, at which point the procedure can begin again, usually on newly chosen random batches. SGD enables backpropagation on much larger data sets.

2. DEEP NEURAL NETWORKS

So, why all the excitement about AI powered by Deep Learning? As mentioned before, the difference of DL is both quantitative (an improvement of 5% in voice recognition makes all the difference between a useful user interface or a useless one) and qualitative (how DL models are trained, the subtle relations they can extract from high-dimensional data and how these relations can be integrate into an unified perspective).

It was long known that ANN with more hidden layers (deeper) could have a higher computational power and be better suited to solve classification or regression problems (D. E. Rumelhart 1986). The challenge was how to train them, i.e., learn the weights or connections that link a layer of neurons to the others. The backpropagation algorithm worked fine for ANN with a single layer, but it strives to generalize for deeper architectures due to the so called vanish gradient problem – i.e., the correction signal from the output was dissipated as it travels to lower layers.

However, in 2006, Hinton et al. proposed an unsupervised learning algorithm using a method called Contrastive Divergence, that was successful in training deep generative models known as Deep Belief Networks (DBN) (R. S. G. E. Hinton 2006). A DBN is composed of a stack of Restricted Boltzmann Machines (RBMs) trained by a greedy, layer-by-layer learning algorithm (contrastive divergence). They are normally used for unsupervised tasks, but that could be fine-tuned to perform supervised learning by attaching a Softmax layer to the top layer.

There are many DL approaches and architectures, but most of the DNNs can be classified into five major categories:

1. Networks for unsupervised learning, designed to capture high-order correlation of data by capturing jointly statistical distributions with the associated classes - when available. Bayes rule can later be used to create a discriminative learning machine.
2. Networks for supervised learning. These networks are designed to provide maximum discriminative power in classification problem are trained only with labeled data - all the outputs should be tagged.
3. Hybrid or semi-supervised networks, where the objective is to classify data using the outputs of a generative (unsupervised) model. Normally, data is used

to pre-train the network weights to speed up the learning process prior to the supervision stage.

4. Reinforcement learning - the agent interact and changes the environment and receives feedback only after a set of actions are completed. This type of learning is normally used in the field of robotics and games.

5. Generative Neural Networks - Deep generative models are a powerful approach to unsupervised and semi-supervised learning where the goal is to discover the hidden structure within data without relying on labels. Since they are generative, such models can form a rich imagery the world in which they are used: an imagination that can harnessed to explore variations in data, to reason about the structure and behavior of the world, and ultimately, for decision-making. A great advantage of these models is there is no need to supplement an external loss function as they learn the structure of the data autonomously.

Despite all the hype around deep learning, traditional models still play an important rule in solving machine learning problems, especially when the amount of data is not very large of the input features are relatively "clean". Also, if the number of variables is large compared with the number of training examples, SVMs or ensemble methods, like Random Forest or Extreme Gradient Boosting trees (XGBoost), may be simpler, faster and better options.

The most popular types of DNN architectures are: stacked denoising autoencoders (SdAE), Deep Belief Networks (DBN), Convolutional Neural Networks (CNN) and Recurrent Neural Networks (RNN). Many advances in machine vision were achieved using CNNs - making this DNN type the standard for image processing. However, there are many flavors of DNNs that are applicable to the various business applications, depending on architecture, connectivity, initialization, training method and loss functions being used.

Figure 4 presents a brief summary of these popular DNN architectures. Following is a brief guideline to the terminology and the most popular types of deep neural networks.

2.1. Convolutional Neural Networks (CNN)

A CNN is composed by several blocks composed by different types of layers. Each module consists of a convolutional layer and a pooling layer. These modules are often stacked up with one on top of another, or with a softmax logistic layer on top of it, to form a deep model. The CNN uses several tricks that makes them well suited for image processing like weight sharing, adaptive filters and pooling. Pooling takes subsamples of the convolutional layer to feed the next layer - acting as a powerful regularizer. Weight sharing and pooling schemes (most usually a

Figure 4. Four of the most popular classes of deep learning architectures in biological data analysis: a) convolutional neural network (CNN) has several levels of convolutional and subsampling layers optionally followed by fully connected layers with deep architecture; b) stacked autoencoder consisting of multiple sparse autoencoders; c) deep belief network (DBN); d) restricted Boltzmann machine (RBM) architecture includes one visible layer and one layer of hidden units

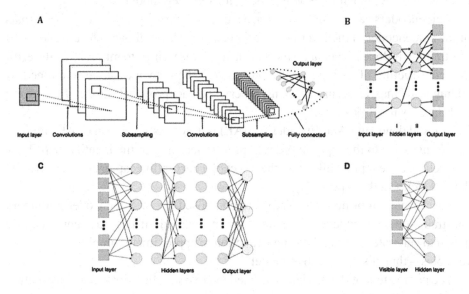

max pooling), allow the CNN to generate conservation properties like translation invariance. CNNs are highly effective and have been commonly used in computer vision and image recognition.

CNNs operate on what should be considered a signal stream rather than a feature vector. That is, fully connected neural nets consist of activation units bound to all inputs of the feature vector. Every unit has a weight specific to each feature in the input. Convolutional layers, on the other hand, utilize weight sharing by sliding a small (trainable) filter of weights across the input vector (or 2D input map, as CNNs are often used on images) and convolving each overlaid region of input with the filter.

CNNs with max-pooling are powerful enough to mimic low-level stages of primates visual cortex having biologically plausible feature detectors, such as Gabor filters. However, once trained, the CNN acts a simple feedforward machine with frozen weights.

2.2. Deep Autoencoders

An autoencoder is a DNN having as outputs the input data input itself. If they are trained with some added noise, these architectures can act as generative models and are called denoising autoencoders. An autoencoder can be trained with a greedy layer-wise mode, much like the DBNs, to form a deep model.

Autoencoders can be stacked to form a deep network by forwarding the outputs of the autoencoder in the layer below as input to the layer above. The unsupervised pre-training is done a layer at a time and each layer is trained to minimizing the error in reconstructing of its input. After pre-trained, the network can be fine-tuned by adding a softmax layer and applying supervised backpropagation - as if they were multilayer perceptrons.

Stacked denoising AutoEncoders (SdAE) is a stochastic version of AE obtained by adding noise to the input in order to prevent learning of the identity map. They try to encode the input while undo the effect of a corruption capturing the statistical dependencies in the inputs.

Variational AutoEncoders (VAE) are composed by an autoencoder with extra constraints on the encoded representations being learned – it learns a latent stochastic model to generate its input data and a function to approximate sampling from latent variables – thus it's a generative model.

The parameters of the model are trained via two loss functions: a reconstruction loss forcing the decoded samples to match the initial inputs (just like a normal autoencoders), and the KL divergence between the learned latent distribution and the prior distribution, acting as a regularization term. You could actually get rid of this latter term entirely, although it does help in learning well-formed latent spaces and reducing overfitting to the training data. See this tutorial and some examples of code applied to the MNIST dataset on the Keras blog.

2.3. Deep Belief Networks

A Boltzmann Machine formed by two layers - one of visible units and other of hidden units with no lateral connections is called a Restricted Boltzmann Machine (RBM). A Deep Belief Network (DBN) is a probabilistic generative model formed by several stacked hidden layers (normally binary). The top two layers are symmetrically connected through indirect connections. Each layer receives a directed connection from the layer below. DBN are trained by greedy layerwise strategy using the Contrastive Divergence (CD) algorithm proposed by Hinton et al. Apart from providing good initialization points for the weights of the network, the DBN also have other interesting properties: 1) we can use all data, even unlabeled datasets; 2) it can be seen as a probabilistic generative model, very useful within the Bayesian framework; and 3) the over-fitting problem, can be effectively alleviated by the pre-training step and other strong regularizers, like dropout.

2.4. Recurrent Neural Networks

Traditional ML methods, like Support vector machines, logistic regression, and feedforward networks, have proved useful without explicitly modeling time in temporal process – by projecting time as space. This assumption, however, is incapable to model long-range dependencies and has limited usability in complex temporal patterns. Recurrent Neutral Networks (RNNs) are a rich family of models differentiable end-to-end, thus amenable to gradient-based training, latter regularized via standard techniques, like dropout or noise injection. Recurrence is key to solve hard problems, like language, as it seems to be present in most of the brain mechanisms.

The first structures of RNN were introduced by Jordan as feedforward networks with a single hidden layer extended with special units. Output node values were fed to the special units, which then feed these values to the hidden nodes at the following time step. If the output values are actions, the special units allow the network to remember actions taken at previous time steps. Additionally, the special units in a Jordan network are self-connected.

RNN are a class of unsupervised or supervised architectures to learn temporal, or sequential, patterns. A RNN can be used to predict the next data point in a sequence using the previous data samples. For instance in text, a sliding window over previous words is used to predict the next word or set of words in the sentence. RNNs are generally trained with Long Short Term Memory (LSTM) algorithm proposed by Schmidhuber (Schmidhuber 2015) or GRU (gated recurrent units). The flip side is that they are difficult to train in capturing long-term dependencies due to the well known gradient vanishing or gradient explosion problems and great care required in optimizing hyper parameters.

RNN have become recently very popular, especially with the introduction of several tricks, like bidirectional learning (forward and backward sequence prediction) and attentive mechanisms that allow the use of dynamic size sliding windows, especially useful to build language models.

2.5. Training DNNs

Almost all DL neural networks are trained evolving the optimizing a loss function, like likelihood maximization. The loss function may assume many forms depending on the problem. The likelihood of a set of parameter values, θ, given outcomes x, is the probability of those observed outcomes given those parameter values, $P(x|\theta)$.

For a classification problem, it's typically defined as the log likelihood, given the observations of labels y, we want to generate a model with a probability distribution than maximizes the log(P(y|x)). This is equivalent to minimizing the cross-entropy, a measure of similarity between two distributions P and Q: the sum of the entropy of P and the Kullback–Leibler divergence between Q and P (also known as the relative entropy of Q with respect to P):

2.5.1. Initialization, Overfitting, and Regularization

Deep Neural Networks are relatively large and complex machines - models with 100 million or even billions of parameters are not uncommon. Models with a large number of free parameters can describe very complex relations within data but extreme caution should be taken that they are able to generalize properly. Traditional ways to regularize DNN include cross validation, noise addition, L2 regularization and, more recently, dropout, i.e., removal of a randomly subset of connections - a very simple but effective technique.

Learning, i.e., adjusting the weights of the neuron connections, is normally performed with backpropagation using Stochastic Gradient Descendent (SGD) in batch mode, with a very small (and decaying) learning rate and a some momentum term. Getting a neural network learning properly is hard. A proper initialization of weights is important to guarantee convergence – normally we should start with a set of small random values in the interval [-1/a, 1/a] where a is the number of connections to the neuron.

The learning rate should be small - depending of the network architecture, complexity of the problem and size of the dataset – the higher the lowest the learning rate. A value between 0.01 and 0.001 is normally a safe choice. The number of epochs is typically in the order of thousands and the batch size not less than 100 – again highly dependent of the problem.

2.6. DL as a Service

2015 may well be considered the year of Deep Learning. Remarkable innovations were achieved, like Microsoft neural net of 152 layers (where 6 or 7 layers was the norm) that lead to the winning of the ImageNet competition - with superhuman accuracy.

At the same time all big players are creating their own DL platforms and open sourcing some of their core algorithms – the era of AI-as-a-service. Amazon, IBM, Google, Facebook, Twitter, Baidu, Yahoo, and Microsoft. Google is offering TensorFlow for free. Next table presents a summary of the principal services offered by these companies.

Table 1. Main machine learning platforms

Company	Cloud-Based ML Platform	DL Technology (Open Sourced)
Amazon	Amazon Machine Learning	DSSTNE
Baidu	-	Deep Speech 2 PaddlePaddle
Facebook	-	TorchNet, FastText
Google	NEXT Cloud	TensorFlow
IBM	Watson	IBM system
Microsoft	Azur	CNTK
Twitter	-	Cortex

Deep Learning is moving to open source and the Cloud. Google, Facebook, IBM, Amazon and Microsoft are trying to establish ecosystems around AI services provided in the cloud. "This technology will be applied in pretty much every industry out there that has any kind of data—anything from genes to images to language"

3. APPLICATIONS TO NATURAL LANGUAGE PROCESSING

Deep Learning is having a tremendous impact in Natural Language Processing (NLP). Language understanding is one of the oldest, and probably the hardest problem for machines. However, as large corpus of data become available on the Internet, DL is a natural option to solve innumerous problems related to understanding human language.

Parsing is a central problem for NLP. It consists in decomposing a sentence in its components (nouns, verbs, adverbs, etc.) and built the syntactic relation between them – the parsing tree. It is a very complex problem due the ambiguity in possible decompositions. For instance the sentence "Alice drove down the street in her car" has at least two possible dependency parses:

Figure 5. Parsing a sentence: two possibilities

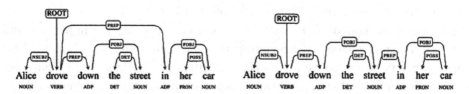

The first corresponds to the (correct) interpretation where Alice is driving in her car; the second corresponds to the (absurd, but possible) interpretation where the street is located in her car. The way humans disambiguate these options is through "common sense" – they know that streets cannot be located in cars. For machines incorporating this world information is very challenging.

Google launched a recent tool SyntaxNet (code based on Tensorflow available at Github SyntaxNet) to solve the hard parsing problem – a 20 to 30 words sentence can have thousands of syntactic structures (see the blog post on Google research Google parser). They used a globally normalized transition-based neural network model that achieves state-of-the-art part-of speech tagging, dependency parsing and sentence compression. The model is a simple feed-forward neural network that operates on a task-specific transition system, yet achieves comparable or better accuracies than recurrent models. The SyntaxNet English language parser, Parsey McParseface, is considered the best parser surpassing, in some cases, human level accuracy. Recently they expand the service to cover about 40 languages.

3.1. Distributed Representations

One of the core problems in NLP is related to the high-dimensionality of data, thus a huge search space) and inference of grammatical rules. Hinton (D. E. Rumelhart 1986) was one of the first to propose the idea that words could be represented via distributed (dense) representations. The advantage of distributed representations is that semantics can easily be accessible and knowledge be transferred from different domains - even on different languages.

Learning a distributed (vectorized) representation for each word is called word embedding. Word2vec is the most popular approach to create a distributed representation of words; It's a publicly available library providing an efficient implementation of skip-gram based vector representations for words. The model and implementation is based on the work of Mikolov et al. (Mikolov & Sutskever 2013). In addition to the implementation, the authors also provide vector representations of words and phrases learnt by training this model on Google News Dataset (about 100 billion words). Vectors can be up to 1000-dimensional containing 3 million words and phrases. An interesting feature of these vector representations is that they capture linear regularities in the language. For example the result of the vectorized words equation: "Madrid" - "Spain" + "France" is "Paris".

After the "bag of words" (BOW) - with the TFIDF trick - Word2vec is probably the most used method for NLP problems since it's relatively easy to implement and very useful in understanding (in an unsupervised way) hidden relations in the data. There is a very good and well-documented Python implementation of word2vec, Gensim. It can be used with pre-trained vectors or trained to learn the embeddings

Figure 6. The schematic representation of word2vec algorithm—word W(t) is used to predict context words W(t-2)...W(t+2)—here a context window of K=5 is considered

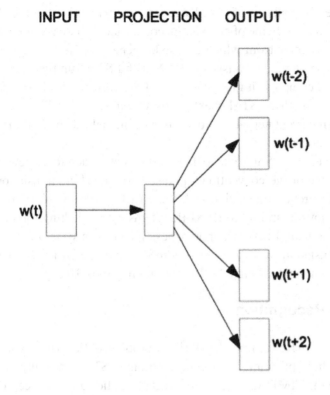

from scratch given a large training corpus - normally on the order of million of documents.

Le et al. also proposed a method to encode whole (variable size) paragraphs using a similar technique; they called it Paragraph Vector. The paragraph vector is shared across all contexts generated from the same paragraph but not across paragraphs. Each word vector is shared across paragraphs. Kiros et al. (R. Kiros 2015) introduced the idea of Skip-Though Vectors using unsupervised learning to encode sentences. The model used a RNN to reconstruct the surrounding sentences of an encoded passage.

3.2. Language Translation

Natural Language Translation is a very hard problem that has been defeating a satisfactory solution since the eve of AI in the 50's. Traditional DNNs have some limitations in dealing with this problem, like the requirement that the inputs and targets should be encoded with vectors of fixed dimensionality. For sequences of arbitrary length this is a serious limitation[2]. Unlike the traditional statistical machine translation, recent DNN models create a single neural network to jointly represent the distributions of both languages and maximize the translation score. Most models use a scheme of encoder–decoders and encode a source sentence into a fixed-length vector from which a decoder generates the respective translation. The most common model consists of RNN with LSTMs unities that process input sequences and compress it into a large, but fixed, dimensional vector. This vector is later used by another LSTM to extract the output sequence. The second LSTM is essentially a recurrent neural network language model except that it is conditioned on the input sequence.

Sutskever et al. (I. Sutskever 2014) used this approach to achieve state-of-the-art performance of the conventional phrase-based machine translation system on an English-to-French translation task - a BLEU score of 34.81, outperforming the best previous neural network NLP systems, and matching the best published results for non-neural network approaches. When their system is used to re-rank candidate translations from another system, it achieved a BLEU score of 36.5. The implementation involved eight GPUS and training took 10 days to complete.

3.3. Voice Recognition

Automatic Speech Recognition (ASR) is the problem of translating voice transcripts into pioneer the application of Deep Bidirectional LSTM to this problem achieving top results in the TIMIT database. Graves et al. applied applied Deep Bidirectional LSTM to this problem achieving top results in the TIMIT database. They used end-to-end designed for discriminative sequence transcription with recurrent neural networks, namely Connectionist Temporal Classification and Sequence Transduction. These methods do not require forced alignments to pre-segment the acoustic data, as they directly optimize the probability of the target sequence conditioned on the input sequence and are able to learn an implicit language model from the acoustic training data.

A Baidu team recently proposed an advanced Automatic Speech Recognition (ASR) system for translating voice into text (Amodei 2015). The improvement performance of the algorithm is due to deep learning replacing feature extraction modules with a single neural model. The Baidu system, called *Deep Speech 2*, consists of a pipeline that approaches the accuracy of humans in several languages. This system was built on end-to-end deep learning using bidirectional RNN trained in clean and noise environments. In English the speech system was trained on 11,940 hours of speech, and in Mandarin for 9,400 hours. Data synthesis was used to augment the data during training. Training a single model at these scales requires tens of exaFLOPs that would require 3-6 weeks to execute on a single GPU. A recent

Table 2. Performance of deep speech 2 compared with humans

	Read Speech		
Test set	DS1	DS2	Human
WSJ eval'92	4.94	3.60	5.03
WSJ eval'93	6.94	4.98	8.08
LibriSpeech test-clean	7.89	5.33	5.83
LibriSpeech test-other	21.74	13.25	12.69

experiment showed that users, using this system on smartphones, input text faster by speaking then typing.

4. APPLICATIONS TO IMAGE AND VIDEO PROCESSING

Probably the area where most advances were made by DL was in image processing. The human visual perceptual system achieves remarkable object recognition performance even in noisy environments or under geometric transformations or background variation. Recent advances in DNN, particularly using Convolutional Neural Networks, lead to a revolution in image processing and analysis achieving, or even surpassing, human level performance. In this section we will show some applications of deep learning into image processing.

4.1. From ImageNet to Caption Generation

CNNs were one of the first deep learning models - biologically inspired by the mammal visual cortex. In a CNN each unit takes its input from a local receptive field on the layer below forcing it to extract local features. Furthermore units within a plane or feature map are constrained to share a single set of weights, this makes the operations performed by a feature map to be shift invariant. The weight sharing technique also reduces the number of free parameters, thus reducing risk of overfiting. The features of CNNs can be summarized as:

- Convolutional neural network with a sequence of convolution and pooling layers.
- Use convolution to extract spatial invariant features.
- Subsample using spatial average of maps.
- Multilayer neural network (MLP) as a final classifier.

- Sparse connection matrix between layers (weigh sharing) to avoid large computational cost and reduce overfitting.

Complete CNNs are formed by stacking together multiple convolutional layers (each with featuremaps planes and local receptive fields). Sub-sampling layers are also added improving invariance to shift and distortions. During 1990's it become evident that deeper networks perform better. However, larger networks required lots of computational resources and overfit easily since not much data was available.

Krizhevsky et al. (A. Krizhevsky 2012, R. Kiros 2015, Amodei 2015) pioneered the use of a graphical processor units (GPUs) for a fast implementation of a CNN containing 650,000 neurons and 60 million parameters – by contrast LeNet-5 had 60,000 - winning with a top-5 error rate of 15.3% - a far better result than the state of the art technique techniques that reached only 26.2%. Besides using larger data set and bigger networks, these authors used aggressive regularizations techniques to avoid overfitting, like data augmentation (applying slight distortions in shapes, rotations and colours) and dropout to shrink co-adaptions of neurons. This last technique allows a single neuron to learn more robust features without relying on other neighbour neurons.

A trained CNN can be used for classification on the ImageNet data set replacing the final classification layer with a regression network. This regression network is simply an MLP with two hidden layers of 4,096 and 1,024 units, connected finally to the output layer of 4 units which predicts the coordinates of the bounding boxes. The final layer is class-specific having 1,000 versions (one for each class) while the rest of the regression network shares weights. During localization only the regression network's weights are updated, and the remaining larger network only acts as a feature extractor.

Figure 7. Image captioning with CNN

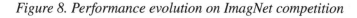

Figure 8. Performance evolution on ImagNet competition

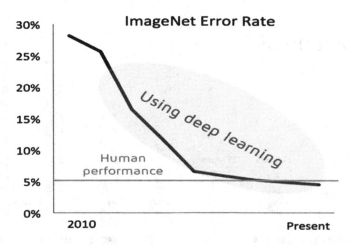

In 2014, Google introduced Inception5 (Google LeNet), a very deep CNN (with 20 layers) that won the ImageNet contest with an error rate of only 6.7% - this work showed the importance of using very deep models to abstract higher level features from the images.

Recently, a Microsoft team achieved a super-human performance on ImageNet with an error rate of only 3.7% with a network named ResNet (residuals network) (K. He 2015) as well as MS COCO data set – the code is available on github. ResNet is based on a simple idea: feed the output of two successive convolutional layer bypassing the input to the next layers - bypassing a single layer did not give much improvements while two layers can be seen as a classifier itself. They were able to train networks of up to 1000 layers.

4.2. Video and Satellite Images

Donahue et al. investigated a CNN model with RNN and proposing a recurrent convolutional architecture for end-to-end large-scale visual challenging task, like activity recognition, image captioning, and video description. This model departs from fixed visual representations and was able to learn compositional representations in space and time. The model is a fully differentiable RNN, capable to learn long-term dependencies, and very appealing since it can map variable-length videos to natural language text. The model is fully trained with backpropagation. The authors show that this model can achieve good results for discriminative or generative text generation tasks. They evaluate the model on TACoS multilevel dataset containing 44,762 video/sentence pairs obtaining a BLUE score of 28.8.

Figure 9. Deep residual learning for image recognition (from He, Zhang, Ren, & Sun, 2016)

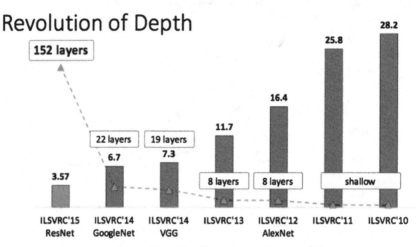

In Mamoshina (2016), the authors combined a CNN and a LSTM for jointly learn the embedding of video and text in order to generate automatic annotation of videos. Due to lack of datasets, the authors relied on photo annotation data and used knowledge transfer techniques. They achieved good accuracy in the subject, verb, and object (SVO) metrics but still far from human level – probably due to the lack of training data.

Satellite image classification is a complex problem involving remote sensing, computer vision, and machine learning. The problem is challenging due to the high variability of the data. Basu et al (S. Basu 2015) proposed a method based on Deep Belief Networks and careful preprocessing of satellite image achieving 97.95% accuracy in two public datasets. One dataset consists of 500,000 image patches covering four broad land cover classes: barren land, trees, grassland and other; 400,000 patches were chosen for training and the remaining 100,000 for testing.

Cargometrics is a startup that uses VHF radio tracking as well satellite images processing through deep learning algorithms to analyze maritime traffic data in order to help predict commodity prices – it tracks the movement of 120 000 ships across the world. Their work is being used by hedge funds to identify pricing and securities opportunities.

Terrapattern uses DL to perform similarity based search for unlabeled satellite photos. It provides an open-ended interface for visual query-by-example, the user clicks in a spot on Terrapattern's map and it will find other locations that look similar.

Vicarious developed deep learning algorithms for vision, language, and motor control. They are mainly focused on visual perception problems, like recognition, segmentation, and scene parsing. They claim that their system requires orders of magnitude less training data than traditional machine learning technique in deploying generative probabilistic models.

5. OTHER APPLICATIONS

5.1. Self-Driven Cars

Deep Learning plays a consider role in Self-driving cars technology by analyzing a disparate set of signals, being video the most challenging. Following the recent success of Google driverless car, almost all carmakers are considering this option in future versions of they cars. Some models under test are Toyota Prius, Audi TT, and Lexus RX450h. Tesla S3 will probably be the first production car with self-driving capabilities included by default. All of these models rely on Deep Learning technology for object recognition, planning, routing and object avoidance.

Google has developed its own custom vehicle relying on a 64-beam laser detector that allows the vehicle to generate a detailed 3D map of its environment. The algorithm use these maps and combines them with high-resolution maps of the world, producing a sufficiently detailed model for self-navigation. Google tested their fleet of vehicles over 2 million km – Tesla tested their own vehicles on more than 130 million km.

Nvidia launched a GPU specific for these cars and Baidu plans to start self-driving cars tests on roads in the United States over 2016 - the core technology is based on DL algorithms. Baidu and Google are pushing towards governmental regulation of self-driven cars claiming it only requires minor changes in actual infrastructure. The goal of Baidu is to run a shuttle service in Chinese cities by 2018.

Autonomous driving requires intuitive psychology. The self-driving car needs to have some common sense understanding or inferring pedestrian behavior and beliefs (do they think it is safe to cross the street? Are they paying attention?) as well as desires (where do they want to go? Are they in a rush?). Similarly, other drivers on the road have similarly complex mental states underlying their behavior (do they want to change lanes or ass another car?). This type of psychological reasoning, along with other types of model-based causal and physical reasoning, are likely to be especially valuable in challenging and novel driving circumstances for which there is little relevant training data.

A recent study concluded that self-driving taxis could reduce the traffic in cities as much as 90%.

5.2. Chatbots

Chatbots, also called Conversational Agents or Dialog Systems, are algorithms designed to have human level conversation capabilities. The goal of bots is to achieve a level of natural conversations indistinguishable from humans. There are two types of bots, Retrieval-based, that use a repository of predefined responses and some heuristics to pick an appropriate response based on the input and context and Generative models that generate automatically responses from past experience and context. Most of the latter rely on Deep Learning technology.

Generative models can be quite sophisticated and learn from creating latent representation of data. They are very flexible but require a large corpus of text (training data). Sequence-to-Sequence learning methods like (I. Sutskever 2014) has a great potential, but most production systems are still based on hard rules for dialogue retrieval. Short text conversations are easier to optimize, especially in closed domain knowledge where the space of possible inputs and outputs is somewhat limited to a specific context.

Vinyals et al. used the sequence-to-sequence framework to create a conversational model able to predict the next sentence given previous sentences in a conversation (O. Vinyals 2015). It was designed as an end-to-end model requiring few crafted features. They trained it in a large conversational dataset and it was competent enough to deliver good advice using an IT helpdesk dataset while showing common sense reasoning in a movie conversational dataset. However, the bot fails to be consistent in the conversations.

Generative models are very powerful, but grammatical mistakes can be costly, so companies still rely on old retrieval technologies. However, as companies get more data, generative models will become the norm - but probably with some human supervision to prevent them from "inappropriate behavior", like happened to the Microsoft Twitter chatbot, Tay

Most big companies are using, testing or considering the implementation of chatbots in their services and operations. Using its experience with its personal assistant Cortana, Microsoft has recently opened a development framework for Chatbots implementation and also released Luis.ai an API for language understanding. Facebook has launched M, a chatbot for its message service and acquired Wit.ai, a company that works on voice recognition technology. IBM has also available a very simple API to embed its powerful knowledge inference machine, Watson, into a conversational bot. Most of these services can be easily incorporated in conversational services like Twitter, Whatsapp, Skype, WeChat, Telegraf or Slack. For instance, Slack allow simple or complex conversation automating based on hard or soft rules.

Retail banks and FinTech start-ups are now exploring the use of Chatbots for digital experiences for checking bank account balances, finding nearby ATMs, making payments and even advising how to spend your money more wisely. Tractica predicts US$ 40.6bn will be spent on artificial intelligence systems for enterprises from 2015 to 2014. Zendesk launched a chatbot to automate answers to customer queries, after other competitors, like Slack, start automate some conversations. Deep learning for chatbots on Wildml, offfers an excellent tutorial on how to build bots from scratch using Ubuntu forum data.

In a recent post (Hybrid Intelligence) Clarie Corthell stated that: "humans will always be part of the system. So we shouldn't focus on how to replace humans in a system, rather how to optimally integrating the contributions of humans and computers." I partially agree: humans will definetly have to be in the loop for the next years, but as technology evolves we have to change.

5.3. Art

Perhaps the most extraordinary achievements of DL were obtained in an unsuspicious area: art. Gatys et al. applied Convolutional Neural Networks to obtain a representation of the style of an artist (input image) using the feature space originally designed to capture texture information. By including the feature correlations of multiple layers, they obtain a stationary, multi-scale representation of the input image. They proved that the representations of content and style in the Convolutional Neural Network are separable. Both representations can be independently manipulated to produce new, perceptually meaningful images. To demonstrate this finding, they generate images that mix the content and style representation from two different source images – see Figure 10 (see a demo online on Ostagram).

A Swedish company, Peltarian, released a neural network that can perform sophisticated computer generated choreography by extracting high-level features from raw sensor data. The system, called chor-rnn, uses Recurrent Neural Networks for generating novel choreographic material in the nuanced choreographic language and style of an individual choreographer. It also can create higher-level compositional cohesion, rather than just generating sequences of movement. The neural network is trained on raw motion capture data and that can generate new dance sequences for a solo dancer.

In literature, Hitoshi Matsubara, used a DL based algorithm to generate a short story that was shortlisted, among 10 others, from more than 1000 human written pieces.

In music, Google Brain's creative AI launched a project Magenta dedicated to the creation of music and art through machine learning. They released the first music track - which show the potential ANN to generate creative music.

Figure 10. Artificial generated images using CNNs trained on two sets of images

5.4. Biomedical

In the era of Big Data, modern biology and medicine are confronted with a massive scale of data that requires novel computational tools for analysis and translation of the results. Success of the analysis depends on the ability to interpret such complex and biased data.

5.4.1. Biomarkers and Genomics

One of the main directions of biomedicine is the transition from biological data to valid biomarkers that reflect phenotype and physical state of the body. Biomarkers are critical in measuring clinical trials outcomes, detecting diseases, and monitoring disease states, particularly for diseases as heterogeneous as cancer (see Mamoshina, 2016, for a review).

Exponential growth in modern genomics technology, particularly with the introduction of Next Generation Sequencing (NGS), allows production of a massive amount of genomics data by reducing cost and time consumption of sequencing. Analysis of sequencing data implies analysis of the function and structure of genome. All of this could be performed *in silico* using modern computational approaches.

Analysis of transcriptomics includes analysis of various types of transcripts (mRNA, IncRNA, miRNA, etc.) that carry various types of functional information, from splicing code to biomarkers of various diseases. Transcriptomics data are often obtained from different types of platforms (various microarray platforms, sequencing platforms) that differ by the gene set measured and method of signal detection. Cross-platform analysis requires normalization techniques, which can be a major challenge[22]. DNNs are particularly well-suited for cross-platform analysis with their generalization ability and as such have great potential to benefit transcriptomics data analysis.

Some startups working on these areas are:

- Stratified medical.
- Atomwise.
- Quantitative Medicine.
- Insillico medicine.
- Deep Genomics.

5.4.2. Healthcare

Deep Learning in already having a strong impact in healthcare industry due to: i) increase capacity and accuracy of learning algorithms and ii) wide availability of large sets of healthcare data – made possible through the digitalization of (structured and unstructured) medical records, as well as personal genetic data and other personalized data originated from mobile devices.

Having achieved human level performance on object identification or facial recognition, DANN have a great potential in processing medical imaging, an area where subjectivity interpretation is common and contextualization is key to disambiguate several possible explanations.

DL is being applied to images—which remains its primary application today. Some companies—like Enlitic—are applying DL to recognize cancer in medical images, like X-rays and many automated image recognition tools are already used in hospitals. Diagnoses based on processing of medical images is, however, just a tiny fraction of the potential of DL in medical sector.

Some startups have emerged to apply deep learning to medical imaging such as BayLabs, Imagia, MD.ai, AvalonAI, Behold.ai or Kheiron Medica. iCarbonX has a near term goal of predicting the onset of diseases from genomic, medical and lifestyle data.

DL was also extensively used for model and understanding complex biomedical processes like protein interactions, RNA decoding.

6. CONCLUSION AND FUTURE DIRECTIONS

We are experiencing a revolution in Artificial Intelligence. This fast-moving wave of technology innovations powered by AI is impacting business and society in such a velocity that is hard to predict its implications. One thing is sure: cognitive computing powered by AI will be able to perform most tasks and empower humans even in creative tasks. AI will impact jobs that had seemed impossible to automate a few years ago, from doctors to legal clerks.

By 2020, the market for machine learning applications will reach $40 billion, IDC, a market research firm, estimates - 60 percent of those applications, the firm predicts, will run on the platform software of four companies (Amazon, Google, IBM and Microsoft) most of it relying on Artificial Intelligence.

Probably the most immediate impact of GAI supported by DNN will not be in self-driving cars or robotics but in customer service. Services like sending a specific email, a mobile push, or a customer pass for a specific shop or event; predictive analytics to help support decisions and call centers. Contact centers deal with very mundane interactions that soon will be serviced through automated messaging like chat bots and personal assistants. AI can help suggest how to deliver a conversation; user interests and product. It can even use the data for secondary proposes, like risk assessment based on previous interactions.

6.1. Research

From the point of view of technology, I would like to highlight three key research areas I found the most promising:

- Deep Generative Adversarial Neural Networks (GANs).
- Recurrent Neural Networks.
- Multimodal learning models.

GANs are a powerful approach to explore unsupervised and semi-supervised learning where the goal is to discover the hidden structure within data without relying on external labels. One of the most interesting models is Generative Adversial Networks (GANs) where a generative networks is trying to confuse a discriminative one in distinguish real data from faked (generated) one (Alexey Kurakin 2016)14]. The Deep generative models have widespread applications including probability density estimation, image denoising and inpainting, data compression, scene understanding, representation learning, 3D scene construction, semi-supervised classification, and hierarchical control.

New methods to train Recurrent Neural Networks and Multimodal Learning (learning from different data types – video, image, voice, text) are presently very active areas of research and very promising in solving problems related with control and object manipulation, image and video caption and text processing.

6.2. Risks

DL is a powering this tremendous transformative AI technology. A study by Carl Benedikt Frey and Michael Osborne, published in 2013, found that 47% of jobs in America were at risk of being replaced in a near term. More recently Bank of America Merrill Lynch predicted that by 2025 the "annual creative disruption impact" from AI could amount to $14 trillion, including a $9 trillion reduction in employment costs thanks to AI-enabled automation of knowledge work; The McKinsey Global Institute says AI is contributing to a transformation of society "happening ten times faster and at 300 times the scale, or roughly 3,000 times the impact" of the Industrial Revolution.

6.3. Startups

In 2015 only 1% of software have AI capabilities. In 2020 that number will be 50%. DL thus represents a huge opportunity for Startups and investors. In a recent review by The Economist, Nathan Benaich stated that "In 2015 a record $8.5 billion was spent on AI companies, nearly four times as much as in 2010, according to Quid, a data-analysis company. The number of investment rounds in AI companies in 2015 was 16% up on the year before, when for the technology sector as a whole it declined by 3%."

Accel, a venture capital firm headquartered in Palo Alto, announced a $500 million fund for early stage companies and $1.5billion fund for late stage businesses. Of their nine areas of focus for the future, Artificial Intelligence topped the list of priorities. New Enterprise Associates, also a worldwide venture capital firm, is the second top investor in Artificial Intelligence. The firm has invested in WellTok's CafeWell.com website which combines social networking technology with knowledge of healthcare, making recommendations based on health goals allowing users to take control of their wellbeing.

Most AI based venture capital deals were in deep learning/machine learning. Naveen Rao, founder and Chief Executive of Nervana Systems explains, "the method allows computers to process tasks through 'neural networks', systems that mimic the structure of the human brain in order to learn, improve and, in the case of AlphaGo, become capable of decision-making that resembles human intuition more than it does brute computation."

REFERENCES

Amodei, D. (2015). Deep Speech 2: End-to-End Speech Recognition in English and Mandarin. *CoRR*.

Basu, Ganguly, Mukhopadhyay, DiBiano, Karki, & Nemani. (2015). DeepSat – A Learning framework for Satellite Imagery. *CoRR*.

Brenden, M. L., Salakhutdinov, R., & Tenenbaum, J. B. (2015). Human-level concept learning through probabilistic program induction. *Science*, 1332. PMID:26659050

Domingos, P. (2012). A few useful things to know about machine learning. *Communications of the ACM*, 55.

Goodfellow, I., Bengio, Y., & Courville, A. (2006). *Deep Learning*. Boston: MIT Press.

He, Zhang, Ren, & Sun. (2015). Deep Residual Learning for Image Recognition. *CoRR*.

Hinton & Salakhutdinov. (2006). Reducing the dimensionality of data with neural networks. *Science*, *313*(5786).

Hinton, G. E., Osindero, S., & Teh, Y. W. (2006). A fast learning algorithm for deep belief nets. *Neural Computation*, *18*(7), 1527–1554. doi:10.1162/neco.2006.18.7.1527 PMID:16764513

Huang, Yu, Liu, Sedra, & Weinberger. (2016). Deep Networks with Stochastic Depth. *CoRR*.

Kiros, Zhu, Salakhutdinov, Zemel, Torralba, Urtasun, & Fidler. (2015). Skip-Thought Vectors. *CoRR*.

Krizhevsky, A., Sutskever, I., & Hinton, G. (2012). Imagenet classification with deep convolutional neural networks. In Advances in Neural Information Processing Systems. Urran Associates, Inc.

Kurakin, Goodfellow, & Bengio. (2016). Adversarial Examples in the Physical World. *CoRR*.

Long, M., Cao, Y., Wang, J., & Jordan, M. I. (2015). *Learning Transferable Features with Deep Adaptation Networks*. ICML.

Mamoshina, P., Vieira, A., Putin, E., & Zhavoronkov, A. (2016). Applications of deep learning in biomedicine. *Molecular Pharmaceutics*, *13*(5), 1445–1454. doi:10.1021/acs.molpharmaceut.5b00982 PMID:27007977

Mikolov & Le. (2014). Distributed Representations of Sentences and Documents. *CoRR*.

Mikolov, T., Chen, K., Corrado, G. S., Dean, J., & Sutskever, I. (2013). Distributed representations of words and phrases and their compositionality.*Proceedings of NIPS*, 3111.

Ribeiro, B., & Lopes, N. (2011). Deep belief networks for financial prediction. *International Conference on Neural Information Processing*. Springer. doi:10.1007/978-3-642-24965-5_86

Rumelhart, D. E., Smolensky, P., McClelland, J. L., & Hinton, G. (1986). Parallel distributed models of schemata and sequential thought processes. In *Psychological and Biological Models* (pp. 5–57). Cambridge, MA: MIT Press.

Schmidhuber, J. (2015). Deep learning in neural networks: An overview. *Neural Networks*, *61*, 85–117. doi:10.1016/j.neunet.2014.09.003 PMID:25462637

Srivastava, R. K., Greff, K., & Schmidhuber, J. (2015). *Highway network.* arXiv preprint arXiv:1505.00387

Sutskever, I., Vinyals, O., & Le, Q. (2014). Sequence to sequence learning with neural networks. *Advances in Neural Information Processing Systems*.

Venugopalan, Xu, Donahue, Rohrbach, Mooney, & Saenko. (2015). Translating Videos to Natural Language Using Deep Recurrent Neural Networks. *CoRR*.

Vieira, A., & Barradas, N. (2003). A training algorithm for classification of high-dimensional data. *Neurocomputing*, *50*, 461–472. doi:10.1016/S0925-2312(02)00635-5

Vinyals & Le. (2015). A Neural Conversational Model. *CoRR*.

ENDNOTES

[1] Regarding these points, note that DL is a very active area of research and many of these difficulties are being addressed – some of them are partially solved while others probably never will be.

[2] The quality of translation is measured by BLUE - it is the geometric mean of the n-gram precisions for all values of n between 1 and some upper limit – typically 4.

Chapter 4

Significance of Affective Sciences and Machine Intelligence to Decipher Complexity Rooting in Urban Sciences

Alok Bhushan Mukherjee
Birla Institute of Technology, India

Akhouri Pramod Krishna
Birla Institute of Technology, India

Nilanchal Patel
Birla Institute of Technology, India

ABSTRACT

An urban system is a complex system. There are many factors which significantly influences the different aspects of it. The influencing factors possess different characteristics as they may be environmental, economical, socio-political or cognitive factors. It is not feasible to characterize an urban system with deterministic approach. Therefore there is a need of study on computational frameworks that can investigate cities from a system's perspective. This kind of study may help in devising different ways that can handle uncertainty and randomness of an urban system efficiently and effectively. Therefore the primary objective of this work is to highlight the significance of affective sciences in urban studies. In addition, how machine intelligence techniques can enable a system to control and monitor the randomness of a city is explained. Finally the utility of machine intelligence technique in deciphering the complexity of way finding is conceptually demonstrated.

DOI: 10.4018/978-1-5225-2545-5.ch004

1. INTRODUCTION

This chapter aims to explain the significance of affective sciences in deciphering the complexity of an urban system. In addition, the pivotal role which machine intelligence techniques are capable of in characterizing an urban system is described. The proposed chapter begins with a note on urban system outlining its various facets. Then "affective science" is explained in detail, and how the idea of affective science is relevant in functioning of an urban system is outlined. Later, the proposed chapter details the applicability of machine intelligence techniques in studying an urban system under the realm of affective sciences. Having provided a detailed description on the significance of machine intelligence techniques, and their utility in understanding a complex system; a research problem on wayfinding using a machine intelligent technique and decision tree is demonstrated. This chapter ends with concluding remarks, and suggestions that can be incorporated to strengthen the present study.

1.1. Urban System: Complexity, Uncertainty, and Randomness

An urban system is characterized by keywords such as complexity, uncertainty, and randomness. (Coffey, 1998) rightly mentioned that the idea of urban system has been existing for centuries. It is perceived as either a pattern or an archetype that can be analyzed from different perspectives. There are different definitions of urban system available in the literature. But the definition by (Bourne, 1998) seems well fitting: an urban system can be considered as a system, or a perception. From a system's perspective, it is an object that connects independent urban clusters. On the other hand, urban system corresponds to a perception that focuses in understanding the process of urbanization. Now people believe in unanimity that investigation on cities is not possible in isolation. The associations of a city with other urban centres need consideration as functioning of a city is dependent on its spatial connections. In addition, attributes pertaining to social and political context should not be ignored. The social and political attributes has significant impact in shaping a city's structural and functional design. However, studying a city from system's approach has never been easy as it requires huge amount of data to perform the investigation. For example, this kind of study requires data related to its link with other surrounding urban centres, and beyond as well. (Randall, 1998) made a significant note regarding the urban systems research. The transitory nature of events due the human component should not be ignored. These events have significant potential to influence the behavior of an urban system.

Urban system is composed of different components such as social components and ecological components. Social components of an urban system comprised of various attributes such as demographic characteristics, transportation system, building types, and its density. While the ecological components of an urban system contain soil, elevation, climate, hydrology, and vegetation as attributes. Since an urban system has attributes from different fields, contribution from different disciplines is required to characterize it. The various disciplines which can make significant contribution are urban geography, urban ecology, urban economics, urban sociology, and urban planning (Gopal et al., 2016). Systems within an urban system such as transportation system are considered as critical infrastructures as its performance is dependent on many interacting factors. That makes it a complex system itself (Zio, 2016). There is a need to understand the fact that an urban system is composed of various attributes and many of which has systems characteristics. Consequently these kinds of attributes escalate the magnitude of complexity in functioning of an urban system. Therefore modern urban theorists advocate planning theories that include factors from different facets of a city. Inclusion of all participatory factors of an urban system helps to reduce randomness and heterogeneity exist in a city (Mosadeghi et al., 2015).

As mentioned earlier, factors representing different aspects of a city should be included in a study pertaining to an urban system. However this inclusive approach to perform investigations on urban system is not an easy task. It has its own share of complexities. There are factors which have direct impact in triggering, or shaping an event. But there can be factors whose impact on an event cannot be comprehended in straightway. Further presence of conditional factors in an urban domain escalates the complexity in characterizing urban events. The conditional factors correspond to those factors which come into existence as a consequence of integration of primary factors responsible for occurrence of an event. There is a need to understand the significance of these conditional factors in increasing the complexity in an urban system. Any model, empirical, or mathematical, can consider factors which has a direct or indirect presence in shaping the functioning of a city. However, if there is a possibility of factors which may come into the circumference of an event in later stage of an urban process, makes a highly uncertain environment for urban studies. It is a very difficult task to determine the variables which may start showing their presence in later stages of a process. There are definitive reasons for the complexity in determining these factors. For example, it is not just the combination of primary, or we can say, direct factors, that lead to the birth of another set of variables that are potential enough to influence an urban process. The intensity of the direct factors with which they combine with each other, has also significance. If a variable, 'A' with participatory value of 'x' combines with another variable, 'B' with participatory value of 'y' may generate a variable, called 'C'. But, if the same variable, 'A' with a different participatory value combines with the variable 'B' may lead to the occurrence of a variable possessing different characteristics from the variable C. Therefore, the range of possible combinations of influencing factors becomes huge. Moreover, the possibility of combinations becomes hugely complex and uncertain. That makes an urban system, dynamic and uncertain. In addition, it needs to be understood in clear terms that the central component of an urban system is the human component. There is no denying in the fact that the components such as environment, infrastructure, and socio-economic, have their role in defining the functions of a city. But all of these components are meant to serve the central component of a city; that is the human component. Therefore, it becomes naïve to ignore the role of human cognition in characterizing a city. In fact, it is one of the most important factors that can influence the different facets of a city. Prevailing complexity in an urban system is not just a consequence of spatial and structural components. Even though physical components of urban landscape may have its contribution in escalating ambiguity and capriciousness in the system, it alone cannot contour the characteristics of a city. Had that been the reality, cities with robust infrastructures would have been sustainable from environmental, economical, and social perspective. But the term, sustainability, is still an unfulfilled aspiration for the urban science fraternity. It needs to be understood that evolution of cities resembles biological organisms in terms of their growth process; it comes into being from a tiny cluster, and then matures with time as a consequence of demographical, socio-political exposure, next it evolves through economic growth, and finally, it degenerates due to its vulnerabilities to environmental, economical, or social disparities. The cognitive aspects of a city should not be ignored; otherwise its ignorance makes a city prey of randomness existing in the operation of an urban system. However it is not easy to represent the cognitive aspect of a city in a definitive way. It does not possess absolute characteristics, as structural components of a city possess. For example, the structural characteristics of an urban landscape can be quantified precisely. There are different landscape indices available in literature which can be used to characterize the landscape of a city. But how a particular landscape is related with the human cognition cannot be determined on the basis of landscape indices. The landscape indices can be helpful in understanding the pattern of a city. But the pattern of a city is a consequence of the process that a city goes through while evolving. The growth process of a city is hugely dependent on its cognitive aspects. Consequently, there is an inevitable need of understanding the significance of spatial cognition in the urban growth process. Moreover, it is absolutely necessary that we dig deep to find various ways of effective representation of cognitive variables in urban research investigations. There are definitive models to effectively represent and characterize the different facets of an urban system ranging from environment to socio-economic dynamics of a city. However the element of spatial cognition in urban studies cannot be handled using deterministic models. Instead there is a need of models that can incorporate dynamic variables. Therefore we can find the application of probabilistic models across the spectrum of urban studies. The limitations of deterministic models in studying cities are overcome by probabilistic models to some extent. The probabilistic models do have success in representing the uncertainty prevailing in the functioning of an urban system. However they are not adequately flexible to incorporate the all possible combinations of factors. Consequently they fail to represent the anomalous behavior of elements existing in an urban system. In addition, these models do not have mechanism to normalize the outliers. That makes the model vulnerable to inaccurate characterization of a city.

1.2. Affective Science: Meaning and Significance

It has been observed that there is an undeniable relationship between emotion and cognition. The way one feels about an entity affects its decision regarding that entity. Therefore the research fraternity felt the need to develop systems which are capable enough to process the inputs erupting from the emotional brain. It needs to be outlined explicitly that the computational systems meant to automatically process the inputs related to emotional states. The domain of affective science confined to investigate emotional states, which in other way, can be rephrased as emotional research. On the other hand, affective computing deals with the development of computational systems that can automatically recognize and process the emotional states. The emotional states are formally termed as affective states (Calvo, 2010). Sabourin & Lester (2014) reiterates the fact that evidence from previous investigations shows that there is a definite relationship between affective state and decision making. In addition, the emotional states also influence the moral reasoning of an individual. Khurshid (2008) highlighted that one's actions or thoughts towards an entity create a certain feeling for that entity, that feeling is called 'affect'. The 'affect' is a representation of one's mood or emotional state. There are different ways in which affect is manifested such as facial expressions, body postures, and language. The language is significant in displaying different states of emotion. It can be either spoken or in written form.

Therefore, nowadays affective computing is a booming research discipline as it significantly bridges the gap between emotion and decision making (Tao & Tan, 2005). As mentioned earlier, the emotional states can be manifested in different ways, one of them is language. Through language, the behavior of user can be mapped. There are different techniques available which can be employed to characterize the behavior such as sentiment mining (Goatly, 2008). Advanced techniques can be effective and efficient in mining opinions. For example, the techniques such as clustering made the process of opinion mining efficient and robust (Gamon). Kim (2011) highlighted the fact that text can be a potential weapon to mine the sentiments of users. The users may be customers, students, or common public using some kind of digital services. In this digital era where a large chunk of information is distributed through text; an opportunity is there to track the text, and extract the possible range of affects of the users. That needs robust algorithms which can classify the text into different classes representing different set of emotions. The emotions can be measured in different ways such as dimensional, or categorical. In the first way of emotion measurement, it is measured through quantitative measures. The quantitative measures use multi-dimensional scaling. On the other hand, in categorical measurements, the emotions are differentiated using labels, that is, different emotions are associated with different labels. Therefore it becomes easy to distinguish between different emotional states. Furthermore, it is easy to understand. However it has some disadvantages such as it is associated with theoretical assumptions, and therefore it can have subjective biases. In addition, there is high likelihood that it can contradict the findings of actual data. That further can create a chaotic situation in terms of clarity on the accuracy and precision of findings. There are different emotion modelling and machine learning methods which can be effective in developing affective computing systems. The systems which are significant in understanding the relationship between affects and cognition. Furthermore the intensity of the impact of emotions in guiding decision making process can be determined decisively. Earlier psychologist have developed many models to characterize the human emotions, those models can be utilized in the affective computing (Kim, unpublished).

1.3. Significance of Affective Science in Investigations Pertaining to Urban Systems

Affective computing can be considered as a potential weapon to counter the challenges which erupt from the circumference of human sciences. It borrows concepts from a number of disciplines such as computer sciences, and cognitive sciences. Cognitive science itself is an interdisciplinary domain involving expertise from the fields such as philosophy, anthropology, psychology, mathematics etc. Then it's obvious to wonder, "Why is there a need of such interdisciplinary expertise to study problems originating from human sciences?" well, answer to this question is not a tough nut to crack, however, if the question is," how, accurately and precisely, the research problems of human science can be tackled?" then there is a need of deep digging not just from the perspective of philosophy, but from the technical perspective as well. It needs to be understood in the right perspective that any research problem involving human component have a high likelihood of unpredictability in terms of causal and consequential factors. Consequently the problems falling in the domain of human sciences are primarily non linear in nature, and hugely dependent on characteristics of the independent factors responsible for shaping an event. Amongst the causal factors instrumental in functioning of an urban system, the most intriguing and complex is cognitive factors. Therefore there arises a situation in urban sciences where factors encompassing from spatial, environmental, socio-economic, to cognitive domain comes to the fore in defining the characteristics of the urban system. Now imagine the complexity in understanding the relative influence of each of the factors on a phenomenon that surfaces in an urban system. The methods and technologies which are effective in assessing the environmental aspects of an urban system have a high likelihood of falling flat in assessing the other aspects of the system such as the spatial aspect of the urban system. This kind of prevailing disjoint characteristics among the causal factors fuels the need of concepts and methods which can simultaneously handle the different facets of an urban system.

Therefore emergence and evolution of affective science is inevitable. Now the question that needs rumination: what are the different methods in affective science which are most compatible with the problems of human sciences, and specifically, in urban sciences? There are numerous methods available under the rein of affective science, such as artificial neural network, genetic algorithm, decision tree, *meta-heuristic optimization* etc. However each method has its own advantages and disadvantages, and thus coupling of various techniques is required to address an urban phenomenon.

As discussed earlier, urban system is comprised of different attributes from different dimensions. Thus it has complex, random, and unpredictable characteristics. The unpredictability in the behavior of an urban system is due to non-linear characteristics of the participating variables. That also makes the system behave randomly at different times. If a system, be it an ecological, biological, or a social system has random characteristics, then it is not consistent, and vulnerable to total breakdown. However, the fact those social systems such as an urban system cannot deny the possibility of randomness in its functioning. That suggests considering the accepted fact that it is an inconsistent system, and therefore it can crumble at any point of time. But this kind of direct inferences is not feasible in case of an urban system. Because it is not easy to put forth predefined principles to define an urban system as a consistent and robust system. There is an absolute necessity of clarity regarding the definition of a consistent system, or say, a robust system. It can be considered as an well accepted fact that a system which is flexible enough to accommodate uncertain elements, and process it using deterministic, or probabilistic algorithms to output accurate results, is consistent. However there is a need of deep digging regarding this hypothesis about the consistency, or robustness of an urban system. Is it fair to expect a system to accommodate uncertainty of any magnitude? In fact, the question is: is it possible to design a system which can accommodate uncertainty of any magnitude? The answer to these questions can be positive, but the answer has obvious conditions. A system can be designed to handle uncertainty of any magnitude if the domain of the possible influencing factor is a closed set. Then the obvious question arises; is every system function with a closet set of variables? Specifically, does urban system have a definitive set of influencing factors? The answer depends upon the context. If an attribute of the urban system is under consideration then the set of influencing factors may or may not be definitive. For example, if there is a study on urban environment, then the factors which can be instrumental in influencing the environmental aspect of the system confined to morphological characteristics of the city. However, how different aspects of a city can affect the environmental sustainability has a chain of potential influencing factors that need consideration. That means, in the former case, we can have a definitive view of the potential variables, but in the later case, the decision regarding all possible factors is not an easy and direct task. Therefore the definition of consistency for an urban system cannot be absolute; instead it needs to be relative. In addition, besides structural factors, there is a huge impact of cognitive factors in influencing different aspects of a city. Thus we can witness rapid emergence of disciplines such as environmental psychology, traffic psychology, urban psychology, spatial cognition etc. It is an absolute necessity to realize the obvious dimension of an urban system i.e. it is a human-centric and human-driven system. Therefore there is a no way of ignoring the most significant factor of this system; human factor. There are innumerable ways by which human induced factors can affect the whole urban system ranging from anthropogenic activities responsible for abrupt land use transformation to the impact of driver's attitude on the traffic flow. Hence it becomes inevitable to understand the need of studying urban systems from a broader perspective. Firstly, it has to be kept in consideration that influencing factors under the realm of urban system possess different characteristics. In addition, the domain of influencing attributes cannot be determined beforehand. The inclusion or exclusion of factors in later stages of the investigation may happen. Furthermore there are attributes in the urban system whose domain cannot be determined at any stage of the investigation. This kind of prevailing uncertainty in urban system makes an uphill task for researchers to define the framework which can justify the meaning of consistency in the perspective of urban system. Therefore aiming for development of computational models which are consistent and robust for studying the behavior of urban system is a bit over-ambitious, and practically, not feasible. Instead we need to focus on the development of computational models that have flexibility of adding user defined variables. It will enable the system to adapt with the requirement of current scenario since the characteristics of a city changes with time. Consequently the number of influential actors and their domain may change. Therefore there must have some mechanism to incorporate the changing scenarios. As discussed earlier, urban system is a human-centric and human-driven system, and therefore, the computational models intended to characterize a city must have a component that can input and process the emotional responses of people. This has to be incorporated in the system since there are many instances in the working of an urban system where the response of people influences the final outcome of an event. For example, if a policy maker has a biased response towards a proposal, then there is a high likelihood that the actual structural characteristics of the city won't be instrumental in devising a policy for the city. Instead the emotional state of the policy maker will influence the decision. The emotional response of the policy makers towards a certain policy may be dependent on many factors. It may have a relation with some past instances, or it may just be the consequence of the present mood of the policy makers. Here in this instance, the proposal act as a 'stimuli' and the mood of the policy maker is the 'affect'. There are various instances where one's emotional state can influence the sustainability of the whole system. For example, in a traffic flow system, there are various influencing actors which are instrumental in influencing the characteristics of traffic flow such as traffic capacity, traffic volume, lane width, number of interactions present in a lane, and the type of land use present along a link. There is a well defined principle to have smooth flow of traffic; the traffic capacity of a link should be greater than the traffic volume. If this principle is followed then the link flow congestion can be contained in a link of a transportation network. To maintain the link flow congestion, other factors such as lane width, number of interactions present in a lane, and the type of land use present along a link, are also considered. However the question that needs to be thought of: does efficient traffic management system ensure smooth traffic flow? In addition, there is a need of elaborate discussion that do we need to see beyond physical factors in regulating traffic flow? The answer to the first question is 'no', and 'yes' to the second question. We need to understand the fact that the transportation infrastructures and traffic management systems do have a significant role in maintaining a smooth traffic flow in a city. Furthermore they do contribute in making the transportation system robust and sustainable. However they alone cannot guarantee a smooth traffic flow. If the physical infrastructures are enough to monitor and control traffic flow, then why is there a huge increase in the research investigations in the traffic psychology? Despite having adequate transportation infrastructure and a robust traffic management system, if the attitude of driver towards driving is not consistent, then there is a high likelihood of point congestions. These point congestions will ultimately affect the link flow. That can further abrupt the normal traffic flow all across the transportation network of a city. That means there is no way we can ignore the cognitive dimension of an urban event, otherwise it may lead to affecting the functioning of other attributes of the urban system. Therefore there is a need of systems that can handle the emotional responses of influencing actors of the system. These emotional responses adds biases to the system which can influence the decision making process. If ignored, it can ultimately break down the whole system, or can affect the performance of the system. Therefore these biases need to be normalized so that the system can function in a normal way.

2. MACHINE LEARNING: MEANING, NEED, AND SIGNIFICANCE

Machine learning techniques enable extraction of useful informative patterns from a web of data. It is noteworthy that retrieval of useful patterns which can be converted into pertinent knowledge, has potential to solve real world problems, such as prediction of real time congestion, weather forecasting, development of early-warning systems for natural disasters, modelling social intelligence, and predictive modelling for urban systems. Further there has been a far and wide research going on the application of machine learning techniques in the field of cognitive sciences. A deep insight into the current status of research investigations on the core, or application of machine intelligence will conform to the fact that it has significant presence across the spectrum of physical sciences, formal sciences, and social sciences. So it can be inferred and established in unanimity that machine learning has been rooting into many disciplines with speed and ease, and thus has omnipresence with irrefutable significance. However there are few things that need to be taken into account regarding the application of machine intelligence techniques in investigations spanning different disciplines. The techniques under the realm of machine intelligence are generally employed to uncover the complexity prevailing in a system. That finally paves way for finding precise and accurate patterns from a set of data. Otherwise it just would not be possible to get anything meaningful out of a data set. The intensity of complexity varies with the nature of study, and is dependent on the interrelationship of participating factors responsible for the eruption and evolution of a phenomenon. Therefore there is an absolute necessity of strong understanding of the variables which are responsible for triggering a phenomenon. Knowledge of causal factors helps to decide the set of machine learning techniques which can be used to investigate a particular event, since same set of methods cannot be used for different events of varying nature. Now the question that needs a serious thought and a clear understanding as well," can't we do without machine learning methods?" answer to the question will address an array of issues pertaining to the significance and utility of machine learning. There cannot be denial in the fact about the phenomenal growth of data as a consequence of information technology revolution across the world. Nevertheless this tremendous growth of data is not the just reason for rise in the application of machine intelligence methods in various studies; there is a tectonic shift in the approach of investigations as well. Nowadays most of the scientific problems are being studied from the perspective of system sciences rather than having a linear approach. When a phenomenon is being investigated from a systems' perspective; the permutation and combination of the causal factors and their impact on different aspects of the system are considered. It generates a huge possibility of combinations from the available data, and combinations breed complexities in understanding the data. Since different combinations can come up with different kind of information for the phenomenon. That makes an uphill task to accurately classify and categorize the derived information on the basis of their utilitarian significance for the research problems being analyzed. Moreover there is a need to understand that there are multitudes of factors which are responsible for shaping up an occurrence. How is it possible to unveil the actual reasons which are responsible for triggering an event or the actual impact of an event on different facets of a system by just eyeing on a few factors? Therefore combinatorial analysis is considered and consequently they need appropriate methods which can tackle such requirements. That results into the ubiquitous machine learning techniques which nowadays are being in use for assessing and modelling of real world applications.

It is well said by John Naisbitt: We are drowning in information and starving for knowledge. This quote beautifully explains the paradox of this digital world. We all are surrounded by the digital data; we can literally access information about any entity existing on this earth. Each and everything which has existence, not just on the surface of this earth but beyond has presence in the digital space. It doesn't matter that whether we look for information about Homo sapiens or Aliens; huge data and information is available, and the only thing which can deprive us from that information is our will. Gone are the days when information used to be a hard earned thing, today information is like a basic need. We are living in an information age where we can go into the world of data through a click. Interestingly, a closer look on the current pattern of this world will leave no doubt in our mind that we all are just a data. We can comfortably say that we all are living in a data forest. And if we don't know how to get out of this data forest: there is a high likelihood that we can get lost. Adding to that, it is an illusion that data about a certain entity is enough in the quest of solution. In fact, it is just the beginning of a long way. There is a hierarchy that needs to follow in the journey of knowledge discovery. Acquisition of data is the first step in this process. Data are just raw facts. These raw facts need to be processed to convert them into meaningful expressions. These meaningful expressions are information. That later need to be converted into knowledge. However, ironically what happens in a general perspective, data is not processed scientifically, and is used as it is, considering it in a final form. That leads to erroneous perception about a certain situation. Because there is no denying in the fact that there is high likelihood of generating wrong perception based on inconsistent fact. It needs to be understood with full clarity that data in their rough forms have inconsistencies. If inconsistencies are not removed and made it smooth, it cannot be used to produce accurate results. In fact, it would just lead to inaccurate and imprecise results. Therefore there is an absolute necessity that data collected from different spaces need to be smoothed and brought into a linear dimension, so that the applicability of data becomes more practical and feasible. Otherwise efficient knowledge discovery is not possible. To achieve the aforementioned stated purpose, there are techniques available in the literature which can be used to refine the data, and make it suitable for application of further processing. In addition, we need methods which can analyze the set of data and discover patterns from it. Then machine learning comes into picture.

Machine learning can be defined as a set of tools or methods which help us to detect underlying patterns. Then these discovered patterns can be used for prediction. Furthermore the discovery of underlying patterns helps us to understand the reasons of uncertainty that exist in a data set (Murphy). It can also be put in this way that machine learning methods helps to train computers to perform certain tasks. Furthermore it needs to be highlighted that there are different ways to define machine learning. For example, it can be defined from the perspective of artificial intelligence, software engineering view, and stats view. From the perspective of artificial intelligence, it provides a framework through which a system automatically learns. The software engineering way insists on programming computer through example rather than coding it. The statistical definition of machine learning can be phrased in this way: in machine learning speed has more significance than accuracy, and it considers factors from different dimensions. It does not confine themselves to conventional statistical techniques (Hertzmann & Fleet, 2010).

It must be clear from the aforementioned points that machine learning methods overcome the limitations of traditional statistical techniques. The conventional statistical models don't follow the principle of training a system and then go for decision making process. Therefore they mainly focus on a one dimensional approach for problem solving. But machine learning trains a system and by reducing the mean square error, it helps to make the system more robust and resilient. Then the trained system process a test data set to aid decision making process. Since it has already been trained on a training data, therefore it is more efficient and effective in extracting useful patterns from the given test data set. Moreover the training process of a data set helps to understand the different aspects of possible injection of uncertainty in a system. Advent and application of machine learning techniques influences the way of problem solving in a significant way. It significantly makes the system more flexible, and accommodating. A set of techniques can be used at a particular instance of time to process the data. Since the application of techniques is from different dimensions of computational sciences, and therefore, it makes the system more effective and efficient in extracting meaningful patterns from the data set. The test data can be viewed from different perspectives, and therefore the possibility of randomness due to the presence of uncertain elements is reduced significantly. That makes the system consistent in terms of flexibility, robustness, accuracy, and precision.

2.1. Types of Machine Learning

There are different types of machine learning approaches are available in the literature such as supervised learning, unsupervised learning, reinforcement learning etc. In supervised learning, the data is trained with reference to the desired outputs. The training data is associated with labels. There are different types of supervised learning such as classification and regression. These two approaches of supervised learning differ in terms of the nature of their output. In the case of classification, the outputs of the training data are in the form of discrete labels. On the other hand, the outputs of the training data in the case of regression are real-valued. Classification is a process in which a classifier divides the data set into different classes. Each data class has some unique characteristics, and the element of the data set is associated to these different data classes on the basis of their characteristics. There are different techniques for classification such as decision tree, Bayes classifier, rule-based classification etc. Decision tree is a framework that resembles tree like structure. It is comprised of root nodes, internal nodes, leaf nodes, and branches. The internal nodes of a decision tree represent testing attributes. The results of these tests are shown through the branches. The leaf nodes are also known as terminal nodes, and they denote the labels for different classes. The inputs required to construct a decision tree are training data, labels for different data classes, list of attributes, attribute selection method and splitting criteria. Bayesian classifier is the consequence of work done by Thomas Bayes. These classifiers are based on Bayes theorem. They work on the basis of subjective probabilities. Each data class is associated with Bayesian probabilities. It can be said with unanimity that these are statistical classifiers. These classifiers consider both prior probabilities and posterior probabilities. The rule-based classifications are easy to implement and understand. These are basically based on if-then rules. Now moving to the unsupervised learning, in unsupervised learning, the data classes' are not associated with any data labels. Without data labels, the underlying patterns in the training data need to discovered, and categorized into different classes. There are basically two types of unsupervised classification that is, dimension reduction and clustering. Clustering corresponds to the process of dividing the data set into different subsets. Each subset is known as cluster. Elements of a cluster possess similar characteristics, but the characteristics of elements of one cluster are different from the characteristics of elements of the other. It needs to be mentioned explicitly that clustering is done using algorithms. There are different methods to perform clustering. Therefore, different clustering methods can produce different clusters on the same data set. Clustering is also known as automatic classification, data segmentation. It can also be applied for outlier detection. As mentioned earlier in this section that there are different clustering methods to perform clustering such as portioning methods, hierarchical methods, density-based methods, and grid based methods. Partitioning methods are capable of finding exclusive clusters. The shape of exclusive clusters is spherical. They are distance based, and find center of the cluster through mean. They are effective when data sets small or medium. The hierarchical methods for clustering divide the data set in multiple levels. It has capability to incorporate other techniques for clustering. The density based methods for clustering is capable of finding outliers. The grid-based methods for clustering are fast in processing. Finally, the reinforcement learning represents those type of learning mechanism where learning is based on the results of the past actions (Hertzmann & Fleet, 2010; Han et al., 2012).

2.2. Different Types of Machine-Learning Techniques

There are different types of machine learning techniques such as artificial neural network, fuzzy logic, genetic algorithm, hybrid systems etc. Each technique has its own advantages and disadvantages. The applicability of these techniques depends upon the context. It may happen that a machine learning technique which is the most feasible option for application in one case, but it is not the best option for some other application.

2.2.1. Artificial Neural Network (Sivanandam & Deepa, 2014)

The artificial neural network can be viewed as an information processing model. The development of an artificial neural network is inspired by the working of brain. It is an attempt to mimic the working of brain. The architecture of the artificial neural network is designed in such a way that it can do parallel processing effectively and efficiently. The artificial neural network model is trained in a specific way to deal with a particular problem. It is learned by example as a biological brain does. There are many advantages of artificial neural network model. As mentioned earlier in this section that an artificial neural network model aims to mimic the way a brain operates. That means it should be capable enough to incorporate the basic tenet of a brain. Characteristics such as fault tolerance, self-organization, adaptive learning should characterize an artificial neural network model. Fault tolerance of an ANN model corresponds to the capability of the model to preserve the properties of the model in the case of sudden and abrupt network damage. If a model can preserve the basic properties of a model after a network breakdown then the system can be restored. The self organization represents the potential of a system to represent the knowledge it learned during learning in its own. This enables a model to evolve in a fast and mature way. Now the most important characteristic of an artificial neural network model is its capability to learn from the training data which can be applied on a test data set.

The neural network model is a powerful tool to analyze data and discover hidden patterns from a data set. Its application can be found in different disciplines across the spectrum of academic studies. It also borrows concepts from these academic fields. For example, its presence can be witnessed in the areas related to cognitive psychology, linguistics, philosophy, computer science, mathematics, physics, and engineering. The utility of artificial neural network model for practical applications can be seen in different fields. For example, it can be significant in investigating fraud detection, it is a potential tool to analyze and model functions of ecosystem as it is effective in extracting non-linear patterns. Further it can be applied for traffic monitoring, be it air traffic control or road traffic control. The utility of ANN models can also be seen in studying physical and chemical systems, music composition, medical diagnosis, and weather prediction studies. Any event which is non-linear in nature and involves factors from different dimensions under an uncertain environment can find ANN suitable for their study.

There are primarily three facets of an artificial neural network model namely interconnections, learning algorithm, and activation functions. Interconnections of an artificial neural network model can also be viewed as weights that are associated with the links. In neural network architecture contains interconnected processing nodes. There are different architectures of artificial neural network model such as feed-forward network, and recurrent network. The feed-forward network may consist of a single layer or multi layer. Similarly the recurrent network can be of a single layer or multi layer. The single layer feed-forward network has only two layers i.e. input layer and output layer. On the other hand, the multi layer feed-forward network consists of minimum three layers i.e. input layer, hidden layer, and output layer. The number of hidden layers may differ according to the context. In these kinds of network architectures, the formation of a layer is done by integrating a neuron of the network with other neurons of the network. In addition, there has to be clarity on the meaning of feed-forward network architecture. Then the difference between feed-forward architecture and feedback architecture need to be understood. The feed-forward network architecture resembles that network in which no processing node of the output layer is connected to itself or to the input layer. While in feedback network architecture, it is possible. Recurrent networks belong to the class of feedback network architectures, but these networks have loops. Now moving on to the next basic characteristics of neural network models; learning algorithms. As it is discussed earlier, the neural network model learns from the training data through learning algorithms. Then the trained neural network model is applied on a test data set to analyze, discover or predict patterns. There are different learning algorithms which are generally used to train the network such as supervised learning, unsupervised learning, and reinforcement learning. Furthermore it needs to be clear about the context so that the decision regarding selection of learning algorithm can be made. Finally the last basic characteristic of neural network architecture is activation functions. The activation function of neural network architecture corresponds to the rules that are used to calculate the output of a neural network. There are different activation functions which are applied over the neural networks such as identity function, binary step function, bipolar step function, sigmoidal function, bipolar sigmoidal function etc. Each activation functions have different set of characteristics and should be used in an appropriate context. If an inappropriate activation function is applied over a neural net then there is likelihood that the trained network can produce inaccurate results.

2.2.2. Fuzzy Logic (Sivanandam & Deepa, 2014)

Primarily, the concept of fuzzy logic is an extension of classical set theory which works on binary values. But fuzzy logic considers the possibilities of values existing between 0 and 1. It was originally proposed by Lotfi A. Zadeh in the year of 1965. As the real world events have a range of possibilities not just in terms of outputs but inputs as well. It is not possible to categorize each and every event occurring in a real world domain into binary classes. There are instances where it is not possible to assign an entity to a particular class in an absolute way. In other words it can be viewed as a situation where a particular entity does not hold the complete characteristics of a class, but it certainly has similarities with the particular class. That means it does possess a certain amount of characteristics of that class. In that case, it generates a possibility that it also holds characteristics of other classes. Thus we can say an entity has characteristics of different classes, and therefore it is not possible to label that entity with a certain class. It has overlapping characteristics. Therefore there must have some mechanism to represent these kinds of circumstances where a particular element cannot be categorized in a rigid manner. Moreover it is a fact that is not convincing to ignore that the domain of real world is full of such possibilities. If we choose to ignore this aspect of real world, then there is a high likelihood that a range of possibilities of combinations of elements would be missed. Consequently there are many events that can erupt in real world domain can never be predicted. That ultimately will affect the consistency, robustness, and reliability of computational systems meant to investigate real world events. Advent of fuzzy logic provides the framework and mechanism that can handle and process effectively such possible scenarios. There are tools and techniques available in fuzzy logic to handle the aforementioned scenarios. Application of fuzzy sets instead of classical sets provides flexibility to represent elements with partial membership values. That helps to include the element of uncertainty and vagueness in the provided framework. Inclusion of uncertain and vague elements in the current framework would ultimately reduce the possible inconsistency that can be generated by the system. It also needs to be considered that we cannot incorporate uncertain and inconsistent element in a system straightway. There must have some mechanism that can make it possible. In fuzzy logic, this can be done through linguistic variables and membership functions.

The conceptual demonstration for studying the wayfinding problem using M-P Neuron model and decision tree is shown in the Figure 1.

Figure 1.

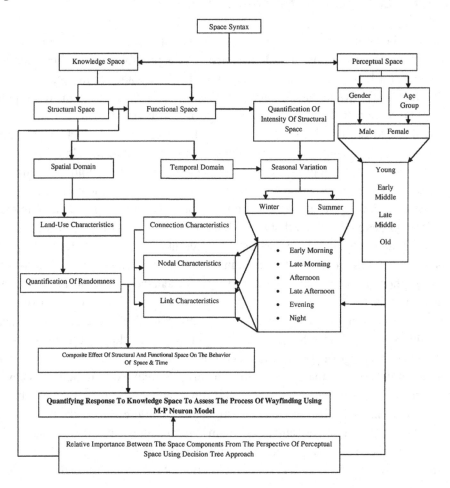

3. FUTURE SCOPE OF THE WORK

The utility of the principles of affective science in urban studies has been discussed in detail. In addition the significant role that machine learning techniques can play in understanding the underlying complexities of an urban system is discussed. This work also discussed and demonstrated the applicability of affective sciences' principles and machine learning in enhancing the decision making process regarding wayfinding research problem. It was highlighted that there are different ways to incorporate the principles of affective sciences such as development of systems that automatically can input and process the response of emotional brain. However it is not always feasible to have such infrastructures that can achieve the aforementioned objectives. Therefore to achieve the same objective, surveys or interviews are conducted. But there is a practical problem in these kind of approaches i.e. inclusion of subjective biases, if subjective biases are not monitored and controlled through proper mechanism then it has potential to make the system inefficient and ineffective in terms of accuracy and precision. Therefore it would be desirable as a future scope of work that there must have a dedicated effort to formulate mathematical algorithms that can identify the subjective biases and can normalize it for further application in understanding an event.

4. CONCLUSION

The proposed chapter explained the underlying complexities of an urban system in detail. It further explains the numerous reasons which are responsible for breeding or escalating complexity in functioning of a city. It is highlighted that an event which surfaces on the circumference of a city is a consequence of many factors. Furthermore it is not just the combination of influencing factors which is responsible for its eruption. Instead the magnitude of their participation should also be considered. Moreover the natures of the significant factors that can influence an urban system have strikingly different characteristics. Therefore it is not an easy task to include them in their raw form in the same framework. Instead they need to be normalized on a same scale and then needs to be processed. However incompatible frameworks would fail to process the data accurately and precisely. That means the selection of computational frameworks have huge significance in studying these data sets. In fact, it needs to be understood that absence of models that are flexible enough to accommodate non linear influencing factors can produce erroneous results. Therefore computational systems that can input and process factors of varying characteristics should be developed. The proposed chapter thus explains the significance of the concept of affective sciences in urban studies. It outlines the basic characteristics of affective sciences. It further highlights the significance of affective sciences. Especially how the principles of affective sciences can be utilized and applied in investigations pertaining to urban systems is explained. The proposed chapter moves on to describe the utility of machine intelligence techniques in deciphering the complexity of an urban system. Different learning algorithms are briefed in this chapter to provide an idea for selecting appropriate learning algorithm to train a particular set of data. Furthermore principles of different machine learning techniques is provided in the proposed chapter aiming that it would help in selecting the appropriate method for different research investigations. The importance of machine learning in the context of affective computing and urban studies is also highlighted in this chapter. This work ends with a conceptual demonstration of understanding a wayfinding problem using the principles of affective science and machine learning. This demonstration is aimed to describe the influence of different factors in a wayfinding problem. The factors can be direct or indirect in their influences. However the significance of many factors in affecting an event is sometimes overshadowed by the presence of factors which are easily perceivable. That creates an erroneous perception regarding the working mechanism of an urban system. There is always a likelihood of presence of those factors that don't have direct presence, but affect the behavior of the system significantly. Therefore the wayfinding problem was chosen for the conceptual demonstration to insist on the fact that each and every factor has a significant role in an urban event. In addition, how the basic principle of affective science and machine learning can be used to aid decision making regarding wayfinding is explained. Therefore wayfinding problem was explained conceptually using M-P neuron model and decision tree.

ACKNOWLEDGMENT

The authors are grateful to the Vice Chancellor, Birla Institute of Technology Mesra, Ranchi for providing necessary facilities to perform the research investigation.

REFERENCES

Bourne, L. S. (1998). *Whither Urban Systems? A commentary on research needs and the marketing of ideas*. The Annual Meeting of the Canadian Regional Science Association, Ottawa, Canada.

Calvo, R. A. (2010). Affect Detection: An interdisciplinary review of models, methods, and their applications. IEEE Transactions on Affective Computing, 1(1).

Coffey, W. J. (1998). Urban systems research: An overview. *The Canadian Journal of Regional Science*.

Gamon, M., Aue, A., Corston-Oliver, S., & Ringger, E. (n.d.). *Pulse: Mining customer opinions from free text*. Academic Press.

Goatly, A. (2008). Metaphor as Resource for the Conceptualization and Expression of Emotion.*Workshop on Emotion, Metaphor, Ontology, and Terminology (EMOT)*.

Gopal, S., Tang, X., Phillips, N., Nomack, M., Pasquaellar, V., & Pitts, J. (2016). Characterizing urban landscapes using fuzzy sets. *Computers, Environment and Urban Systems, 57*, 212–223. doi:10.1016/j.compenvurbsys.2016.02.002

Han, J., Kamber, M., & Pei, J. (2012). *Data mining concepts and techniques*. Waltham, MA: Morgan Kaufmann Publishers.

Hertzmann, A., & Fleet, D. (2010). *Machine Learning and Data Mining Lecture Notes*. Computer Science Department, University of Toronto.

Khurshid, A. (2008). Introduction:*Affect Computing and Sentiment Analysis. Workshop on Emotion, Metaphor, Ontology, and Terminology (EMOT)*.

Kim, K. (n.d.). *Emotion modeling and machine learning in affective computing*. Unpublished manuscript.

Kim, S. M. (2011). *Recognizing emotions and sentiments in text* (Thesis). School of Electrical and Information Engineering, The University of Sydney.

Mosadeghi, R., Warnken, J., Tomlinson, R., & Mirfenderesk, H. (2015). Comparison of Fuzzy-AHP and AHP in a spatial multi-criteria decision making model for urban land-use planning. *Computers, Environment and Urban Systems*, *49*, 54–65. doi:10.1016/j.compenvurbsys.2014.10.001

Murphy, K.P. (n.d.). *Machine learning a probabilistic perspective*. The MIT Press.

Randall, J. E. (1998). *Reflections on Urban Systems Research*. The Annual Meeting of the Canadian Regional Science Association, Ottawa, Canada.

Sabourin, J. L., & Lester, J. (2014). Affect and engagement in game-based learning environments. IEEE Transactions on Affective Computing, 5(1).

Sivanandam, S. N., & Deepa, S. N. (2014). *Principles of soft computing*. New Delhi: Wiley India Pvt. Ltd.

Tao, J., & Tan, T. (2005). Affective computing: A review. LNCS, 3784, 981 – 995.

Zio, E. (2016). Challenges in the vulnerability and risk analysis of critical infrastructures. *Reliability Engineering & System Safety*, *152*, 137–150. doi:10.1016/j.ress.2016.02.009

Chapter 5

Coronary Heart Disease Prognosis Using Machine-Learning Techniques on Patients With Type 2 Diabetes Mellitus

Angela Pimentel
FCT-UNL, Portugal

Hugo Gamboa
FCT-UNL, Portugal

Isa Maria Almeida
APDP-ERC, Portugal

Pedro Matos
APDP-ERC, Portugal

Rogério T. Ribeiro
APDP-ERC, Portugal

João Raposo
APDP-ERC, Portugal

ABSTRACT

Heart diseases and stroke are the number one cause of death and disability among people with type 2 diabetes (T2D). Clinicians and health authorities for many years have expressed interest in identifying individuals at increased risk of coronary heart disease (CHD). Our main objective is to develop a prognostic workflow of CHD in T2D patients using a Holter dataset. This workflow development will be based on machine learning techniques by testing a variety of classifiers and subsequent selection of the best performing system. It will also assess the impact of feature selection and bootstrapping techniques over these systems. Among a variety of classifiers such as Naive Bayes (NB), Random Forest (RF), Support Vector Machine (SVM), Alternating Decision Tree (ADT), Random Tree (RT) and K-Nearest Neighbour (KNN), the best performing classifier is NB. We achieved an area under receiver operating characteristics curve (AUC) of 68,06% and 74,33% for a prognosis of 3 and 4 years, respectively.

DOI: 10.4018/978-1-5225-2545-5.ch005

1. INTRODUCTION

About 387 million people worldwide have diabetes. In 2014 diabetes was the direct cause of 4.9 million deaths (WHO, 2015). The prevalence of diabetes is increasing in developed and developing countries and is predicted to achieve 7,7% worldwide by 2030 (Shaw, 2010). Within Europe, Portugal is reported as having the highest prevalence of diabetes. Over 1 million Portuguese have diabetes, with almost half of these still undiagnosed (Gardete-Correia, 2010). Diabetes increases the risk of heart disease and stroke. In a multinational study, 50% of people with type 2 diabetes (T2D) die of cardiovascular disease (primarily heart disease and stroke) (Morrish, 2001). The cardiovascular events associated with T2D and the high incidence of other macrovascular complications, such as peripheral vessel disease and amputations, are a major burden of disease and a huge economic determinant. Clinicians and health authorities for many years have expressed interest in identifying individuals at increased risk of CHD. The underlying cause of CHD is a slow buildup of plaques after fatty deposits on the inner wall of the blood vessels that supply the heart muscle with blood (the coronary arteries). These fatty deposits gradually obstruct the arteries, sometimes clogging them and subsequently reduce the flow of blood to the heart. There is no single cause for CHD, but there are risk factors that increase the chance of developing it. A useful clinical diagnostic tool for following cardiac diseases evolution is with the electrocardiogram (ECG)-Holter records. Long term Holter monitoring is used for patients with heart conditions such as arrhythmias. Heart beats with unusual timing or unusual ECG morphology can be very helpful in early diagnosis of hearts with damaged electrophysiology.

In clinical training and practice, prognosis typically receives less attention than diagnosis and disease treatment. Yet many clinical decisions are not fully useful unless the patient's prognosis is considered (Gill, 2012) (Lan, 2012).

The healthcare industry has generated large amounts of data, driven by record keeping, compliance and regulatory requirements, and patient care (Raghupathi, 2016). With the potential to improve the quality of healthcare delivery, while reducing costs, these massive quantities of data (known as 'big data') supports a wide range of medical and healthcare functions, which includes clinical decision support, disease surveillance, and population health management. (Burghard, 2012). Machine learning enables the extraction of implicit, previous unknown and potentially useful information from data (Witten, 2011). With machine learning techniques, supervised or unsupervised methods are applied in order to extract and evaluate data patterns which can be used to take better decisions and to present the knowledge we extracted in a better way.

This paper proposes a new prognostic approach of CHD for T2D patients based on a Holter dataset. This approach, based on machine learning methods, supports the applicability of using the Holter dataset, to efficiently predict T2D patients that are likely to develop CHD. We also highlight the importance of using feature selection algorithms for the construction of our predictive model. A drawback of this study is the low number of patients that evolve to CHD, therefore the use of boostrapping technique. The result is a prognostic tool that allows the identification of high-risk subjects in the diabetic population. The entire data set captures 8 years (2006-2014) of clinical visits, and a CHD prognosis can be made with intervals for time windows of 3 and 4 years, with AUC values of 68,06% and 74,33%, respectively using a Naïve Bayes classifier. We also show that our predictive model outperforms the Framingham study (D'Agostino, 2000) for this population. We present a solution with a higher number of features than the Framingham, but with a higher precision on the prognostic of the CHD. We present a novel work that provides a risk indicator of CHD in T2D patients just by performing a Holter exam. Ultimately, our goal is to improve clinical decision making, and, ultimately patient clinical outcomes.

2. DATA AND METHODS

2.1. Dataset

Monitoring the ECG during normal activity using Holter devices is a standard procedure for detection of cardiac arrhythmias, transient ischemic episodes and silent myocardial ischemia (Jovanov, 1999). ECG-Holters are portable, battery operated, devices for monitoring ECG signals (Levin, 1986). Ambulatory ECGHolter recordings were made with a 7-electrode recorder for 24 hours and with 10 mVolts resolution. This dataset contains 8 years (2006-2014) of clinical visits at the APDP – Diabetes Portugal. A total of 711 Holters were used for this analysis of T2D patients, with ages between 23 and 89 years. We only used patients that performed the Holter more than once since it will allow us to apply a temporal analysis as future work. Overall, 505 are male and 206 are female. The following coronary heart diseases were the only ones present in the dataset and were considered for analysis: coronary disease, ischemic cardiopathy, myocardial infarction and coronary insufficiency (decreased supply of blood to the myocardium resulting from constriction or obstruction of the coronary arteries, but not accompanied by necrosis of the myocardial cells). In order to provide a prognosis analysis, the year of diagnosis of the CHD is fundamental. However this information was not available on the Holter dataset, requiring an extensive inspection on each patient clinical file in order to obtain this parameter.

Afterwards, the dataset was rearranged to provide a prognosis on different time windows. Prognostic windows between 0 to 4 years spaced by one year were selected in order to be comparable with the Framingham study. Two classes were defined:

CHD that manifests in T2D patients during a defined time window and CHD that does not manifest in T2D patients.

Also, any data that was obtained after the diagnosis was discarded, since it was irrelevant for the prognosis analysis. This reduced our dataset to 597 Holters. Table I shows the class distributions for the different time windows used. It is also important to mention that these patients performed the ECG-Holter because they already had some symptoms that could indicate the presence of a cardiac disease. Authorization to access the data was obtained from the APDP internal Ethics Committee. Data collection was performed by the clinical staff. Confidentiality of individual data was ensured.

2.2. Feature Extraction

We proceeded to the feature extraction in order to provide an informative dataset to the classification. The Holter device provides time and frequency parameters that contribute for the prognosis of CHD. Some of the features are: heart rate; number of bradycardias, tachycardia, missed beats, pauses, bigeminy and trigeminy; square root of the mean squared difference (RMSSD) between adjacent RR intervals; standard deviation of RR intervals (SDNN); very low frequency (VLF); low frequency (LF) and high frequency (HF); We have divided the dataset preparation in three major steps as seen in Figure 1: 1) dataset confirmation; 2) redundant parameters cleaning and 3) addition of new features.

In step 1, age was confirmed with the exam date and birth date performed; gender was confirmed with the patient ID; pacemaker was confirmed with features that provide pacemaker rhythm. In step 2, 40 features were not considered for having unique values for all patients which would be redundant for the classification analysis. In step 3 new features were included in the dataset. Medication was described in the dataset as a comment and sometimes with misspelling. Therefore we extended

Table 1. Class distributions for different time windows. Number of patients that evolve (evolution) and do not evolve (no evolution) to CHD condition. For each time window, there are a total of 597 holters.

Window (Years)	Evolution	No Evolution
0	15(2.51%)	582(97.49%)
1	31(5.19%)	566(94.81%)
2	42(7.04%)	555(92.96%)
3	49(8.21%)	548(91.79%)
4	52(8.71%)	545(91.29%)

Figure 1. Feature extraction scheme for data preparation

each medication name according to their active principle level as a new feature with binary values, where 1 means medication is being taken by the patient; we also created 4 groups of medications: statins, antiplatelet agents, beta-blockers and antiarrhythmics. Overall 145 features for medications were included and confirmed with the National Authority of Medicines and Health Products, IP (INFARMED) (INFARMED, 2015); bradycardia and tachycardia are classified if the heart rate is under 60 bpm and above 100 bpm respectively. Frequency values between those limits are not characterized for this analysis. Therefore we created 4 new features that groups the frequencies from 60 to 100 bpm with a step of 10 bpm. In the end, the data comprises information from 2006 to 2014 with the evolution feature as our target class as described in II-A. The training set will be represented by 70% of the original data, and the testing set with the remaining data (30%). There are 241 features for 579 Holters recordings. The programming language used for this processing was Python.

2.3. Classification

After preprocessing the data we proceeded to the CHD diabetes prognosis by assessing different classifiers. Standard classifiers were used. These include: Naive Bayes (NB) (John, 1995),

Alternating Decision Tree (ADT) (Freund, 1999), Random Forest (RF) (Breiman, 2001), Random Tree (RT), k-Nearest Neighbour (KNN) (Aha, 1991) and Support Vector Machine (SVM) with a polynomial kernel implementation and complexity parameter 1 (Platt, 1998). These classifiers were selected in order to assess different models: numerical (SVM), symbolic (ADT,RF,RT), instance-based (KNN) and probabilistic (NB). The predictive models were built using 5x10-fold cross-validation (CV) with random seeds (1,11,21,31,41) on the training data (Kohavi, 1995). The classifier's parameters were optimized using a meta-classifier that performs CV given a list of possible parameters (Kohavi, 1997). Also, knowing that the classes are unbalanced, we used another technique - Bootstrapping. This technique is applied in each CV train fold and produces random sub-samples of the dataset with replacement to bias the class distribution toward a uniform distribution. We also tested other techniques, such as Synthetic Minority Over-sampling Technique

(SMOTE) (Chawla, 2011) that is responsible for over-sampling the minority class by creating synthetic examples. However, bootstrapping performed better.

Final classification is based on a mid-point threshold (50%) on the probability output by the classifier. Due to the unbalanced dataset and according to (Grzymala-Busse, 2005), better sensitivity values can be achieved by changing this threshold. Therefore we also improved the sensitivity outcomes by changing this threshold to 45%. Given the high number of used features in this study (241), we proceeded to a feature selection (FS) analysis in order to verify if, in fact, some of the original features would be discarded as being irrelevant to the classification. The correlation-based feature selection (CfsSubsetEval) evaluator was used with a Best First search method from the Weka package. This algorithm evaluates the worth of a subset of attributes by considering the individual predictive ability of each feature along with the degree of redundancy between them. The Weka machine learning package was used to test the machine learning algorithms (Hall, 2009).

2.4. Comparison With Framingham

In order to confirm that our risk assessment outcome provides practicable results, the outcomes were compared with the Framingham Heart Study - a risk assessment tool for CHD. The objective of the Framingham Heart Study was to identify the common factors or characteristics that contribute to cardiovascular disease (CVD) by following its development over a long period of time in a large group of participants who had not yet developed overt symptoms of CVD or suffered a heart attack or stroke (D'Agostino, 2000). There are different risk functions, however we used the CHD - second event function, which provides a risk prediction probability estimates for any time between 0 to 4 years. The predictive factors for man are: 1) age; 2) systolic blood pressure (SBP); 3) smoking status; 4) fasting lipid levels (total and HDL cholesterol); 5) physician diagnosis of diabetes at the current or a previous examination; 6) use of antihypertensive medication (yes/no). The predictive factors for women are the same as man with the addition of: 7) menopause (yes/no); 8) alcohol consumption (oz/week) and 9) triglycerides; other existing tools were found in the literature (HeartScore (Heartscore, 2015), QRISK (QRISK, 2015), ASSIGN (Assign score, 2015)), however, these are 10-year risk tools, for which we do not have enough longitudinal data for comparison. The disadvantage of using the Framingham tool is that it is based on a population from the United States, meaning that the risk functions are not adapted for the Portuguese population. As future work, we intend to update our risk assessment outcome to provide a prognosis of 10 years and then compare with the HeartScore tool, which is based in an European population and has been already approved by the Portuguese Directorate-General of Health (DGS).

To summarize, in our workflow we tested different classifiers for different time windows on the original data (OD) and on the selection features (FS) from the dataset. Bootstrapping was applied in order to provide a more balanced training data. Regarding performance evaluation, several metrics were retrieved, such as the receiver operating characteristic (ROC) area (AUC), sensitivity and specificity (Fawcett, 2006). Afterwards, the best classifier was chosen based on the best metrics obtained and applied on the test data. Comparison with an existing CHD risk tool was made - the Framingham Heart Study risk tool. Our predictive model will then allow a prognostic of CHD in T2D patient's when a new Holter is performed.

3. RESULTS AND DISCUSSION

In this section we present and discuss the results of the predictive models on the training set (70% of initial dataset). Afterwards we show the performance evaluation of the best predictive model on the test set (remaining 30%) and compare our probability outputs with the Framingham study. Given that the classes are unbalanced (see Table 1), stratification was ensured when splitting the training and testing set.

3.1. Training Set

The results are shown in Tables 2, 3 and 4, for the AUC, sensitivity and specificity, respectively, after applying 5 x 10-fold CV on the training set for different classifiers. The bold values represent percentages higher than 70%. We notice that the classifiers behave as random predictors of CHD for time windows of 0 and 1 year, since the AUC values are near 50%. Even though AUC values improve with increasing time windows, we wanted to ensure that this improvement was not accidental. Therefore, for this test, we edit the evolution class by randomly selecting who will develop CHD. The AUC values for all classifiers were near

50,21±2,74%, meaning the classifiers lost their predictive ability. Hence we can validate this improvement. Also, according to (Cook, 2008), AUC values for models predicting 10 years risk of CHD are often in a range of 75 - 85%. Therefore we suggest that time windows higher than 3 years are preferred for the prognosis of CHD with this dataset. Regarding the remaining time windows, the low classification outcomes may be justified by the exclusive use of a holter dataset, that may not be sufficient to provide a prognostic in a short time. Therefore we believe that with the inclusion of more features, that are independent of the holter dataset (e.g x-ray, blood tests), we could improve this prognostic outcomes for these time windows. Sensitivity values from Table 3 are highly improved with bootstrapping for all classifiers, although specificity decreases - Table 4.

Table 2. AUC values obtained from the train set in percentage (stratified 5 x 10-fold CV). OD is original data; FS is after applying feature selection; RF is Random Forest. NB is Naive Bayes. SVM is Support Vector Machine. ADT is Alternating Decision Tree. RT is Random Tree and KNN is K-Nearest Neighbour.

Window (Years)	Bootstrapping	Data	AUC (%)					
			RF	NB	SVM	ADT	RT	KNN
0	No	OD	57.02±6.55	47.97±0.28	50.0±0.0	68.71±1.71	50.5±12.23	55.81±3.5
		FS	38.44±2.98	54.49±0.29	50.0±0.0	34.58±0.42	33.95±0.39	33.86±0.44
	Yes	OD	66.89±7.87	**77.25±0.99**	49.64±0.11	50.91±8.03	53.82±7.67	61.02±4.05
		FS	26.29±4.0	73.98±0.31	67.31±4.08	35.8±7.57	25.73±4.64	29.96±5.18
1	No	OD	55.2±2.37	56.56±0.43	50.0±0.0	53.48±2.94	50.0±3.08	62.01±1.6
		FS	56.28±2.17	62.26±0.95	50.0±0.0	39.81±1.35	57.94±1.49	57.5±1.82
	Yes	OD	60.31±4.14	64.45±1.73	54.43±1.36	67.21±6.11	54.58±2.15	62.87±4.71
		FS	61.0±1.91	70.26±1.72	59.28±0.92	52.41±2.95	54.34±3.45	62.72±1.28
2	No	OD	50.45±4.2	60.4±0.67	50.0±0.0	48.92±5.63	51.32±2.7	60.05±2.35
		FS	55.35±0.91	59.4±1.62	49.96±0.77	54.87±3.37	54.22±1.53	54.21±1.87
	Yes	OD	62.7±4.02	68.35±1.44	56.28±1.87	69.96±4.12	53.73±5.21	62.69±4.24
		FS	78.38±1.05	83.76±0.73	70.25±1.84	79.83±2.01	63.59±3.1	**83.17±1.2**
3	No	OD	57.27±2.31	67.09±1.58	50.16±0.59	**80.29±1.41**	51.67±3.34	68.73±1.78
		FS	68.64±0.89	**80.21±0.78**	50.0±0.0	78.59±0.4	58.97±3.99	**79.0±0.96**
	Yes	OD	67.28±3.19	71.27±1.57	63.36±3.44	77.92±2.37	53.59±2.28	69.99±6.59
		FS	72.43±1.36	82.35±1.12	65.73±1.5	83.01±1.83	62.95±2.55	**72.34±2.93**
4	No	OD	58.62±3.25	66.53±1.33	50.87±0.95	77.38±2.48	57.25±4.59	65.61±3.1
		FS	**70.8±0.68**	**80.38±1.62**	50.0±0.0	**78.27±1.92**	62.93±3.15	**78.21±2.71**
	Yes	OD	69.45±2.91	74.36±1.53	61.19±2.68	75.11±2.53	58.16±3.99	66.44±3.1
		FS	74.39±1.44	83.89±1.29	68.87±1.17	82.46±1.8	67.49±3.0	**74.78±1.44**

However, improvements on sensitivity values are preferred, since this metric represents the percentage of T2D patients correctly identified among all patients that will develop CHD. Overall NB presents better results. It is also visible that classification improves with FS for the NB classifier. The main features selected by the CfsSubsetEval evaluator with a BestFirst search are visible in Table 5 for different time windows, indicating that the isolated supraventricular ectopic beats events (SVPB) is the most important parameter for time windows of 3 and 4 years.

Performance between each time window was made with a Friedman test (Demšar, 2008). Statistically significant differences occurred between the different time windows. Using pairs comparison, with significance values corrected for multiple testing, we found that windows 2 to 4 performed significantly better than the remaining ones. And, according to the mean test rank, the top performance window

Table 3. Sensitivity values obtained from the train set in percentage (stratified 5 x 10-fold CV). OD is original data; FS is after applying feature selection; RF is Random Forest. NB is Naive Bayes. SVM is Support Vector Machine. DT is Alternating Decision Tree. RT is Random Tree and KNN is K-Nearest Neighbour.

Sensitivity (%)								
Window (Years)	Bootstrapping	Data	RF	NB	SVM	ADT	RT	KNN
0	No	OD	0.0±0.0	0.0±0.0	0.0±0.0	0.0±0.0	0.0±0.0	20.0±6.13
		FS	0.0±0.0	0.0±0.0	0.0±0.0	0.0±0.0	0.0±0.0	0.0±0.0
	Yes	OD	0.0±0.0	77.5±5.0	0.0±0.0	5.0±6.13	25.0±13.7	10.0±5.0
		FS	12.5±7.91	65.0±5.0	45.0±6.13	7.5±6.13	7.5±10.0	20.0±6.13
1	No	OD	0.0±0.0	12.39±2.34	0.0±0.0	0.0±0.0	1.91±2.34	0.0±0.0
		FS	0.0±0.0	0.0±0.0	0.0±0.0	0.0±0.0	0.0±0.0	0.0±0.0
	Yes	OD	16.2±2.34	79.05±3.81	12.39±2.34	37.15±7.62	41.91±5.56	54.29±8.84
		FS	68.58±2.34	45.72±2.34	29.53±1.91	18.1±5.56	58.1±7.0	33.34±0.0
2	No	OD	0.0±0.0	16.56±1.38	0.0±0.0	2.07±4.14	4.83±1.69	6.9±3.78
		FS	2.07±1.69	0.0±0.0	0.69±1.38	0.0±0.0	2.07±1.69	0.0±0.0
	Yes	OD	33.11±7.11	77.94±1.69	18.63±3.52	51.73±7.56	44.83±9.51	45.52±4.03
		FS	46.21±6.4	80.0±2.59	46.21±3.52	86.21±2.19	41.38±6.17	88.28±2.76
3	No	OD	0.0±0.0	15.43±1.4	0.58±1.15	8.58±3.62	5.15±2.14	18.29±6.67
		FS	5.15±2.14	16.0±1.4	0.0±0.0	3.43±2.14	7.43±2.29	0.58±1.15
	Yes	OD	36.58±7.54	76.0±2.92	33.72±7.1	74.86±6.86	40.58±4.2	58.29±8.97
		FS	59.43±3.34	72.58±1.4	49.15±4.2	85.15±7.96	59.43±3.34	66.29±4.2
4	No	OD	0.53±1.06	17.37±2.11	2.11±1.97	18.95±2.58	7.37±4.22	20.53±3.07
		FS	4.22±3.16	10.53±1.67	0.0±0.0	12.11±4.28	10.53±2.36	0.0±0.0
	Yes	OD	38.95±3.07	81.58±1.67	31.06±5.87	54.22±7.92	47.9±5.37	53.16±1.06
		FS	64.22±2.69	79.48±3.07	54.74±1.06	72.11±4.28	64.22±3.57	75.79±6.95

was for a 4-years prognosis. Statistical comparisons were also made between each data type with a Wilcoxon-signed rank test as suggested from (Demšar, 2008) for 3 and 4 years' time windows. We found that the use of the bootstrapping technique statistically significant improves the AUC values ($p \leq 0{,}042$). In order to compare the performance of the different classifiers, we applied the Friedman test, suggested in (Demšar, 2008), using the IBM SPSS Statistics Editor. The results show that there are statistically significant differences between the classifiers for the AUC values. We analyzed the pairs comparison, with significance values corrected for multiple testing and found that the NB, ADT and KNN performed significantly better than SVM and RT ($p \leq 0{,}006$). Moreover we verified that the top performing classifier, according to the mean test rank, was NB. We have chosen the NB for the construction of our predictive model due to its performing metrics outputs and statistical analysis.

Table 4. Specificity values obtained from the train set in percentage (stratified 5 x 10-fold CV). OD is original data; FS is after applying feature selection; RF is Random Forest. NB is Naive Bayes. SVM is Support Vector Machine. DT is Alternating Decision Tree. RT is Random Tree and KNN is K-Nearest Neighbour.

Window (Years)	Bootstrapping	Data	RF	NB	SVM	ADT	RT	KNN
					Specificity (%)			
0	No	OD	100.0±0.0	98.4±0.12	100.0±0.0	99.96±0.1	99.27±0.27	96.69±0.12
		FS	99.96±0.1	100.0±0.0	100.0±0.0	100.0±0.0	99.91±0.2	99.91±0.2
	Yes	OD	97.18±0.4	60.83±0.25	99.27±0.22	87.61±1.29	77.86±2.83	89.08±1.12
		FS	98.35±0.29	90.25±0.71	89.61±3.46	96.0±0.83	98.98±0.55	99.27±0.01
1	No	OD	99.9±0.21	96.18±0.11	100.0±0.0	98.85±0.47	96.98±0.23	99.25±0.32
		FS	100.0±0.0	99.45±0.11	100.0±0.0	99.1±0.21	99.85±0.31	99.8±0.3
	Yes	OD	89.12±1.16	44.94±0.81	96.48±1.0	84.14±1.58	64.99±5.29	69.43±1.13
		FS	49.63±2.81	88.17±0.93	89.02±0.61	85.9±1.05	55.47±4.84	87.66±0.43
2	No	OD	99.85±0.13	95.63±0.37	100.0±0.0	97.74±0.6	96.56±0.93	94.92±0.77
		FS	98.87±0.21	98.82±0.27	99.23±0.29	99.08±0.63	98.36±0.27	99.65±0.13
	Yes	OD	85.04±1.12	51.01±1.95	93.94±1.03	77.13±2.49	65.66±3.46	80.67±1.51
		FS	89.31±0.79	68.44±0.48	94.3±0.53	65.56±1.69	86.28±0.71	68.33±1.1
3	No	OD	99.69±0.11	95.57±0.44	99.74±0.29	98.07±0.86	95.15±0.87	93.69±0.45
		FS	98.02±0.27	98.54±0.27	100.0±0.0	97.66±0.97	95.88±1.38	99.59±0.32
	Yes	OD	82.88±1.34	54.1±2.14	93.01±1.37	67.58±1.6	65.38±4.57	80.53±1.59
		FS	75.78±1.07	74.94±1.0	82.3±1.72	67.05±1.79	66.48±2.22	73.63±1.0
4	No	OD	99.85±0.22	95.0±0.8	99.64±0.27	95.95±1.08	93.85±0.66	93.27±0.72
		FS	97.53±0.62	98.01±0.13	100.0±0.0	97.43±0.43	94.79±1.06	99.74±0.34
	Yes	OD	82.27±1.15	53.43±0.73	91.32±0.69	84.48±1.66	66.95±4.61	79.27±1.2
		FS	76.74±2.44	67.95±0.94	83.0±2.55	78.9±2.26	68.85±2.29	64.37±1.86

However, this classifier has other advantages: it is virtually non-parametric, and returns a numerical confidence on the result, which can be used by the clinician as a risk measure. We also wish to highlight that this Bayesian approach has already been used in this area (Lee, 2016) (Orphanou, 2016). For these reasons, we proceeded to the test set with the NB classifier.

3.2. Test Set

After choosing the best classifier based on the training set, we proceeded to analyze its performance on the test set. The entire training set was used on the NB classifier to build our predictive model and then the test set was used and the AUC, sensitivity and specificity metrics were retrieved as seen in Table 6 These results will allow

Table 5. Features selected from the CfsSubsetEval evaluator with a BestFirst search for the different time windows. SVPB is isolated supraventricular ectopic beats events. SVBG is number of bigeminy supraventricular events. VPB is isolated ventricular ectopic beats events. V run is the number of runs of ventricular ectopic beats events. V. Bigeminy is bigeminy ventricular events. V. Trigeminy is trigeminy ventricular events. Max H.R. is maximum heart rate (bpm). Night: HR is heart rate in bpm during the night. Night: VarIndex is the percentage of delta of RR, where deltaRR: RR(i) - R(i - 1). SVBG is the number of bigeminy supraventricular event.

Selected Features				
0	**1**	**2**	**3**	**4**
Clopidrogel	VPB	Age	SVPB	SVPB
VRun	clopidrogel	SVBg	Age	Age
Indapamida	Canef	V.Bigeminy	SVBg	SVBg
Actonel	Varimine	clopidrogel	Max. H.R.	V.Trigeminy
Zanitek	Varimine	Max H.R.	V.Trigeminy	Max. H.R
Aprovel	Aprovel	Adalat	clopidrogel	Clopidrogel
	Actonel	Canef	Night: HR	Night: HR
	Zanitek	Varimine	adalat	Night: VarIndex
		indapamida	canef	24h QT Lead B Total QRS
		diclofenac	varimine	Adalat
		Zanitek	triatec	Canef
		Actonel	diclofenac	Varimine
			dancor	Triatec
			zanitek	Diclofenac
			actonel	Zanitek
				Dancor
				Actonel

us to know what to expect with the NB prediction, when dealing with new and unknown patient's information.

Comparing the results with the training set, we find that most of the test metrics are below the confidence interval (mean ± standard deviation), although some are between or above. However, these are slight deviations that should not compromise our analysis. Another interesting fact, for the AUC outcomes, is that the best performing values occur after using bootstrapping and FS, which is in agreement with our training conclusions. These models can be very useful in clinical practice, especially when using the NB classifier, which can be robust enough to ignore serious deficiencies in its underlying naive probability model (Rish, 2001).

Table 6. Results in percentage obtained from the test set using the NB classifier. OD is original data; FS is after applying feature selection; NB is Naive Bayes.

NB					
Window (Years)	**Bootstrapping**	**Data**	**AUC**	**Sensitivity**	**Specificity**
0	No	OD	50.09	28.58	93.03
		FS	57.94	0.0	100.0
	Yes	OD	65.41	42.86	70.35
		FS	53.49	0.0	94.77
1	No	OD	47.11	20.0	89.35
		FS	68.26	0.0	100.0
	Yes	OD	62.99	80.0	51.48
		FS	65.98	0.0	94.68
2	No	OD	54.55	23.08	88.56
		FS	67.75	7.7	98.8
	Yes	OD	69.79	84.62	48.2
		FS	60.48	46.16	75.91
3	No	OD	55.29	21.43	87.88
		FS	68.84	21.43	96.37
	Yes	OD	68.66	71.43	53.34
		FS	**68.06**	**42.86**	**80.61**
4	No	OD	56.41	28.58	89.7
		FS	73.12	21.43	96.97
	Yes	OD	65.55	78.58	46.07
		FS	**71.74**	**71.43**	**64.85**

3.3. Comparison With Framingham

The Framingham Heart Study for CHD is described in detail in (D'Agostino, 2000). We applied the Weibull model on the test set in order to obtain a probability estimate for a CHD risk. The features used for this model are described in II-D and were not used on our original dataset, with exception to age and hypertensive medication. These features were obtained from the patient's clinical file according to their ID and exam date performed. Since some features were not performed on the same day of the Holter exam, we obtained the nearest exam without exceeding a 6 months interval between the Holter exam and the parameters exam. Afterwards we applied our predictive model on the test set and estimated the probability to have a CHD. Regarding features 3) smoking status, 7) menopause and 8) alcohol consumption, described on II-D, these were not available on the patient's clinical file. Our solution was to obtain this information by contacting each patient that belongs to the test set. For those that we could not reach (37% of the test set) we classified them as missing values. We tested for time windows of 3 and 4 years, however, only a window of 4 years is shown - Figure 2. Comparing the probabilities for each test patient by using the Framingham tool and our predictive model, we found that our classification system identified correctly T2D that will manifest a CHD (red cluster identified in Figure 2) while the Framingham underestimated the results for this population.

The probability values for the Framingham do not show any relation with our outcomes or any trend with patients that manifests CHD. Although we present a solution with a higher number of features (that is obtained from the Holter dataset) than the Framingham, our results present a higher precision on the prognostic of the CHD. Moreover, Framingham studies in European population have already been tested and the main conclusion is that it should be used with caution and specific populations risk functions should be implemented (Menotti, 2000) (Empana, 2003).

Figure 2. Comparison between Framingham risk tool with our predictive model: Naive Bayes, for a prognosis of 4 years with bootstrapping and FS on the training set. Probability results in percentage. Red dots are T2D patients with a CHD and blue dots are T2D patients without CHD.

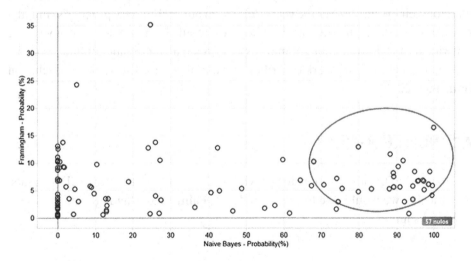

4. CONCLUSION

In this paper we propose a new approach for CHD prognostic prediction on T2D patients, given a Holter dataset. FS was applied given the high number of available features. Bootstrapping was used to provide a more balanced training data. We applied 5x10-fold CV on the training set for different classifiers and selected the classifier that presented the best metrics: AUC, sensitivity and specificity. Following, the test set was applied on the best model - the NB classifier. We achieved an AUC performance of 68,06%, 74,33% for a 3 and 4-years risk prognosis respectively using the data comprising the years from 2006 to 2014 to predict diabetic patients that will evolve to CHD. A drawback of this study is the low number of patients that will evolve to CHD; therefore we used the bootstrapping technique and threshold selector. Also, it is important to mention that supplementary exams can be performed (e.g. echocardiography, chest X-Ray, blood tests) in order to confirm that the patient is actually in risk of CHD.

As future work we aim to include a temporal analysis, meaning we want to add new features to the classification that will represent their evolution over time, and could therefore improve our predictive model. This is a data enrichment which is used to investigate possible improvements on classification. We also want to test other machine learning packages such as Theano - it will allow to attain speeds rivalling hand-crafted C implementations for problems involving large amounts of data. We will also compare our predictive model with other existing tools for CHD as mentioned in II-D; however this will only be possible when we reach enough longitudinal data. We will classify new patients with our predictive model and monitor their evolution over the years to confirm our preliminary prognosis. Finally, we also believe that our prognostic methodology could later be adapted to any Holter software as an additional plugin in order to provide an automatic prognostic to the clinician. The following work describes an example of a software plugin inclusion (Pimentel, 2015).

ACKNOWLEDGMENT

We thank APDP organization for providing the Holter dataset of T2D patients. Specifically, we would like to thank Frederico Palma and Magda Rosado for their technical support.

CONFLICTS OF INTEREST

Pimentel, R. T. Ribeiro, I. Almeida, P. Matos, J. Raposo and H. Gamboa declare that they have no conflict of interest.

HUMAN STUDIES

All procedures followed were in accordance with the ethical standards of the responsible committee on human experimentation (institutional and national) and with the Helsinki Declaration of 1975, as revised in 2000 (5). Informed consent was obtained from all patients for being included in the study.

REFERENCES

Aha, D. W., Kibler, D., & Albert, M. K. (1991). Instance-based learning algorithms. *Machine Learning*, 6(1), 37–66. doi:10.1007/BF00153759

Assign Score - Prioritising Prevention of Cardiovascular Disease. (n.d.). Retrieved March 2015 from http://assign-score.com/

Breiman, L. (2001). Random forests. *Machine Learning*, 45(1), 5–32. doi:10.1023/A:1010933404324

Burghard, C. (2012). *Big Data and Analytics Key to Accountable Care Success*. I. H. Insights.

Chawla, N. V., Bowyer, K. W., Hall, L. O., & Kegelmeyer, W. P. (2011). SMOTE: Synthetic minority over-sampling technique. *Journal of Artificial Intelligence Research*, 16, 321–357.

Cook, N. R. (2008). Statistical evaluation of prognostic versus diagnostic models: Beyond the ROC curve. *Clinical Chemistry*, 54(1), 17–23. doi:10.1373/clinchem.2007.096529 PMID:18024533

DAgostino, R. B., Russell, M. W., Huse, D. M., Ellison, R. C., Silbershatz, H., Wilson, P. W., & Hartz, S. C. (2000). Primary and subsequent coronary risk appraisal: New results from the Framingham study. *American Heart Journal*, 139(2), 272–281. doi:10.1016/S0002-8703(00)90236-9 PMID:10650300

Demšar, J. (2006). Statistical comparisons of classifiers over multiple data sets. *Journal of Machine Learning Research*, 7(Jan), 1–30.

Empana, J. P., Ducimetiere, P., Arveiler, D., Ferrieres, J., Evans, A., & Ruidavets, J. B. et al.. (2003). Are the Framingham and PROCAM coronary heart disease risk functions applicable to different European populations? *European Heart Journal, 24*(21), 1903–1911. doi:10.1016/j.ehj.2003.09.002 PMID:14585248

Fawcett, T. (2006). An introduction to ROC analysis. *Pattern Recognition Letters, 27*(8), 861–874. doi:10.1016/j.patrec.2005.10.010

Freund, Y., & Mason, L. (1999, June). The alternating decision tree learning algorithm. In ICML (Vol. 99, pp. 124-133). Academic Press.

Gardete-Correia, L., Boavida, J. M., Raposo, J. F., Mesquita, A. C., Fona, C., Carvalho, R., & Massano-Cardoso, S. (2010). First diabetes prevalence study in Portugal: PREVADIAB study. *Diabetic Medicine, 27*(8), 879–881. doi:10.1111/j.1464-5491.2010.03017.x PMID:20653744

Gill, T. M. (2012). The central role of prognosis in clinical decision making. *Journal of the American Medical Association, 307*(2), 199–200. doi:10.1001/jama.2011.1992 PMID:22235093

Grzymala-Busse, J. W., Stefanowski, J., & Wilk, S. (2005). A comparison of two approaches to data mining from imbalanced data. *Journal of Intelligent Manufacturing, 16*(6), 565–573. doi:10.1007/s10845-005-4362-2

Hall, M., Frank, E., Holmes, G., Pfahringer, B., Reutemann, P., & Witten, I. H. (2009). The WEKA data mining software: an update. *ACM SIGKDD Explorations Newsletter, 11*(1), 10-18.

Heartscore. (n.d.). Retrieved March 2015 from http://www.heartscore.org/Pages/welcome.aspx

INFARMED National Authority of Medicines and Health Products. (n.d.). Retrieved March 2015 from http://www.infarmed.pt/portal/page/portal/INFARMED

John, G. H., & Langley, P. (1995, August). Estimating continuous distributions in Bayesian classifiers. In *Proceedings of the Eleventh conference on Uncertainty in artificial intelligence* (pp. 338-345). Morgan Kaufmann Publishers Inc.

Jovanov, E., Gelabert, P., Adhami, R., Wheelock, B., & Adams, R. (1999, August). Real time Holter monitoring of biomedical signals. In DSP Technology and Education conference DSPS (Vol. 99, pp. 4-6). Academic Press.

Kohavi, R. (1995, August). A study of cross-validation and bootstrap for accuracy estimation and model selection. In IJCAI (Vol. 14, No. 2, pp. 1137-1145). Academic Press.

Kohavi, R., & John, G. H. (1997). Wrappers for feature subset selection. *Artificial Intelligence, 97*(1), 273–324. doi:10.1016/S0004-3702(97)00043-X

Lan, G.-C., Lee, C.-H., Lee, Y.-Y., Tseng, V., Chin, C.-Y., Day, M.-L., & Wu, J.-S. et al. (2012November) Disease risk prediction by mining personalized health trend patterns: A case study on diabetes. In *2012 Conference on Technologies and Applications of Artificial Intelligence* (pp. 27-32). IEEE. doi:10.1109/TAAI.2012.53

Lee, B. J., & Kim, J. Y. (2016). Identification of Type 2 Diabetes Risk Factors Using Phenotypes Consisting of Anthropometry and Triglycerides based on Machine Learning. *IEEE Journal of Biomedical and Health Informatics, 20*(1), 39-46.

Levin, R. I., Cohen, D., Frisbie, W., Selwyn, A. P., Barry, J., Deanfield, J. E., & Campbell, D. Q. et al. (1986). Potential for real-time processing of the continuously monitored electrocardiogram in the detection, quantitation, and intervention of silent myocardial ischemia. *Cardiology Clinics, 4*(4), 735–745. PMID:3096569

Menotti, A., Puddu, P. E., & Lanti, M. (2000). Comparison of the Framingham risk function-based coronary chart with risk function from an Italian population study. *European Heart Journal, 21*(5), 365–370. doi:10.1053/euhj.1999.1864 PMID:10666350

Morrish, N. J., Wang, S. L., Stevens, L. K., Fuller, J. H., & Keen, H. (2001). Mortality and causes of death in the WHO Multinational Study of Vascular Disease in Diabetes. *Diabetologia, 44*(2), S14–S21. doi:10.1007/PL00002934 PMID:11587045

Orphanou, K., Stassopoulou, A., & Keravnou, E. (2016). DBN-Extended: A Dynamic Bayesian Network Model Extended With Temporal Abstractions for Coronary Heart Disease Prognosis. *IEEE Journal of Biomedical and Health Informatics, 20*(3), 944-952.

Pimentel, A., Gomes, R., Olstad, B. H., & Gamboa, H. (2015). A New Tool for the Automatic Detection of Muscular Voluntary Contractions in the Analysis of Electromyographic Signals. *Interacting with Computers, 27*(5), 492–499. doi:10.1093/iwc/iwv008

Platt, J. (1998). *Sequential minimal optimization: A fast algorithm for training support vector machines*. Academic Press.

QRISK - Cardiovascular Disease Risk Calculator. (n.d.). Retrieved March 2015 from http://www.qrisk.org/

Raghupathi, W. (2016). Data Mining in Healthcare. *Healthcare Informatics: Improving Efficiency Through Technology, Analytics, and Management*, 353.

Rish, I. (2001, August). An empirical study of the naive Bayes classifier. In IJCAI 2001 Workshop on Empirical Methods in Artificial Intelligence (Vol. 3, No. 22, pp. 41-46). IBM.

Shaw, J. E., Sicree, R. A., & Zimmet, P. Z. (2010). Global estimates of the prevalence of diabetes for 2010 and 2030. *Diabetes Research and Clinical Practice*, *87*(1), 4–14. doi:10.1016/j.diabres.2009.10.007 PMID:19896746

WHO. (n.d.). Retrieved January 2015 from http://www.who.int/en/

Witten, I. H., Frank, E., & Hall, M. A. (2011). *Data Mining: Practical Machine Learning Tools and Techniques*. Elsevier.

APPENDIX A: FEATURE DESCRIPTIONS

Tables 7 and 8 presents all features used for classification. Table 7 shows the features provided by the Holter, and Table 8 the created features for medication.

Table 7. Feature descriptions without medication

Feature	Description	Feature	Description
PATIENT_ID	patient id	24h QT Lead C QTa (ms)	
EXAM_DATE	exam date	24h QT Lead C QTe (ms)	
Birth date	birth date	24h QT Lead C QTac (ms)	
Age	Age	24h QT Lead C Slope (mV/s)	
Gender	Gender	24h QT Lead C Total QRS	
Pacemaker	pacemaker - yes or no	24h QT Lead C Nb. QRS	
Number of day	nr of days that performed exam	24h QT Lead C Amplitude (V)	
Number of Day Recorded		24h QT Lead C QTec (ms)	
Average	heart rate average in bpm	24h QT Lead C SD RR (ms)	
Max. H.R (bpm)	max heart rate in bpm	24h QT Lead C Mean RR (ms)	
Min. H.R (bpm)	min heart rate in bpm	24h QT Lead M Total QRS	
Mean day H.R. (bpm)	mean heart rate during day in bpm	24h QT Lead M Nb. QRS	
Mean Night H.R. (bpm)	mean heart rate during night in bpm	24h QT Lead M SD RR (ms)	
Max. RR (ms)	max RR in ms	24h QT Lead M Mean RR (ms)	
Min. RR (ms)	min RR in ms	LF/HF	ratio between low frequency high frequency for 24 hours
Total no.of QRS	total nr of QRS complexes	EV	ventricular extra-systole
BRADYCARDIA	nr of bradycardias	TV	ventricular tachycardia
PAUSE	nr of pauses	ESV	supraventricular extra-systole
MISSED BEATS	nr of missed beats	TSV	supraventricular tachycardia

continued on next page

Table 7. Continued

Feature	Description	Feature	Description
VPB	nr of isolated ventricular ectopic beats events	NORMAL	
V_COUPLET	nr of couplet ventricular ectopic beats events	ritmo_circadiano	circadian rhythm (normal or abolished)
V_RUN	nr of runs ventricular ectopic beats events	24h HR (bpm)	heart rate for 24 hours in bpm
V. Bigeminy	nr of bigeminy ventricular events	PNN50	percentage of the normal heartbeat intervals (NN) > than 50 ms
V.Trigeminy	nr of trigeminy ventricular events	24h PNN30 (perc)	percentage of the normal heartbeat intervals (NN) > than 30 ms
V_TACHYCARDIA	nr of tachycardias ventricular events	RMSSD	square root of the mean of the squares of the successive differences between adjacent NNs during 24h
SVPB	nr of isolated supraventricular ectopic beats events	24h VarIndex (perc)	percentage of delta of RR. Delta RR: RR(i)-R(i-1) for 24 hours
SV_COUPLET	nr of couplet supraventricular ectopic beats events	24h ASDNN/5mn (ms)	average of all 5-min standard deviation of all NN intervals for 24h
SV_RUN	nr of runs supraventricular ectopic beats events	24h SDANN/5mn (ms)	standard deviation of the average NN intervals over 5 min interval for 24h
SVBg	nr supraventricular events bigeminy	SD/SDNN	ratio standard deviation with standard deviation of all NN intervals
SVTg	nr supraventricular events trigeminy	24h Total Power (ms)	total power of FFT between 0Hz and 2Hz in ms for 24h
SVT	nr supraventricular events tachycardia	24h VLF (ms)	very low frequency in ms for 24h
RR INSTABILITY	nr of supraventricular events for RR instability	LF	low frequency in ms
Acceleration		HF	high frequency in ms
Deceleration		Day: HR (bpm)	heart rate in bpm during day
EPISODES OF ST SEGMENT DEVIATION		Day: PNN50 (perc)	percentage of NN > than 50ms during day
Minimum pause duration (ms)	minmum value to count for a pause in ms	Day: PNN30 (perc)	percentage of NN > than 30ms during day

continued on next page

Table 7. Continued

Feature	Description	Feature	Description
Supraventricular prematurity < (perc)	limit value to count a supraventricular prematurity in percentage	Day: RMSSD (ms)	square root of the mean of the squares of the successive differences between adjacent NNs during the day
Bradycardia < (bpm)	limit value to count a bradycardia in bpm	Day: VarIndex (perc)	percentage of delta of RR. Delta RR: RR(i)-R(i-1) during day
Ventricular tachycardia > (bpm)	limit value to count a ventricular tachycardia in bpm	Day: ASDNN/5mn (ms)	average of all 5-min standard deviation of all NN intervals during day
Deceleration (perc)		Day: SDANN/5mn (ms)	standard deviation of the average NN intervals over 5 min interval during day
Spontaneous Rhythm	spontaneous rythm in percentage	Day: SD (ms)	standard deviation during day
avP	pacemaker rhythm in percentage	Day: Total Power (ms)	total power of FFT between 0Hz and 2Hz in ms during day
aP		Day: VLF (ms)	very low frequency in ms during day
vP		Day: LF (ms)	low frequency in ms during day
Fp		Day: HF (ms)	high frequency in ms during day
Define VLF	limit for very low frequency in Hz	Night: HR (bpm)	heart rate in bpm during night
Define LF	limit for low frequency in Hz	Night: PNN50 (perc)	percentage of NN > than 50ms during night
Define HF	limit for high frequency in Hz	Night: PNN30 (perc)	percentage of NN > than 30ms during night
24h QT Lead A QTa (ms)		Night: RMSSD (ms)	square root of the mean of the squares of the successive differences between adjacent NNs during the night
24h QT Lead A QTe (ms)		Night: VarIndex (perc)	percentage of delta of RR. Delta RR: RR(i)-R(i-1) during night
24h QT Lead A QTac (ms)		Night: ASDNN/5mn (ms)	average of all 5-min standard deviation of all NN intervals during night
24h QT Lead A Slope (mV/s)		Night: SDANN/5mn (ms)	standard deviation of the average NN intervals over 5 min interval during night

continued on next page

Table 7. Continued

Feature	Description	Feature	Description
24h QT Lead A Total QRS		Night: SD (ms)	standard deviation in ms
24h QT Lead A Nb. QRS		Night: Total Power (ms)	total power of FFT between 0Hz and 2Hz in ms during night
24h QT Lead A Amplitude (V)		Night: VLF (ms)	very low frequency in ms during night
24h QT Lead A QTec (ms)		Night: LF (ms)	low frequency in ms during night
24h QT Lead A SD RR (ms)		Night: HF (ms)	high frequency in ms during night
24h QT Lead A Mean RR (ms)		MedHyper	medication for hypertension - yes or no
24h QT Lead B QTa (ms)		Statins	medication that are in statins groups - yes or no
24h QT Lead B QTe (ms)		Antiagregant	medication that is antiplatelet agents - yes or no
24h QT Lead B QTac (ms)		Betablockers	medication that is betablockers - yes or no
24h QT Lead B Slope (mV/s)		Antiarrythmic	medication that is antiarrythmic -yes or no
24h QT Lead B Total QRS		freq6070	heart rate average between 60 and 70 -yes or no
24h QT Lead B Nb. QRS		freq7080	heart rate average between 70 and 80 - yes or no
24h QT Lead B Amplitude (V)		freq8090	heart rate average between 80 and 90 - yes or no
24h QT Lead B QTec (ms)		freq90100	heart rate average between 90 and 100 -yes or no
24h QT Lead B SD RR (ms)		Evolution	evolution to CHD - yes or no
24h QT Lead B Mean RR (ms)			

Table 8. Medication used according to their active principle level

Livetan	Glucovance	Crestor	Magnesium
Diovan	Supralip	Trajenta	Aas
Cloretotrospio	Blopress	Niaspan	Semi-Daonil
Singulair	Atacand	Pariet	Actrapid
Cozaar	Elugel	Lantus	Loftyl
Rivotril	Pantoprazol	Cartia	Pentoxifilina
Indapamida	Amizal	Pritor	Silodyx
Sertralina	Dilamax	Dancor	Irbesartan
Salazopirina	Ramipril	Januvia	Captopril
Glucobay	Amoxicilina	Adalat	Thyrax
Lyrica	Furosemida	Valdoxan	Gradumet
Mixtard	Lortaan	Lercanidipina	Diazepam
Rasilez	Folicil	Pulmicort	Duagen
Lopresor	Diclofenac	Lescol	Zolnor
Lisinopril	Seroxat	Hyperium	Varfine
Cervoxan	Diamicron	Tromalyt	Euritox
Micardis	Proaxen	Tecnosal	Nexium
Nebivolol	Glucophage	Humalog	Simvastatina
Alprazolam	Xanax	Zolpidem	Aspegic
Aldactone	Praxilene	Norvasc	Conversyl
Pradaxa	Ever-Fit-Cardioantioxidante	Ticlopidina	Medipax
Zyloric	Isoptin	Lanoxin	Socian
Canef	Metformina	Zestoretic	Olsar
Preterax	Atenolol	Triatec	Adalgur
Vitalux	Maxilase	Concor	Inegy
Venex	Diltiazem	Bromazepam	Preslow
Fluoxetina	Monoket	Tricef	Daflon
Clopidogrel	Co-Diovan	Amlodipina	Icandra
Glimepirida	Doxi-Om	Carvedilol	Atorvastatina
Daonil	Morfex	Filotempo	Hytacand
Catalip	Triapin	Varimine	Beta-Histina
Cipralex	Indur	Ezetrol	Cyclo
Persantin	Venlafaxina	Viartril	Letter
Omeprazol	Inderal	Visacor	Amiodarona
Brufen	Lendormin	Salofalk	Pravastatina

continued on next page

Table 8. Continued

Ranitidina	Olmetec	Zofenopril	Sintron
Zurim	Alfuzosina	Enalapril	Tecnolip
Vipocem	Nitroglicerina	Avandamet	Tansulosina
Sinemet	Gabapentina	Permixon	Actonel
Fosavance	Janumet	Ferro	Difrarel
Losartan	Combodart	Zanitek	Aprovel
Co-Aprovel			

APPENDIX B: CLASSIFIERS PARAMETERS OPTIMIZATION

Table 9 shows the best parameters obtained after applying CV on each classifier for different values. We have provided this table in order to facilitate its reproducibility.

Table 9. CV parameters optimization. RF presents the best number of trees after testing values from 10 to 1000. SVM presents the best complexity parameter after testing values from 0.1 to 10. ADT presents the best number of boosting iterations after testing values from 5 to 50. KNN presents the best number of nearest neighbours after testing values from 1 to 10.

Window (Years)	Data	RF	SVM	ADT	KNN
0	OD	10	0.1	5	2
	FS	10	0.1	5	1
1	OD	10	0.1	10	4
	FS	10	2.3	25	1
2	OD	10	0.1	10	2
	FS	230	1.2	5	9
3	OD	10	0.1	5	2
	FS	890	0.1	5	4
4	OD	10	0.1	20	2
	FS	10	0.1	10	7

Chapter 6

Application of Machine Learning Techniques for Software Reliability Prediction (SRP)

Pradeep Kumar
Maulana Azad National Urdu University, India

ABSTRACT

Software reliability is a statistical measure of how well software operates with respect to its requirements. There are two related software engineering research issues about reliability requirements. The first issue is achieving the necessary reliability, i.e., choosing and employing appropriate software engineering techniques in system design and implementation. The second issue is the assessment of reliability as a method of assurance that precedes system deployment. In past few years, various software reliability models have been introduced. These models have been developed in response to the need of software engineers, system engineers and managers to quantify the concept of software reliability. This chapter on software reliability prediction using ANNs addresses three main issues: (1) analyze, manage, and improve the reliability of software products; (2) satisfy the customer needs for competitive price, on time delivery, and reliable software product; (3) determine the software release instance that is, when the software is good enough to release to the customer.

DOI: 10.4018/978-1-5225-2545-5.ch006

INTRODUCTION

Reliability is increasingly becoming more important during the design of software systems, as our daily lives and schedules are more dependent than ever before on the satisfactory functioning of these systems. The common examples of such systems are computers, critical safety system, automobiles, aircraft, and space satellites. Some of the specific factors that are playing a key role in increasing the importance of reliability in designed systems include system complexity and sophistication, global market competition, increasing reliability and quality-related issues, high acquisition cost, the past well-publicized system failures, and loss of prestige. On the other hand, the importance of quality in business and industry is increasing rapidly due to market competition, growing demand from customers for better quality, increasing various quality-related lawsuits, and the global economy.

Today, billions of dollars are being spent annually to produce new products using modern information and communication technologies. Many of these products are highly sophisticated and contain millions of parts. For example, a Boeing 747 jumbo jet is made up of approximately 4.5 million parts including fasteners. Therefore, reliability and quality of software systems have become more important than ever before. Moreover, global competition and other factors are forcing software practitioners and industry professionals to produce highly reliable and good quality software. That is why, there is a definite need for the reliability and quality professionals to work closely during testing and other phases of SDLC.

BACKGROUND

In literature, many empirical studies based on multivariate linear regression and neural network methods have been carried out for prediction of software reliability growth trends. Although, multivariate linear regression method can address linear relationship but require large sample size and more independent variables (Jung-Hua 2010). The use of support vector machine (SVM) approach in place of classical techniques has shown a remarkable improvement in the prediction of software reliability in the recent years (Xiang-Li 2007). The design of SVM is based on the extraction of a subset of the training data that serves as support vectors and therefore represents a stable characteristic of the data. SVM can be applied as an alternative approach because of their generalization performance, ease of usability and rigorous theoretical foundations that practically can be used for regression solving problems (Ping and Lyu 2005). However, the major limitation of support vector machines is the increasing computational and storage requirements with respect to the number of training examples (Chen 2005). The group method of data handling (GMDH) network based on the principle of heuristic self-organization has also been applied for predicting future software failure occurrence time and the optimal cost for software release instant during the testing phase (Dohi et al., 2000). They numerically illustrated that GMDH networks are capable to overcome the problem of determining a suitable network size in multilayer perceptron neural network. GMDH also can provide a more accurate measure in the software reliability assessment than other classical prediction methods. Another reliability prediction method, neural network based approach for predicting software reliability using Back-Propagation Neural Network (BPN) has been applied for estimating the failures of the software system in the maintaining phase (Chen et al, 2009).

Therefore it is quite natural for software practitioners and potential users to know that which particular method tend to work well for a given type of dataset and up to what extent quantitatively (Aggarwal and Singh, 2006). The objective of our study is to assess the effect of past and present failure data detected during software testing using soft computing techniques in a realistic environment. That will help project managers in optimizing the testing efforts to market the product on time leading to maximize the profit.

The reliability (Zuzana, 2007) is one of the major issue of electronic device, hardware and application software. Over the years many software reliability growth models have been employed for predicting reliability. Yet, there is no universal agreement among the researchers in the field of software reliability modeling that a correct or best model can exist. Because one modeller might consider certain aspects of reality very important thus giving them significant weight in his model On the other hand another modeller may have dissimilar views which result in a different model.

Mathematically reliability R (t) is the probability that a system will be successful in the interval from time 0 to time t:

$$R(t) = P(T \succ t), t \geq 0 \tag{1}$$

where T is a random variable denoting the time-to-failure or failure time.

Alternatively, the failure rate F(t), can be defined as the probability that the system will fail by time t can be expressed as:

$$F(t) = P(T \leq t), t \geq 0 \tag{2}$$

In other words, F (t) is the failure distribution function and the relationship between reliability and failure rate can be defined as follows:

$$R(t) = 1 - F(t) \tag{3}$$

Software Reliability Prediction Models play an important role in developing software systems and enhancing computer software. The classical software reliability theory deals with probabilistic methods applied to the analysis of random occurrence of failures in a given software system. In general, software reliability models fall into two categories depending on the operating domain. The most popular category of models depends on time, whose main feature is that probability measures, such as the mean time between failures and the failure intensity function depend on failure time. The second category of software reliability models measures reliability as the ratio of successful runs to the total number of runs.

This section introduces some fundamental definitions, important terms, concepts, and notations which are frequently used in this chapter.

TERMS AND DEFINITIONS

There are a large number of terms and definitions used in software reliability engineering. This section presents some of the commonly used terms and definitions used in this thesis taken from the published literature (1–29). This section presents several statistical measures considered useful in classical and modern reliability theory.

Probability Definition and Properties

Probability may be defined as likelihood of occurrence of a given event. Mathematically, it can be expressed as:

$$P = \frac{\text{Total number of ways an event occurs}}{\text{Total number of occurrence possibilities}} \tag{4}$$

where P is the probability.

Some of the most important event-related properties of probability are described as follows:

1. The probability of occurrence of event, say Y, is $0 \leq P(Y) \leq 1$
2. The probability of occurrence and non-occurrence of an event, say Y, is always $P(Y) + P(\bar{Y}) = 1$ where $P(Y)$ is the probability of occurrence of event Y and $P(\bar{Y})$ is the probability of non-occurrence of event Y.
3. The probability of the union of m mutually exclusive events is given by

$$P\left(Y_1 + Y_2 + \ldots + Y_m\right) = \sum_{i=1}^{m} P\left(Y_i\right)$$

where $P(Y_i)$ is the probability of occurrence of event Y_i for $i = 1, 2, 3, m$

Random Variables

Random Variables (RV) is a variable quantity which denotes the result of a given experiment known as stochastic variable. RV is denoted by upper case letters and their realizations by the corresponding lower case (Aggarwal & Singh, 2008). A random variable may be either discrete or continuous. A random variable X is known as discrete if its range forms a discrete (countable) set of real numbers. On the other hand, random variable X is known as continuous if its range forma a continuous set of real numbers and the probability of X equalling any single value in its range is zero.

Here we consider a variable X that can take on only the values $x_1, x_2, \ldots, x_n$ with the respective probabilities $P(x_1), P(x_2), \ldots, P(x_n)$ then the variable X over its complete range of values can be written as:

$$\sum_{i=1}^{n} P(x_n) = 1 \tag{5}$$

where x is called a random variable. The function P(x) which takes on the discrete values at the given points is called the probability frequency or probability density function i.e.,

$$P(x_i) = \Pr ob(x = x_i) \tag{6}$$

The probability distribution function is defined as follows:

$$P(x) = \Pr ob(X \leq x) = \sum_{i=1}^{n} \left\{ P(x_i), x_i \leq x \right\} \tag{7}$$

where X refers to the set of all x_i, $p(x)$ – probability frequency function and $P(x)$ is probability distribution function. The functions can be discrete or continuous. In reliability applications small x refer to time that is a random distribution of the failure times.

Probability Density and Cumulative Distribution Functions

This section presents several mathematical definitions considered useful to perform various types of software reliability studies such as:

For a continuous random variable, the probability density function is defined by

$f(t) = \dfrac{dF(t)}{dt}$ where, t is the time (i.e., a continuous random variable) and

f(t) = probability density function (it is often referred to as failure density function)

F(t) = cumulative distribution function and is expressed by: $F(t) = \displaystyle\int_{-\infty}^{t} f(x)dx$ and

$F(\infty) = 1$

or $F(t) = \displaystyle\int_{0}^{t} f(x)dx$ (8)

Expected Value

Expected value of a random variable (the mean value or the average value) defined as follows:

$$E\left[x\right] = \sum_{i=1}^{n} x_i * p(x_i)$$ (9)

In general case, the expected value of a deterministic function of x may be defined by the equation:

$$E\left[f(x)\right] = \sum_{i=1}^{n} f(x_i) * p(x_i)$$ (10)

Alternatively, the expected value E(t), of a continuous random variable t is defined by

$$E(t) = m = \int_{-\infty}^{\infty} tf(t)dt \qquad (11)$$

where E(t) is the expected value of the continuous random variable t and m is the mean value.

Variance

The variance $\sigma^2(t)$ of a random variable t is expressed by

$$\sigma^2(t) = E(t^2) - \left[E(t)\right]^2 \qquad (12)$$

In reliability theory, the variance is commonly known as mean time to failure (MTTF).

Statistical Distributions

This section presents the most commonly used statistical or probability distributions useful for performing various types of reliability computations described as follows:

Exponential Distribution

A continuous random variable having the range of $0 \leq x \prec \infty$ is said to have an exponential distribution if it has the probability-density function of the form:

$$f(x) = \begin{cases} \lambda e^{-\lambda x}, 0 \prec x \prec \infty \\ 0, x \prec 0 \end{cases} \qquad (13)$$

where λ is a positive constant. The corresponding distribution function can be written as

$$F(x) = \begin{cases} (1 - \lambda e^{-\lambda x}), 0 \leq x \prec \infty \\ 0, x \prec 0 \end{cases} \qquad (14)$$

In reliability theory, the exponential distribution function plays an important role while modeling complex failure behavior of software. Thus, exponential distribution function is one of the simplest continuous random variable distributions widely used in reliability studies.

MEASURES OF RELIABILITY

Some important key functions to describe the failure process of a software system can be defined as follows:

1. Probability density of failures, p (t).
2. Cumulative failure probability, P (t).
3. Failure rate λ (t).

The equations relating these functions are:

$$P(t) = \int_0^t p(x)dx \tag{15}$$

$$\overline{P(t)} = 1 - P(t) \text{ or } \overline{P(t)} = e^{-\left[\int_0^t \lambda(x)dx\right]} = R(t) \tag{16}$$

The reliability, R (t) of a software is defined as the probability that the software will operate correctly until time t, given that it was operational at time t = 0. The failure density of the software component, p (t) can also be expressed in terms of reliability as:

$$p(t) = -\frac{d}{dt}\left[R(t)\right] \tag{17}$$

The instantaneous failure rate function λ (t), is given by:

$$\lambda(t) = \frac{p(t)}{R(t)} \tag{18}$$

The choice of this density leads to a constant failure rate (or hazard rate) function λ (t) = λ.

The unreliability of the system, Q (t) is the probability that the component will fail in the time interval from zero to t, given by:

$$Q(t) = \int_0^t p(\tau)d\tau = 1 - R(t) \tag{19}$$

MTTF (Mean Time to Failure) is given by: $MTTF = \int_0^\infty tp(\tau)d\tau$ (20)

The Probability Density Function (PDF)

The probability density function $f(t)$, the cumulative distribution function $F(t)$, the reliability function $R(t)$ and the failure rate function $\lambda(t)$ are closely related to each other. Under general conditions, any one of these functions can be determined from the others given the failure rate function $\lambda(t)$, and the reliability function $R(t)$. Failure rate function may be computed by:

If the intensity function increases, then the probability of failure over a specific interval of time becomes greater as long as time proceeds. This trend indicates that the software system deteriorates. On the contrary, if the intensity function decreases, this indicates that the software reliability is growing. Although, in software systems it is reasonable to assume that the intensity function may change only when the program undergoes some modification in its codes (addition of new codes in the program or fault removal, and so on). The time interval under which the system software will be used is important. Thus, in order to achieve a required outcome, it is essential that the system software involves functions properly with an extremely high reliability during a short time interval, which is usually shorter than other phases of software development. For software in commercial and industry applications, the time interval for which software is designed is supposed to be much longer.

PARAMETER ESTIMATION TECHNIQUES

In order to validate the software reliability prediction model precisely we need to estimate the model's parameters accurately. Two well-known and broadly used method of parameter estimation are least square estimation (LSE) and maximum likelihood estimation (MLE). The method of least squares minimizes the sum of squares of deviations between what is expected and what we observe from the experiment. Also, fitting the present model to actual error data we required to estimate the model's parameters from failure data sets of real-life software projects. MLE is the direct approach which allows estimating the parameters through input the data directly into equations for the parameters. LSE, another alternative approach is fitting the curve described by the function to the data and estimating the parameters from the best fit to the curve.

Maximum Likelihood

The maximum likelihood method consists of solving a set of simultaneous equations for parameter values. The equations of software reliability prediction model define parameter values that maximize the likelihood from the observed data extracted from a distribution with those parameter values. MLE satisfies several important statistical conditions for an optimal estimator and therefore considered to be the best statistical estimator for large sample sizes. However, the set of simultaneous equations defined through MLE are very complex and consumes more efforts to be solved numerically (Musa, 87).

Least Squares Estimation

The LSE curve-fitting find the parameter values that minimize the difference between the data and the function fitting the data, where the difference is defined as the sum of the squared errors. The classical least squares method involves log likelihood functions. The least squares method solves the model equation for parameter values by picking the values that best fit a curve to the data. LSE method is generally considered to be the best for small to medium sample sizes failure datasets for realistic predictions.

SOFTWARE RELIABILITY PREDICTION MODELS USING SOFT COMPUTING TECHNIQUES

Soft computing introduced by Zadeh (1994) is an approach which exploits the tolerance for imprecision, uncertainty, and partial truth to achieve tractability, robustness, low solution cost, and better rapport with reality. Madsen et al. (2005) conducted a study on the usage of soft computing techniques for software reliability engineering and proposed a framework in order to support fuzzy approaches, evolutionary computing and data mining techniques (Madsen et al., 2005).

Here we are focusing on the soft computing techniques evolved in last two decades to assess and predict the present and future failure behaviour of software systems. Marcia et al., (2010) reviewed various soft computing approaches for reliability modelling and analysis of repairable systems. They pointed out that several soft computing techniques such as neural networks and fuzzy systems and even stochastic methods have been employed for solving many different engineering complex problems. Yet, it is quite difficult to capture the changes in software characteristics precisely that can help software developers in preventing failures and improve the system performance resulting in better quality software.

They pointed out the new challenges of reliability modelling in terms of analyzing failure and repair data. Their study of soft computing techniques was particularly concerned with the modelling of repairable systems (Marcia et al. 2010). An overview of software reliability prediction method using soft computing techniques is shown in Figure 1.

Figure 1. Overview of software reliability prediction model

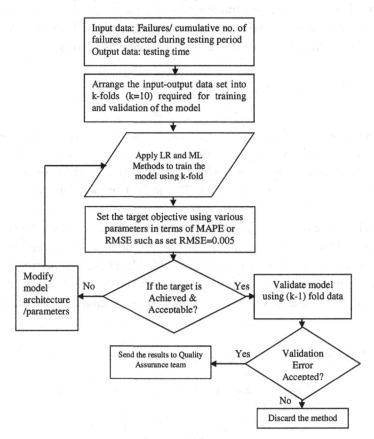

Software Reliability Prediction Models Using ANNs

The ability of ANNs to model complex non-linear relationships and capability of approximating any measurable function make them attractive prospects for solving complex tasks without having to build an explicit model of the system. In this section we present a brief description of some well-known ANNs applied for software reliability prediction includes as: (1) Feed forward back propagation neural network, (2) radial basis function network, (3) Elman network, (4) Generalized neural networks

We describe a multilayer feed forward neural network referred to as M-H-Q network with M source nodes, H hidden nodes and Q nodes in the output layer (Aggarwal et al. 2007). The input nodes are connected to every node of the hidden layer but not connected directly to the output node. The ANN repetitively adjusts different weights until the difference between estimated output and actual output from the network is minimized. The network gets trained by finding a vector of connection weights minimizing the sum of squared errors applied to all data sets. Thus mathematically, multilayer neural network architecture can be defined as follows:

$$net_k = b_k + \sum_{i=1}^{n} x_i w_{ki} \text{ and } y_k = f(net_k) \tag{21}$$

where n is no. of input elements i.e., $x_1, x_2, x_3, \ldots x_n$, w_{ki} -a set of connecting links associated with weighs $w_{k1}, w_{k2}, w_{k3}, w_{k4}, \ldots\ldots\ldots w_{kn}$, y_k - output of the previous layer of network and b_k - is the bias which acts exactly as a weight on a connection from a unit whose activation is always 1. The non-linear model of a neural network is shown in Figure 2.

The architecture of radial basis function network consists of three layers namely input layer, hidden layer and output layer. RBFN composed of n number of input neurons and m number of neurons with the hidden layer existing between the input and output layer. The interconnection between the input layer and hidden layer forms hypothetical connection and between the hidden and output layer forms weighted

Figure 2. Non-linear Model of a Neuron

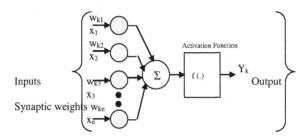

connections. The training algorithm is used for updating of weights in all the interconnections. Elman networks are two-layer back propagation networks, with addition of a feedback connection from the output of the hidden layer to its input. This feedback path allows Elman networks to recognize and generate temporal & spatial patterns. A simple recurrent network (Elman, 1990) has activation feedback, which embodies short-term memory. A state layer is updated not only with the external input of the network but also with activation from the previous forward propagation. This feedback is modified by a set of weights as to enable automatic adaptation through back propagation learning. The Elman network approach to retain a memory of previous events is to copy the activations of nodes on the hidden layer. After feeding the forward values from input to output a copy of the activations of the hidden layer replaces the value in the copy or context nodes.

Generalized Regression Neural Network (GRNN)

Generalized Regression Neural Network (GRNN) is another popular ANNs for predicting software reliability more realistically. The GRNN consists of a radial basis layer and a special linear layer used for function approximation with sufficient number of hidden neurons. GRNN was introduced by Specht (1991) as a normalized radial basis function (RBF) network in which there is a hidden unit centred at every training level. The radial basis function employs some probability density function such as the Gaussian function called kernel. The main drawback of GRNN is that it suffers badly from the curse of dimensionality. That is GRNN cannot handle irrelevant inputs without major modifications to the basic algorithm. General regression neural network (GRNN) is an extended form of probabilistic neural network based on mathematical statistics theory.

In literature, Karunanithi, Whitley, & Malaiya applied various neural networks for predicting software reliability with the help of feed-forward neural networks (FFNN), recurrent neural networks, Elman neural networks and Jordan neural networks. They investigated that neural network can construct models with varying complexity which are adaptable to different datasets in a realistic computing environment. They also discussed various issues of data representation and architecture of neural network (Karunanithi et al., 1990). Khoshgoftar et al. (1992), Khoshgoftar and Szabo (1996) studied the usefulness of connectionist models for software reliability growth prediction. R. Sitte (1999) compared the predictive performance of two methods of software reliability prediction based on neural networks and recalibration for parametric models. Adnan et al. (2000) investigated that neural network approach is capable of learning a function that maps input to output and encodes it in the magnitudes of the weights in the network's connection. Thwin and Quoh (2002, 2005) applied neural network for predicting software development faults using object-oriented design metrics and presented the approximation of any non-linear continuous function with arbitrary accuracy. Kai-Yuan Cai, Lin Cai, Wei-Dong Wang, Zhou-Yi Yu, David Zhang (2001) investigated the effectiveness of neural back-propagation network method (BPNN) for software reliability assessment and prediction using multiple recent inter-failure times as input to predict the next failure time.

S.L. Ho, M. Xie and T.N. Goh (2003) pointed out that in a dynamic reliability growth-modeling environment, the connectionist approach using neural network could be used as a general-purpose growth prediction model. Liang Tian and Afzel Noore (2005) proposed an evolutionary neural network modeling method for software reliability estimation and prediction based on multiple-delayed-input and single-output architecture. Y. S. Su and C. Y. Huang (2007) used a dynamic weighted combinational model (DWCM) for software reliability prediction based on neural network approach to study the effects of various activation functions along with the conventional software reliability growth models. Jung Hua Lo (2009) implemented the artificial neural networks to software reliability models and examined several conventional software reliability growth models by eliminating some unrealistic assumptions. Aljahdali et al. applied ANN for predicting software reliability with a slightly different configuration from that proposed in previous models. They proposed a model using the number of accumulated failures in a determined time interval with the help of a feed forward neural network. They numerically considered the number of neurons in the input layer representing the number of delay in the input data (Aljahdali et al., 2001).

Software Reliability Prediction Models Using Support Vector Machines

Support Vector Machine (SVM) is an elegant and highly principled learning method for the design of a feed forward network with a single hidden layer of nonlinear function (Vapnik, 1960). The design of SVM is based on the extraction of a subset of the training data that serves as support vectors and therefore represents a stable characteristic of the data. SVM has robust theoretical foundations which can be practically applied for pattern-recognition and regression solving problems (Ping and Lyu, 2005). However, the major limitation of support vector machines is the increasing computing and storage requirements with respect to the number of training examples (Chen, 2005). These severe requirements tend to leave many large-scale learning problems beyond the reach of support vector machines. However, the application of SVM based approach in place of traditional statistical techniques has shown a remarkable improvement in the prediction of software reliability in the recent years (Xiang-Li, 2007).

Vladimir Vapnik (1960) invented support vector machine (SVM) algorithm based on statistical learning theory that constructs the set of hyperplanes in a high dimensional space which can be used for classification and regression. Fei-Xing and Ping Guo suggested a novel technique to predict software quality by adopting SVM for the classification of software modules based on complexity metrics (Ping06). That can be used for early software quality predictions particularly applicable to small size sample data. Ping-Feng Pai and Wei-Chiang Hong investigated the capabilities of SVMs for predicting software reliability with the help of simulated annealing algorithms (SA). They pointed out that SVM model with simulated annealing algorithms (SVMSA) results in better predictions than other existing techniques in practice. Bo Yang, Xiang Li (2007) suggested an SVM-based model for predicting software reliability and pointed out that recent failure data is more appropriate to be used which affect prediction accuracy significantly. They also compared the capabilities of various approaches and found that SVM-based software reliability prediction model achieve a higher prediction accuracy than ANN-based existing models. Xingguo Li Xiaofeng Li Yanhua Shu (2007) investigated the status of early prediction methods for software reliability by introducing support vector machine (SVM). They identified that early prediction model based on SVM is more accurate in its prediction with better capacity in generalization.

Genetic Algorithms

Genetic algorithms (GA) are basically biologically inspired learning methods. In GA, a target function is represented as string of bits. The searching process starts using a population of initial hypotheses, the crossover and mutation operations. The members of current population give rise to the next generation of population. The search process terminates when some hypothesis having some fitness value reaches to the threshold level. Genetic algorithms are useful in searching which starts with a set of solutions called population. The search is performed based on the principle of survival of the fittest for several generations. In each generation based on the fitness function, the better solution is selected to form a new population with the help of reproduction, crossover and mutation operators. Reproduction operator is the combined process of evaluation and selection activities. The crossover operator takes two or more chromosomes and by swapping information between them generates one or more chromosomes. The mutation operator is the process that randomly modifies a part of chromosome's information. This process is repeated for several generations until some termination criteria is satisfied. Here, we explore genetic-based approach as one of the computational intelligence techniques applied for predicting software reliability using past failure dataset observed during the software testing process.

Jung-Hua compared the capabilities of SVM and Genetic Algorithm (GA) for predicting software reliability. They determined the parameters of SVM by using GA and suggested that only recent failure data is sufficient for training the model providing software developers and testers to obtain general ideas about software reliability in early phase. They applied genetic algorithm, an efficient, parallel, and global optimal solution searching method based on the principle of the survival of the fittest. During the process of solution searching, it attempts to retain genetic information from generation to generation leading to the global optimal solution (Jung-Hua, 2010).

Genetic Programming

In Genetic programming (GP), a target function is represented as programs. GP is based on the extended capability of genetic algorithms to structure the search spaces. Genetic programming is useful to accomplish the regression of any practical function. GP is a machine learning technique proposed by (Smith, 1980) useful for optimal searching based on the principles of natural selection and genetics. The population structures in GP are represented in terms of programs which upon execution are solutions to the problem. Thus, GP is a systematic, domain-independent method applied for solving problems automatically. The programs in GP are expressed as syntax trees containing nodes which represents executable instructions known as functions. The tree leaves consist of independent variables and constants of the problem are known as terminals. GP iteratively transforms the population of computer programs into a new generation of programs using different genetic operators. GP includes several operators such as crossover, mutation and reproduction.

Eduardo et al. explored the characteristics of Genetic Programming (GP) as an alternative approach to model complex software failure phenomena. The idea behind choosing GP for predicting software reliability was to exploit its capability of learning from historical data, discovering pattern with different variables and operators. They applied GP for predicting software reliability on sixteen failure datasets of DACS and compared the performance measures with other traditional and non-parametric models. They introduced Genetic Programming and Boosting (GPB) approach using boosting techniques to enhance the performance of GP algorithms for predicting software reliability (Eduardo et al., 2005, 2007, 2010). Wasif et al. (2008) applied GP for modeling software reliability growth based on weekly fault count data using three different industrial projects. The predictive capability of their model has shown statistically significant improvement in terms of goodness of fit and predictive accuracy (Wasif et al., 2008).

Support Vector Regression

Support vector regression (SVR) is an extended form of support vector machine proposed by Vapnik's with the help of e-insensitive loss function to solve nonlinear regression estimation problems. However, it has been rarely applied for software reliability prediction in realistic conditions. Wang and Chen (2005) in their study compared the capabilities of neural network approaches and Support Vector Regression (SVR) methods with the traditional NHPP models for the prediction of software reliability. Based on the criteria of Mean Absolute Deviation (MAD) and Directional Change Accuracy (DCA) they empirically suggested that SVR outperforms both NN models and NHPP models. Another software failure model based on least squares support vector regression machines (LSSVRM) also can be used to reduce the fitting error during reliability prediction (Zhu et al., 2010). The LSSVRM was optimized using simulated annealing algorithm to overcome the problem of free parameters in LSSVRM to be modified manually.

Fei and Ping applied support vector regression (SVR) to build software reliability growth model known as SVRSRG (Fei et al., 2005). Software reliability growth models (SRGMs) is another mathematical tool applied for measuring, assessing, and predicting software reliability quantitatively (Pham, 2006). SRGMs measure and predict the improvement of reliability programs through the testing process. Thus, reliability growth can be represented as the reliability or failure rate of a system as a function of time or the number of test cases. The basic idea of support vector regression was to map the input data into another higher dimensional feature space through a nonlinear mapping function so that we get a linear regression problem and solve using this feature space. SVRSRG is a new technique for software reliability growth modeling and prediction. SVR was adopted to build SRGM in order to improve the performance of conventional classical SRGMs.

Gene Expressing Programming

Gene Expression Programming (GEP) introduced by Candida Ferreira is a new technique for the creation of computer programs (Ferreira01). The GEP uses chromosomes composed of genes organized in a head and a tail. The chromosomes are subjected to modification by means of mutation, inversion, transposition, and recombination. This technique performs with high efficiency that greatly surpasses existing adaptive techniques. The fitness function measures the number of correct predictions in terms of MSE. GEP is a method applied for creating a computer program for modeling software failure phenomenon. In gene expression programming, symbols are the basic unit consist of functions, variables and constants. The symbols used for variables and constants are called terminals, because they have no arguments. A gene is an ordered set of symbols whereas an ordered set of genes form a chromosome. In GEP programs, the range of genes typically varies from 4 to 20 symbols, and chromosomes are typically built from 2 to 10 genes. Chromosomes may consist of only a single gene also.

Fuzzy Inference System (FIS)

Fuzzy inference system is similar to a neural network type structure capable of mapping inputs through input membership functions and associated parameters. The parameters associated with the membership functions and corresponding associated output parameters are used to interpret the final output of the system. Fuzzy inference system is capable of making decisions under uncertainty which can be used for reliability prediction when applied to unknown datasets. Fuzzy logic has the capability of modeling highly nonlinear and multidimensional processes. The fuzzy model for predicting software reliability composed of three components namely model structure, parameter estimation and model validation. The structure of fuzzy model is represented by the model type, the number of rules and the positions of the fuzzy sets in the domain of each variable. A Model structure can be defined by the number ad arrangements of membership functions associated to the fuzzy model such as one membership function per input variable. The parameter of fuzzy model can be estimated using least-square method and the model is validated using unknown failure dataset collected during testing phase.

Adaptive Neuro- Fuzzy Inference System (ANFIS)

In fuzzy inference system the membership functions are chosen arbitrarily or made fixed. But, in case of ANFIS the membership functions and associated parameters can be chosen automatically which results in better prediction accuracy of the system. ANFIS supports only to Sugano-type system and cannot accept all customization options allowed by fuzzy inference system. The adaptive neuro-fuzzy inference system can establish an input-output relation with the help of Backpropagation algorithm using connectionist approach. Thus, ANFIS is a hybrid intelligent system model which combines the low-level computational power of connectionist approach and high level reasoning capability of a fuzzy inference system. This way, neuro-fuzzy inference system is an adaptive model which is used to fine-tune the parameters of fuzzy inference systems for predicting software reliability based on statistical failure data.

Ensemble Software Reliability Prediction Models

An ensemble approach can provide better predictive accuracy than its component functions provided: (1) the individual functions disagree with each other; (2) individual functions have a predictive accuracy that is slightly better than random classification; (3) individual functions' errors are at least somewhat uncorrelated. Generally, two methods are applied for designing the ensembles. First approach is to combine the component functions which are homogeneous (derived using the same learning algorithm) and weak (slightly better than random guessing). Second approach is to combine component functions that are heterogeneous (derived by different learning algorithms) and strong (each of the component function performs relatively well in its own right).

The basic idea behind introducing ensemble systems is to exploit each component model's unique features to characterize different patterns of complex failure datasets. In literature, many theoretical and empirical ensembles have been design to improve the accuracy of reliability prediction models. Pelikan et al. (1992) combined different feed-forward neural networks to improve the reliability prediction in time series problems. Some of the well-known and widely used ensemble techniques applied for reliability prediction with continuous dependent variable include linear ensemble (Beneditktsson et al., 1997), weighted average (Perrone and Cooper, 1993), stacked regression (Breiman, 1996), non-linear ensemble such as neural-network-based nonlinear ensembles (Yu et al., 2005) and linear ensembles based on average, weighted mean, weighted median and neural network based non-linear ensembles (Raj Kiran N. and Ravi V, 2007). Aljahdali et al. (2008) applied GAs for optimizing ensembles of models for predicting software reliability. They evaluated the predictive capability of constructed ensemble using GA on three failure datasets taken from DACS compiled by Musa in 1970s. They suggested that weighted average method for ensemble shows better results in comparison to average method (Aljahadi et al., 2008).

Further, in order to improve the usability of the SRGMs Li (2009) suggested a combination of neural network method to build accurate and adaptive SNN (Selective Neural Network) model (Li et al., 2009). Thus, the newly designed model avoids relying on a single model and reduces the risk to produce inaccurate predictions and improves the average performance in accuracy. Therefore, based on the results of empirical studies in literature, it can be concluded that multi-criteria model selection strategy contribute to the adaptability and accuracy of the model leading to more accuracy of predicted models for software reliability growth.

Particle Swarm Optimization

Particle Swarm Optimization (PSO) proposed by Bratton and Kennedy (2007) can be used for optimizing complex failure behaviour of software during testing. That is, PSO is an optimization probabilistic heuristic approach well-suited to deal with continuous variables, based on the behavior of biological organisms that move in groups such as birds. In modeling the software failure phenomena, the concepts of cognition and socialization are translated in mathematical formulations for updating particles velocities and positions throughout the search space towards an optimum solution. The two commonly used network communication models among particles include gbest and lbest. In gbest model, all particles are connected to each other and in case of lbest all particles are able to communicate only with some of them. Although, there are several probabilistic approach to solve the optimization problem such as Genetic Algorithm (GA) (Goldberg, 1989) and Support vector machines. GA is a computational method usually applied for optimization tasks and attempts to mimic the natural evolution process. GA is based on various operators such as crossover and mutation which are computationally more expensive in comparison to PSO. SVMs assume the parameters as discrete values within a range and all possible combinations of them are assessed. The main drawback of SVM is the discretization of the search space as well as in the large number of possibilities to be evaluated when there are several parameters to adjust.

Particle Swarm Optimization (PSO) and Ant Colony (ACO) algorithms are two optimization techniques applied for solving problems based on the social behavior of birds. Thus, each individual in the population is called particle, and several particles together form particle swarm. Each particle has its position which can be adjusted depending on its own current position and on the position of its neighbours. On the other hand, ant colony optimization method is based on the food searching process adopted by ants for the shortest path to a food source.

MEASUREMENT OF SOFTWARE RELIABILITY MODELS

Over the years a significant number of software reliability models (SRM) have been developed in the literature. Therefore, it is essentially required to measure what has been achieved in order to test the finished product and estimate reliability from the failures observed. Thus, reliability measurement is an essential component of developing quality software. Moreover, it is very difficult to control what we cannot measure. IEEE Standard Glossary (IEE93) defines software metrics as "a quantitative measure of the degree to which a system, component, or process processes a given attribute". Here, we consider three main parameters (reliability, cost and fitness for release) for measuring the capability of software reliability prediction models from both the customer and developers point of view as follows:

Reliability is the probability of mission success that is how likely an accident due to software failure is. For any commercial software application this is important for user-perceived reliability that how likely is the user's work to be affected by failure in operational phase. Cost is another crucial component that is, the vendor's maintenance workload would be increased drastically if the product is less reliable and sold in its present state. This is the basis for all commercial decisions regarding maintenance contracts and warranty of the products. Fitness for release, based on the evaluation criteria of achieving a predefined level of reliability within budget limits can we release the product to the customer or we need to go for further testing leading to overhead the budget.

EMPIRICAL DATA COLLECTION

The challenge of collecting software failure data is to make sure that collected data can provide useful information for potential users and quality managers. In software reliability engineering mainly two types of failure data namely time-domain data and interval-domain data has been widely used. The category of time-domain data is characterized by recording the individual times at which the failure occurred. The interval-domain data are characterized by counting the number of failures occurring during a fixed period. However, time-domain data provide better accuracy for the parameter estimation in comparison with existing software reliability models in practice but require more efforts for data collection than the interval domain approach (17). Some of the widely used datasets of public domain are described in Table 1.

TOOLS FOR SOFTWARE RELIABILITY MODELING

Over the years a significant number of software reliability tools have been developed for reliability prediction in the field. These tools provide a general framework for reliability estimation and prediction. Here we categorize the reliability tools available in the market based on their functionality, capability, availability, applicability & user interface. Software reliability tools can also be characterized using parameters such as: collection of failure data, estimation of model parameters, testing the fit of a model against the collected information and application of the model. Some well-known and widely used software reliability prediction tools are summarized in Table 2.

Table 1. Empirical failure datasets

Datasets	Description	No. of Failures/ Defects	Sources
DS1	DACS: Software failure data of sixteen projects collected from Software Life Cycle Empirical/ Experience Database (SLED) compiled & published by Data & Analysis Center for Software (DACS). In software reliability theory, this dataset has been applied successfully for many real-life applications in practice.	831 (Maximum)	Musa (1970)
DS2	On-line IBM entry software package: In software reliability modeling, this is the most commonly used data set. A small on-line data entry software package test data, available since 1980 in Japan (Ohba 1984a). The size of the software is approximately 40,000 LOC. The testing time was measured in terms of the number of shifts spent running test cases and analyzing the results. This is another category of failure dataset used by majority of researchers for testing and validating software reliability prediction models.	46	Ohba (1984)
DS3	On-line Communication System (OCS): The On-line Communication System (OCS) project at ABC Software Company was completed in 2000 (Pham 2003a). The project consisted of one unit-manager, one user interface software engineer, and ten software engineers/testers. The overall effort was divided into four phases in the software development process of the project such as analysis, design, coding and testing respectively.	55	Pham (2003)
DS4	This set of failure data is taken from Misra (1983), consists of three types of errors: critical, major, and minor. The observation time (week) and the number of failures were recorded weekly.	86	Misra (1983)
DS5	US Naval Tactical Data Systems (NTDS): This failure dataset is extracted from the development of software for the real-time multi-computer complex of the US Naval Fleet Computer Programming Center of the US Naval Tactical Data Systems (NTDS) (Goel 1979a). The software consists of 38 different project modules. The time horizon is divided into four phases: production phase, test phase, user phase, and subsequent test phase. The 26 software failures were found during the production phase, five during the test phase and; the last failure was found on 4 January 1971. One failure was observed during the user phase, in September 1971, and two failures during the test phase in 1971.	34	Goel (1979)
DS6	Tandem Computers Software Data Project: This failure dataset from Release #1 has been taken from one of the four major releases of software products at Tandem Computers (Wood 1996).	100	Wood (1996)
DS7	On-Line Data Entry IBM Software Package: This failure dataset was reported by Ohba (1984a) and recorded from testing the on-line data entry software package developed at IBM.	15	Ohba (1984a)
DS8	AT&T System Project: The AT&T's System is a network-management system developed by AT&T that receives data from telemetry events, such as alarms, facility-performance information, and diagnostic messages, and forwards them to operators for further action. This failure dataset data has been collected by Ehrlich in 1993.	22	Ehrlich (1993)
DS9	Real-Time Control Systems (Hou et al., 1997): The software for monitor and real-time control systems (Tohma 1991) consists of about 200 modules and each module has, on average, 1000 lines of a high-level language like FORTRAN. The software failure records were detected during the 111-day testing period. This failure dataset was recorded with several up and downs reflecting different clusters of detected faults.	481	Hou et. al. (1997)
DS10	The Real-time Control System Data: This failure dataset was documented in Lyu (1996). There are in total 136 faults reported and the time-between failures (TBF) in second during testing.	136	Lyu (1996)
DS11	Real-Time Command and Control System: This failure dataset was reported by Musa (1987) based on failure data from a real-time command and control system, which represents the failures observed during system testing for 25 hours of CPU time. The delivered umber of object instructions for this system was 21700 and was developed by Bell Laboratories.	136	Musa (1987)
DS12	This failure data set was reported by Zhang (2002) based on system test data for a telecommunication system. System test data was reported in two releases (Phases 1 and 2). In the tests, automated test and human- involved tests were executed on multiple test beds.	43	Zhang (2002)

SUMMARY

As the cost of software application failures grows tremendously, its impact on business performance and software reliability has become more important. Thus, project managers and industry professionals need to employ effective software reliability

Table 2. Software reliability modeling tools

SNo	Reliability Tools		Description and Application
1	AT&T	AT&T Software Reliability Engineering Toolkit	The AT&T Software Reliability Engineering Toolkit is a command line driven system which executes Musa basic and Musa-Okumoto software reliability models. This tool can be applied for both time-domain and interval-domain failure datasets for predicting software reliability.
2	SMERFS	Statistical Modeling and Estimation of Reliability Functions for Software	This tool is basically applied for Statistical Modeling and Estimation of Reliability Functions for Systems. SMERFS was designed by William Farr (1982) and it has been utilized in many areas of software reliability engineering ever since. SMERFS is a program for estimating and predicting the reliability of software during the testing phase. It uses failure count information to make reliability predictions. SMERFS allows the user to perform risk analysis and to determine the optimum release time of the software.
3	SRMP	Statistical Reliability and Modeling Programs	The Statistical Reliability and Modeling Program was developed by reliability and statistical consultant in 1988. SRMP is a command-line interface tool which contains nine models for predicting software reliability from failure datasets. The parameters are estimated using Maximum Likelihood Estimation (MLE) method in order to provide the reliability information such as failure rate, mean time to failure, median time to failure etc. SRMP accepts only time-domain input data for making predictions.
4	ESTM	Economic Stop Testing Model	Economic Stop Testing Model is a command-line interface tool which can be applied for releasing the software. That is, it determines the optimal stopping time using a birth-death model for the introduction of faults and a cost-benefit model to measure the trade-off between whether software can be released or further testing is required. Moreover, it helps the user when to stop the testing and release the product for operational use based on reliability achieved.
5	SoRel	Software Reliability Program	Software Reliability Program is a measurement tool developed by Lab of The National Center For Scientific Research, France in 1991. The SoRel has the capability of testing and analyzing the data for making predictions with better accuracy. Several types of tests can be conducted using SoRel leading to more accurate reliability estimation and predictions. It allows various models to accept both time-domain and interval-domain input data which can be applied for predicting software reliability growth.
6	SARA	Software Assurance Reliability Automation	Software Assurance Reliability Automation (SARA), also known as Non-Parametric Software Reliability tool is a comprehensive system for predicting software reliability. SARA incorporates both reliability growth model metrics and design code metrics for analyzing the software applicable to time between failure data. Initially, SARA was a research project funded by the NASA and supported by Software Assurance Technology Center (SATC).
7	CASRE	Computer-Aided Software Reliability Estimation	Computer-Aided Software Reliability Estimation Tool is well-known and widely used software which was developed by Jet Propulsion Laboratories in 1993. CASRE is a user friendly tool with GUI features which runs on Windows operating system. CASRE is capable to customize the user's model using in-build models and can be applied to time-domain failure datasets.

continued on next page

Table 2. Continued

SNo	Reliability Tools		Description and Application
8	RGA ReliaSoft	RGA: Reliability Growth Analysis and Repairable System Analysis Software Tool	RGA is product of ReliaSoft's, particularly applied to software reliability growth models for analyzing data from both developmental testing and fielded repairable systems. In the development stage, RGA can be utilized to quantify the reliability growth achieved with each successive design prototype and also provides advanced methods for reliability growth projections, planning and management. RGA also supports fielded repairable system analysis, including a Design of Reliability Test (DRT) utility and a method for analyzing the system's reliability behavior in order to calculate the optimum overhaul times and other useful metrics of interest.
9	Weka	WaiKato Machine Learning Tool	The Waikato Environment for Knowledge Analysis (Weka), a comprehensive tool composed of Java class libraries has been applied for implementing several machine learning algorithms. Weka is freely available open source suite which can be accessed from http://www.cs.waikato.ac.nz of "Machine Learning Group", University of Waikato.
10	DTReg	Classification and Regression Tool	DTREG is predictive modeling software developed by Phillip H. Sherrod (2003). DTREG has a huge capability of modeling various classification and regression decision trees using neural networks, support vector machine (SVM), GMDH polynomial networks, gene expression programs, K-Means clustering, discriminant analysis and logistic regression models that describe data relationships and can be used to predict values for future observations. DTREG can also be applied for time series analysis. The details of DTReg can be accessed through www.dtreg.com
11	Salford System SPM	Software Predictive Model suite	Salford System: SPM is a software predictive modeling site with a proven record of technical and practical excellence. SPM suite offers a highly accurate predictive analytics and data mining platform for developing models from databases of variable size, complexity, or organization. SPM suite support several data mining techniques such as classification, regression, missing value analysis, and clustering/segmentation. SPM suite contains four basic modules including CART, MARS, TreeNet and RandomForests. Further details can be found at http://www.salford-systems.com
12	SVM Tools	Support Vector Machine Tools	The university of Wisconsin, Madison provides several effective support vector machines (SVM) classification software that has been developed by researchers at the Data Mining Institute as well as a data generator. A list of support vector machine tools such as SSVM, PSVM, LSVM, NDC and other useful tools can be found at http://www.research.cs.wisc.edu/dmi/svm

prediction techniques to improve the product and process reliability. In this paper, we have reviewed the software reliability prediction techniques focusing on methods, metrics and failure databases, the current trends and existing issues. In particular, we have laid out the current and possible future trends for reliability prediction in terms of methods, metrics and databases in order to meet the industry and customer needs. The applications of soft computing techniques for the prediction of software reliability in place of traditional statistical techniques have shown remarkable improvement in recent years. In this paper we extensively reviewed the study of software reliability prediction methods using statistical and machine-learning techniques. The goal of our study was to help researchers and industrial professionals for relevant expert estimation and prediction of software reliability realistically.

FUTURE RESEARCH DIRECTIONS

This chapter on software reliability prediction methods may be improved further by incorporating the following issues:

- The current practices of software reliability engineering (SRE) collect the failure data during integration testing or system testing phases. Failure data collected during the late testing phase may be too late for fundamental design changes.
- Secondly, the failure data collected in the in-house testing may be limited, and therefore, it may not represent failures that would be uncovered under actual operational environment. This is particularly required for high-quality software system, which requires extensive and wide-range testing. The reliability estimation and prediction using the restricted testing data may cause accuracy problems. Although, it is understood that exhaustive testing is not feasible.
- Thirdly, the current practices of SRE are based on various unrealistic assumptions that make the reliability estimation too optimistic relative to real situations. Thus, although SRE has been around for decades, credible software reliability modeling techniques are still urgently needed, particularly for modern software systems using more intelligent soft computing techniques.

CONCLUSION

Software reliability growth models have been proved to be very effective technique for quantitative measurement of software quality particularly non-parametric software reliability prediction method based on ANN approach. We also have discussed the usefulness of connectionist approach using neural network models which is more flexible with less restrictive assumptions in a more realistic environment. The use of ANNs technique requires only failure history as input and then develops its own internal model of failure process by using back-propagation learning algorithm in which the network weight are adapted using errors propagated back through output layer of the network. Therefore the ability of neural networks to model nonlinear patterns and learn from the statistical failure data makes it a valuable alternative methodology for characterizing the failure process which generates less prediction errors realistically over the conventional parametric models.

ANNs have less prediction errors realistically over conventional parametric models. Specifically from researcher's point of view the artificial neural network approach offers a distinct advantage for software reliability assessment that the model development is automatic by using a training algorithm such as back propagation using feed forward neural network.

REFERENCES

Aggarwal, K. K., Singh, Y., Kaur, A., & Malhotra, R. (2008). Empirical analysis for investigating the effect of object-oriented metrics on fault proneness: A replicated case study. *Software Process Improvement and Practice*, *14*(1), 39–62. doi:10.1002/spip.389

Breiman, L. (2001). Random Forests. *Machine Learning*, *35*(1), 5–32. doi:10.1023/A:1010933404324

Funatsu. (2011). *Knowledge-Oriented Applications in Data Mining*. In Tech.

Han, J., & Kamber, M. (2006). *Data Mining: Concepts and Techniques*. Morgan Kaufmann Publishers.

Hastie, T., Tibshirani, R., & Friedman, J. (2001). *The Elements of Statistical Learning: Data Mining, Inference, and Prediction*. New York: Springer. doi:10.1007/978-0-387-21606-5

Ho, S., Xie, M., & Goh, T. (2003). A study of the connectionist models for software reliability prediction. *Computers & Mathematics with Applications (Oxford, England)*, *46*(7), 1037–1045. doi:10.1016/S0898-1221(03)90117-9

Karunanithi, N., Whitley, D., & Malaiya, Y. (1992). Prediction of software reliability using connectionist models. *IEEE Transactions on Software Engineering*, *18*(7), 563–574. doi:10.1109/32.148475

Kohavi, R. (1995). The power of decision tables. *The Eighth European Conference on Machine Learning (ECML-95)*, 174-189.

Kuei, C., Yeu, H., & Tzai, L. (2008). A study of software reliability growth from the perspective of learning effects. *Reliability Engineering & System Safety*, *93*(10), 1410–1421. doi:10.1016/j.ress.2007.11.004

Lyu, M. R. (1999). *Handbook of Software Reliability Engineering*. McGraw Hill.

Malhotra, R., Singh, Y., & Kaur, A. (2009). Comparative analysis of regression and machine learning methods for predicting fault proneness models. *International Journal of Computer Applications in Technology*, *35*(2), 183–193.

Mueller, J., & Lemke, F. (1999). Self-Organizing Data Mining: An Intelligent Approach to Extract Knowledge from Data. Academic Press.

Musa, D. (2009). *Software Reliability Engineering: More Reliable Software Faster and Cheaper* (2nd ed.). McGraw-Hill.

Raj, K., & Ravi, V. (2008). Software reliability prediction by using soft computing techniques. *Journal of Systems and Software*, 576–583. doi:10.1016/j.jss.2007.05.005

Ross, Q. (1993). *C4.5: Programs for Machine Learning*. San Mateo, CA: Morgan Kaufman Publishers.

Salford Predictive Modelling System. (n.d.). Retrieved from http//www.salford-systems.com

Scott, E., & Christian, L. (1991). *The Cascade-Correlation Learning Architecture. CMU-CS-90-100*. School of Computer Science Carnegie Mellon University Pittsburgh.

Sherrod, P. H. (2003). *DTReg predictive modeling software*. Available at http://www.dtreg.com

Singh & Kumar. (2010). Application of feed-forward networks for software reliability prediction. *ACM SIGSOFT Software Engineering Notes, 35*(5), 1-6. DOI: 10.1145/1838687.1838709

Singh, Y., Kaur, A., & Malhotra, R. (2009). Application of support vector machine to predict fault prone classes. *ACM SIGSOFT Software Engineering Notes*, *34*(1). http://doi.acm.org/10.1145/1457516.1457529, 2009.

Singh, Y., & Kumar, P. (2010). A software reliability growth model for three-tier client-server system. *International Journal of Computers and Applications*, *1*(13), 9–16. doi:10.5120/289-451

Singh, Y., & Kumar, P. (2010). Determination of software release instant of three-tier client server software system. *International Journal of Software Engineering*, *1*(3), 51–62.

Singh, Y., & Kumar, P. (2010). Prediction of Software Reliability using Feed Forward Neural Networks. *Proceedings of Computational Intelligence and Software Engineering (CiSE), 2010 International Conference*. doi:10.1109/CISE.2010.5677251

Sitte, R. (1999). Comparison of software reliability growth predictions: Neural Networks vs. Parametric Recalibration. *IEEE Transactions on Reliability*, *48*(3), 285–291. doi:10.1109/24.799900

Software Life Cycle Empirical/Experience Database (SLED). (n.d.). Retrieved from http://www.dacs.org

Witten, I., & Frank, E. (2011). Data Mining: Practical Machine Learning Tools and Techniques with Java Implementations (3rd ed.). Morgan Kaufman.

Zheng, J. (2009). Predicting software reliability with neural network ensembles. *Expert Systems with Applications*, *36*(2), 216–222. doi:10.1016/j.eswa.2007.12.029

KEY TERMS AND DEFINITIONS

Availability: The probability that a system or a capability of a system is functional at a given time in a specified environment or the fraction of time during which a system is functioning acceptably.

Basic Failure Intensity: Failure intensity that would exist at start of system test for new operations for a project without reviews (requirement, design, or code) or fault tolerance.

Bugs: Are the mistakes committed by the developers while coding the program(s).

Client: A node that makes request of services in a network or that uses resources available through the servers.

Client-Server Computing: Defined as processing capability or available information distributed across multiple nodes.

Constant Failure Rate: The period during which failures of some units occur at an approximately uniform rate.

Corrective Action: A documented design process or materials changes implemented and validated to correct the cause of a failure.

Correlation: A statistical technique that determines the relationship between two variables (dependent and independent).

Data: The representation of facts or instructions in a manner suitable for processing by computers or analyzing by human.

Debugging: The process of detection, location, and correction of errors or bugs in hardware or software systems.

Dependent Variable: The variable quantity in an experimental setting that depends on the action of the independent variable.

Developed Code: New or modified executable delivered instructions.

Developer: A person or an individual or team assigned a particular task.

Deviation: Any departure of system behavior in execution from expected behavior.

Error: Incorrect or missing action by a person or persons that causes a fault in a program. Error may be a syntax error or misunderstanding of specifications, or logical errors. An error may lead to one or more faults.

Errors: Are human actions that result in the software containing a fault. Examples of such faults are the omission or misinterpretation of the user's requirements, a coding error etc.

Estimation: Determination of software reliability model parameters and quantities from failure data.

Execution Time: The time a processor(s) is / is executing non-filler operations in execution hour.

Failure: A failure occurs when a fault executes. It is the departure of output of the program from the expected output. Thus, failure is dynamic.

Failure Category: The set of failures that have the same kind of impact on users such as safety or security.

Failure Density: At any point in the life of a system, the incremental change in the number of failures per associated incremental change in time.

Failure Intensity: Failures per time unit, is an alternative way of expressing reliability.

Failure Rate: At a particular time, the rate of change of the number of units that have failed divided by the number of units surviving.

Failure Time: Accumulated elapsed time at which a failure occurs.

Fault: Defect in system that causes a failure when executed. A software fault is a defect in the code. Thus, a fault is the representation of an error, where representation is the mode of expression such as narrative text, data flow diagrams,

Entity-Relationships diagrams, or source code. Moreover, a fault may lead to many failures. That is, a particular fault may cause different failures depending on how it has been exercised.

Prediction: The determination of software reliability model parameters and quantities from characteristics of the software product and development process.

Probability: The fraction of occasions on which a specified value or set of values of a quantity occurs, out of all possible values for that quantity.

Product: A software system that is sold to the customers.

Program: A set of complete instructions (operators with operands specified) that executes within a single computer and relates to the accomplishment of some major function.

Reliability: Reliability is the probability or the capability of a system that will continue to function without failure for a specified period in a specified environment. The period may be specified in natural or time units.

Software Engineering: A systematic approach to the development and maintenance of software that begins with analysis of the software's goals of purposes.

Software Error: An error made by a programmer or designer, e.g., a typographical error, an incorrect numerical value, an omission, etc.

Software Failure: A failure that occurs when the user perceives that the software has ceased to deliver the expected result with respect to the specification input values. The user may need to identify the severity of the levels of failures such as catastrophic, critical, major or minor, depending on their impact on the systems.

Software Fault: An error that leads to a software fault. Software faults can remain undetected until software failure results.

Chapter 7
Feature Selection Algorithms for Classification and Clustering

Arvind Kumar Tiwari
GGS College of Modern Technology, India

ABSTRACT

Feature selection is an important topic in data mining, especially for high dimensional dataset. Feature selection is a process commonly used in machine learning, wherein subsets of the features available from the data are selected for application of learning algorithm. The best subset contains the least number of dimensions that most contribute to accuracy. Feature selection methods can be decomposed into three main classes, one is filter method, another one is wrapper method and third one is embedded method. This chapter presents an empirical comparison of feature selection methods and its algorithm. In view of the substantial number of existing feature selection algorithms, the need arises to count on criteria that enable to adequately decide which algorithm to use in certain situation. This chapter reviews several fundamental algorithms found in the literature and assess their performance in a controlled scenario.

INTRODUCTION

The feature selection problem is inescapable in inductive machine learning or data mining setting and its significance is beyond doubt. The main benefit of a correct selection is the terms of learning speed, speculation capacity or simplicity of the induced model. On the other hand there are the straight benefits related with a smaller

DOI: 10.4018/978-1-5225-2545-5.ch007

number of features: a reduced measurement cost and hopefully a better understanding of the domain. A feature selection algorithm (FSA) is a computational solution that should be guided by a certain definition of subset relevance although in many cases this definition is implicit or followed in a loose sense. This is so because, from the inductive learning perspective, the relevance of a feature may have several definitions depending on precise objective (Caruana and Freitag, 1994). Thus the need arises to count on common sense criteria that enable to adequately decide which algorithm to use or not to use in certain situation (Belanche and González, 2011). The feature selection algorithm can be classified according to the kind of output one are giving a (weighed) linear order of features and second are giving a subset of the original features. In this research, several fundamental algorithms found in the literature are studied to assess their performance in a controlled scenario. This measure computes the degree of matching between the output given by a FSA and the known optimal solution. Sample size effect also studied. The result illustrates the strong dependence on the particular conditions of the FSA used and on the amount of irrelevance and redundancies in the data set description, relative to the total number of feature. This should prevent the use of single algorithm even when there is poor knowledge available about the structure of the solution. The basic idea in feature selection is to detect irrelevant and/or redundant features as they harm the learning algorithm performance (Lee and Moore, 2014). There is no unique definition of relevance, however it has to do with the discriminating ability of a feature or a subset to distinguish the different class labels (Dash and Liu, 1997). However, as pointed out in the paper (Guyon and Elisseeff, 2003a), an irrelevant variable may be useful when taken with others and even two irrelevant variables that are useless by themselves can be useful when taken together.

Figure 1. Feature selection criteria

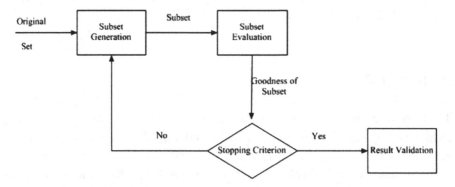

The Feature Selection Problem

Let X be the original set of features which cardinality $|X| = n$. The continuous feature selection problem (also called feature weighing) refers to the assignment of weights w_i to each feature $x_i \in X$ in such a way that the order corresponding to its theoretical relevance is preserved. The binary feature selection problem (also called feature subset selection) refers to the choice of a subset of feature that jointly maximizes a certain measure related to subset relevance. This can be carried out directly as many FSA (Almuallim and Dietterich, 1991: Caruana and Freitag, 1994) or setting a cut point in the output of this continuous problem solution. Although both types can be seen in a unified way (the latter case corresponds to the assignment of weights in {0, 1}), these are quite different problems that reflect different design objectives. In the continuous case, one is interested in keeping all the features but in using them differentially in the learning process. On the contrary in the binary case one is interested in keeping just a subset of the features and (most likely) using them equally in the learning process.

A common instance of the feature selection problem can be formally stated as follows. Let J be a performance evaluation measure to be optimized (say to maximize) defined as $J : P(X) \rightarrow R^+ \cup \{0\}$. This function accounts for a general evaluation measure that may or may not be inspired in a precise and previous definition of relevance. Let $C(x) \geq 0$ represent the cost of variable x and call $C(X') = \sum_{x \in X'} c(x)$

for $X' \in p(X)$. Let $Cx = C(X)$ be the cost of the whole feature set. It is assumed here that c is additive, that is, $C(X' \cup X'') = C(X') + C(X'')$ (Belanche and González, 2011).

Relevance of a Feature

The purpose of a FSA is to identify relevant feature according to a definition of relevance. However, the notion of relevance in machine learning has not yet been rigorously defined on a common agreement (Bell and Wang, 2000). Let E_i, with $1 \leq i \leq n$, be domains of feature $X= \{x_{1,........,} x_n\}$: an instance space is defined as $E= E_1 \times ....\times E_n$. where an instance is a point in this space. Consider P a probability distribution on E and T a space of labels (classes). It is desired to model or identify an objective function c: $E \rightarrow T$ according to its relevant feature. A data set S composed by $|S|$ instances can be seen as the result of sampling E under p a total of $|S|$ times and labeling its element using c.

A Primary definition of relevance(Blum and Langley, 1997) is the notion of being "relevant with respect to an objective". It is assumed here to be classification objective.

Definition 1 (Relevance With Respect to an Objective)

A feature $x_i \in X$ is relevant to an objective c if there exist two examples A, B in the instance space E such that A and B differ only in their assignment to x_i and $c(A) \neq c(B)$. In other words, if there exist two instances that can only be classified thanks to x_i. This definition has the inconvenience that the learning algorithm can not necessarily determine if a feature x_i is relevant or not, using only a sample S of E. Moreover, if a problem representation is redundant (e.g. some features are replicated), it will never be the case that two instance differ only in one feature. A proposal oriented to solve this problem (John et al., 1994) include two notions of relevance, one with respect to a sample and another with respect to distribution.

Definition 2 (Strong Relevance With Respect to S)

A feature $x_i \in X$ is strongly relevant to the sample S if there exist two examples A, $B \in S$ that only differ in their assignment to x_i and $c(A) \neq c(B)$. That is to say, it is the same definition 1, but now A, $B \in S$ and the definition is respect to S.

Definition 3 (Strong Relevance With Respect to P)

A feature $x_i \in X$ is strongly relevant to an objective c in the distribution p if their exist two examples A, $B \in E$ with $p(A) \neq 0$ and $p(B) \neq 0$ that only differ in their assignment to x_i and $c(A) \neq c(B)$.

This definition is natural extension of definition 2 and contrary to it, the distribution p is assumed to be known.

Definition 4 (Weak Relevance With Respect to S)

A feature $x_i \in X$ is weakly relevant to the sample S if there exist a proper $X' \supset X(x_i \in X')$ where x_i is strongly relevant with respect to S. A weakly relevant feature can appear when a subset containing at least one strongly relevant feature is removed.

Definition 5 (Relevance as a Complexity Measure)

Given a data sample *S* and an objective *c*, define *r(S,c)* as the smallest number of relevant feature to *c* using Definition 1 only in *S*, and such that the error in *S* is the least possible for the inducer. In other words, it refers to the smallest number of features required by a specific inducer to reach optimum performance in the task of modeling *c* using *S* *(John et al., 1994)*.

Definition 6 (Incremental Usefulness)

Given a data sample *S*, a learning algorithm *L*, and subset of feature *X'*, the feature x_i is incrementally useful to *L* with respect to *X'* if the accuracy of the hypothesis that *L* produces using the group of features $\{x_i\} \cup X'$ is better than the accuracy reached using only the subset of features *X'*. This definition is especially natural n FSAs that search in the feature subset space in an incremental way, adding or removing features to a current solution. It is also related to a traditional understanding of relevance in the philosophy literature (Caruana and Freitag, 1994).

Definition 7 (Entropic Relevance)

Denoting the Shannon entropy by *H(x)* and the mutual information by $I\left(x;y\right) = H(x) - H(x\ y)$ (the difference of entropy in *x* generated by the knowledge of *y*), the entropic relevance of *x* to *y* is defined as $r\left(x:y\right) = I\left(x:y\right)\ H\left(y\right)$. Let *X* be the original set of feature and let *C* be the objective seen as a feature, a set $X' \supset X$ is sufficient if $I\left(X':C\right) = I\left(X,C\right)$. For a sufficient set *X'* it turns out that $r\left(X';C\right) = r\left(X;C\right)$. The most favorable set is that sufficient set $X' \supset X$ for which *H(X')* is smaller.

Feature Selection

The main objective of feature selection are that it reduces the dimensionality of feature space, speedup and reduce the cost of learning algorithms, improve the predictive accuracy of classification algorithm, and also improve the visualization and the comprehensibility of the induced concepts. The feature selection algorithm may be based on three major criterions such as based on some evaluation measure, based on search organization and based on the generation of successors (Guyon and Elisseeff, 2003a).

Table 1. Feature selection methods characterizations based on different criterion and their types

Characterization Criterion	Types
Evaluation measure	Distance Based
	Divergence Based
	Information theoretic based
	Dependence measure based
	Accuracy based
Search Organization	Exponential
	Sequential
	Random
Generation of successors	Forward selection
	Backward selection
	Compound selection
	Random selection
	Weight based selection

GENERAL METHODS FOR FEATURE SELECTION

The relationship between a FSA and the inducer chosen to evaluate the usefulness of the feature selection process can take three main forms such as Filter, Wrapper and Embedded.

Filter Methods

These methods select features based on discriminating criteria that are relatively independent of classification. Several methods use simple correlation coefficients similar to Fisher's discriminant criterion. Others adopt mutual information or statistical tests (t-test, F-test). Earlier filter-based methods evaluated features in isolation and did not consider correlation between features. Recently, methods have been proposed to select features with minimum redundancy. The methods proposed use a minimum redundancy-maximum relevance (MRMR) feature selection framework. They supplement the maximum relevance criteria along with minimum redundancy criteria to choose additional features that are maximally dissimilar to already identified ones. By doing this, MRMR expands the representative power of the feature set and improves their generalization properties (Guyon and Elisseeff,2003a).

Figure 2. Filter methods

Wrapper Methods

Wrapper methods utilize the classifier as a black box to score the subsets of features based on their predictive power. Wrapper methods based on SVM have been widely studied in machine-learning community. SVM-RFE (Support Vector Machine Recursive Feature Elimination), in each recursive step, it ranks the features based on the amount of reduction in the objective function. It then eliminates the bottom ranked feature from the results. A number of variants also use the same backward feature elimination scheme and linear kernel (Kohavi and John, 1997a).

Embedded Method

The inducer has its own FSA (either explicit or implicit). The methods to induce logical conjunctions provide an example of this embedding. Other traditional machine learning tools like decision trees or artificial neural networks are included in this scheme (Guyon and Elisseeff, 2003a)

FILTER-BASED FEATURE SELECTION METHOD

Filter based feature selection methods may be broadly categorized into two categories-:

Figure 3. Wrapper methods

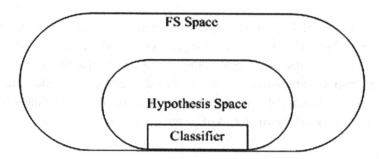

Figure 4. Embedded methods

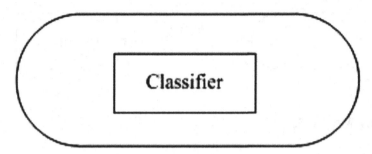

Supervised

In supervised learning, the data is assigned to be known before computation and are used in order to learn the parameters that are really significant for clusters. Each object in supervised learning comes with a pre assigned class label.

Unsupervised

In unsupervised learning the datasets are assigned to segments without the cluster being known. Supervised and Unsupervised learning approaches further classified in univariate and Multivariate data. In univriate data analysis it is assumed that the response variable is influenced only by one other factor whereas in multivariate data analysis it is assumed that the response variable is influenced by multiple factors and even combination of factors (Guyon and Elisseeff, 2003a). Classification of filter based feature selection methods on the basis of supervised and unsupervised learning is shown below in Table 2, evaluation function used by filter based feature selection method is shown in Table 3 and brief description of filter based feature selection methods is shown in Table 4.

WRAPPER-BASED FEATURE SELECTION METHOD

Wrapper methods (Hall, 1999) are feedback methods which merge the machine learning algorithm in the feature selection process. Wrapper method search through the space of feature subset using a learning algorithm to guide the search. A search algorithm "wrapped" around the classification model. In search procedure the space of possible feature subset is defined and generated various subsets of features. Wrapper method can be divided in two groups these are deterministic and wrapper methods.

Table 2. Classification of filter-based feature selection methods on the basis of supervised and unsupervised learning

Filter-Based Feature Selection Methods	Supervised		Unsupervised	
	Univariate	Multivariate	Univariate	Multivariate
Relief F(Robnik-Šikonja and Kononenko, 2003)	No	Yes	No	No
mRmR(Peng, Long, and Ding, 2005)	No	Yes	No	No
FCBF(Yu and Liu, 2003)	No	Yes	No	No
Fisher score(Duda, Hart, and Stork, 2001)	Yes	No	No	No
SVM-RFE(Furey et al., 2000)	No	Yes	No	No
t-test(Duda, Hart, and Stork, 2001)	No	No	Yes	No
Entropy based(Duda, Hart, and Stork, 2001)	No	No	Yes	No
Laplacian Score(He, Cai, and Niyogi, 2005)	No	No	Yes	No
PCA(Duda, Hart, and Stork, 2001)	No	No	No	Yes

Table 3. Evaluation function used by filter-based feature selection method

Basic Criterion/Evaluation Function Used	Examples
Distance based measures	Euclidean distance
Information theory based measure	Entropy, Information gain, mutual information
Data dependency measure	Correlation coefficient
Consistency based measure	Minimum feature bias

Deterministic Wrapper Method

This method searches through the space of available feature either forward or backward. In forward selection single attribute are added to initially an empty set of attributes.

Randomized Wrapper Method

Randomized wrapper algorithms search the next feature subset partly at random. Single feature or several features at once can be added, removed or replaced from various feature set. The brief descriptions of wrapper based feature selection methods are shown in Table 5.

Table 4. Brief description of filter-based feature selection methods

Filter-Based Feature Selection Method		Basic Criterion
Supervised feature selection method	Fisher Score (Duda, Hart, and Stork, 2001)	Distance based, univariate filter method evaluating each feature individually
	Relief F (Robnik-Šikonja and Kononenko, 2003)	A multivariate filter taking into account dependencies between features
	mRmR (Peng, Long, and Ding, 2005)	Information theory based uses mutaual information
	FCBF (Yu and Liu, 2003)	Based on information gain, Fast correlation based filter
	SVM-RFE (Furey et al., 2000)	Ranks features based on their coefficients in the SVM classifier.
Unsupervised rank based feature selection methods	t-test score (Duda, Hart, and Stork, 2001)	Statistical, rank based feature selection approach
	Bhattacharya distance	
	Entropy rank feature	
	Principal component analysis (PCA)	PCA finds a linear projection of high dimensional data into lower dimensional subspace
	Laplacian score based	It is unsupervised feature selection algorithm. It is based on Laplacian Eigen maps.

Table 5. Brief description of wrapper-based feature selection methods

Wrapper	Deterministic	Simple, Interact with the classifier, Models feature dependencies, Less computationally intensive than randomized method	Risk of over fitting, More prone than Randomized algorithm to getting stuck in a local optimum(Greedy Search), Classifier dependent Selection	Sequential forward selection(SFS), Sequential backward elimination(SBE), Plus L Minus R, Beam Search
	Randomized	Less prone to local optima, Interact with the classifier, Model feature dependencies	Computationally Intensive, classifier dependent selection, High risk of over fitting than deterministic algorithms	Simulated annealing, Randomized hill climbing, Genetic algorithms

Embedded Feature Selection Method

Embedded method (Saeys, Inza, and Larrañaga, 2007) sometime also referred as nested subset method. It acts as an integral part of machine learning algorithm itself. During the operation of classification process, the algorithm itself decides which attribute to use and which to ignore. Embedded approach depends on a specific learning algorithm. Embedded methods are faster than wrapper methods. Decision trees are the best example of embedded method.

FEATURE SELECTION ALGORITHMS

CHI (χ^2 Statistics)

This method measure the lack of independence between a term and category. CHI-Squared is the common statistical test that measures divergence from the distribution expected if one assumes the feature occurrence is actually independent of class value. The χ^2 test is applied to test the independence of two events, where two events A and B are defined to be independent if $P(AB) = P(A)P(B)$ or equivalently $P(A \mid B) = P(A)$ and $P(B \mid A) = P(B)$ (Liu and Setiono 1995). Feature selection using the χ^2 statistics is analogous to performing a hypothesis test on the distribution of the class as it relates to the values of the feature in question. Under the null hypothesis, if p of the instance have a given value and q of the instances are in a specific class, $(p.q) / n$ instances have a given value and are in a specific class(n is the total number of instances in the data set) (Liu and Motoda, 2007). This is because p / n instances have the value and q / n instances are in the class, and if the probabilities are independent their joint probability is their product. Given the null hypothesis, the χ^2 statistic measure how far away the actual value is from the expected value:

Euclidian Distance

Euclidian Distance is the most common use of distance. In most cases when we talk about distance refer to Euclidian Distance. It examines the root of square differences between coordinates of a pair of object. For each feature X_i calculate Euclidian distance from it to all other features in sample. Euclidian distance $d(X_i; Y_i)$ between features X_i and Y_i is calculated using the formula (Dash and Liu, 1997):

$$distance\left(x, y\right) = \{\sum_i (x_i - y_i)^2 \}^{\frac{1}{2}}$$

This distance generally computed from raw data and not from standardized data.

t-Test

The t-test assesses whether the means of two groups are statistically different from each other. This analysis is appropriate whenever you want to compare the means of two groups, and especially appropriate as the analysis for the posttest-only two-group randomized experimental design. The formula for the t-test is a ratio. The top part of the ratio is just the difference between the two means or averages. The bottom part is a measure of the variability or dispersion of the scores (Guyon and Elisseeff, 2003b).

Information Gain

Information gain, of a term measures the number of bits of information obtained for category prediction by the presence or absence of the term in a document. Information Gain measures the decrease in entropy when the feature is given vs absent. This is the application of a more general technique, the measurement of informational entropy, to the problem of deciding how important a given feature is(Kira and Rendell, 1992). Informational entropy, when measured using Shannon entropy, is notionally the number of bits of data it would take to encode a given piece of information. The more space a piece of information takes to encode, the more entropy it has. Intuitively, this makes sense because a random string has maximum entropy and cannot be compressed, while a highly ordered string can be written with a brief description of the string's information. In the context of classification, the distribution of instances among classes is the information in question. If the instances are randomly assigned among the classes, the number of bits necessary to encode this class distribution is high, because each instance would need to be enumerated. On the other hand, if all the instances are in a single class, the entropy would be lower, because the bit-string would simply say "All instances save for these few are in the first class" (Joachims 1998) Therefore function measuring entropy must increase when the class distribution gets more spread out and be able to be applied recursively to permit finding the entropy of subsets of the data. The following formula satisfies both of these requirements:

$$H\left(D\right) = -\Sigma\left(n_i / n\right) \, log\left(n_i / n\right) \; i = 1, \ldots l$$

where dataset D has $n = |D|$ instances and n_i members in class c_i, $i = 1,..., 1$.

The entropy of any subset is calculated as:

$$H(D \mid X) = -\Sigma \left(|Xj| / n \right) H(D \mid X - Xj)$$

where $H(D \mid X = Xj)$ is the entropy calculated relative to the subset of instances that have a value of Xj for attribute X. If X is a good description of the class, each value of that feature will have little entropy in its class distribution; for each value most of the instances should be primarily in one class. The information gain of an attribute is measured by the reduction in entropy (Kira and Rendell, 1992) defined as:

$$IG(X) = H(D) - H(D \mid X)$$

The greater the decrease in entropy when considering attribute X individually, the more significant feature X is for prediction.

Correlation-Based Feature Selection (CFS)

Correlation based feature selection (CFS) searches feature subsets according to the degree of redundancy among the features. The evaluator aims to find the subsets of features that are individually highly correlated with the class but have low inter-correlation(Hall, 1999). The subset evaluators use a numeric measure, such as conditional entropy, to guide the search iteratively and add features that have the highest correlation with the class (Saeys, Inza, and Larrañaga, 2007). The downside of univariate filters for example information gain is, it does not account for interactions between features, which is overcome by multivariate filters for example CFS. CFS evaluates the worth of a subset of attributes by considering the individual predictive ability of each feature along with the degree of redundancy between them. Correlation coefficients are used to estimate correlation between subset of attributes and class, as well as inter-correlations between the features. Relevance of a group of features grows with the correlation between features and classes, and decreases with growing inter-correlation. CFS is used to determine the best feature subset and is usually combined with search strategies such as forward selection, backward elimination, bi-directional search, best-first search and genetic search (Yu and Liu, 2004).

Equation for CFS is given:

$$r_{zc} = \frac{k \, \overline{ri}}{\sqrt{k + k(k-1) \, \overline{r_u}}}$$

where r_{zc} is the correlation between the summed feature subsets and the class variable, k is the number of subset features, r_{zi} is the average of the correlations between the subset features and the class variable, and r_{ii} is the average inter-correlation between subset features.

Fast-Correlation-Based Feature Selection (FCBF)

Fast Correlation based Feature Selection (FCBF) (Yu and Liu, 2003) uses also the symmetrical uncertainty measure. But the search algorithm is very different. It is based on the "predominance" idea. The correlation between an attribute $X*$ and the target Y is predominant if and only if $\rho_{y,x}{}^* \geq \delta$ for all

$$X(X \neq X^*), \rho_{X,X}{}^* < \rho_Y, x *$$

Concretely, a predictor is interesting if its correlation with the target attribute is significant (delta is the parameter which allows assessing this one); there is no other predictor which is more strongly correlated to it.

Algorithm for FCBF

1. S is the set of candidate predictors, $M = \emptyset$ is the set of selected predictors
2. Searching $X*$ (among S) which maximizes its correlation with $Y \rightarrow \rho y, x*$
3. If $\rho y, x* \geq \delta$ add $X*$ into M and remove $X*$ from S
4. Remove also from S all the variables X such $\rho x, x* \geq \rho y, x*$
5. If $S \neq \emptyset$ then GOTO (2), else END of the algorithm

This approach is very useful when we deal with a dataset containing a very large number of candidate predictors. About the ability to detect the "best" subset of predictors and it is similar to CFS.

Sequential Forward Selection (SFS)

Sequential Forward Selection (Jain and Zongker, 1997) is the simplest greedy search algorithm. Starting from the empty set, sequentially add the feature x+ that results in the highest objective function $J(Y_k+x+)$ when combined with the features Y_k that have already been selected.

Algorithm

1. Start with the empty set $Y_0 = \{\phi\}$
2. Select the next best feature $X^+ = argmax \left[J(Y_k - X)\right]; x \notin Y_k$
3. Update $Y_{k+1} = Y_k + X^+; \; K = K+1$
4. Goto 2

SFS performs best when the optimal subset has a small number of features. When the search is near the empty set, a large number of states can be potentially evaluated. Towards the full set, the region examined by SFS is narrower since most of the features have already been selected. The search space is drawn like an ellipse to emphasize the fact that there are fewer states towards the full or empty sets. As an example, the state space for 4 features is shown. Notice that the number of states is larger in the middle of the search tree. The main disadvantage of SFS is that it is unable to remove features that become obsolete after the addition of other features.

Sequential Backward Elimination (SBE)

Sequential Backward Elimination(Mao, 2004) works in the opposite direction of SFS. It also referred to as SBS (Sequential Backward Selection). Starting from the full set, sequentially remove the feature $x-$ that results in the smallest decrease in the value of the objective function $J(Y-x-)$. Notice that removal of a feature may actually lead to an increase in the objective function $J(Yk-x-)>J(Yk)$. Such functions are said to be non-monotonic.

Algorithm

1. Start with the full set $Y_0 = X$
2. Remove the worst feature $X^- = argmax \left[J(Y_k - X)\right]; x \; Y_k$
3. Update $Y_{k+1} = Y_k - X^-; k = k+1$
4. Goto 2

SBS works best when the optimal feature subset has a large number of features, since SBS spends most of its time visiting large subsets. The main limitation of SBS is its inability to reevaluate the usefulness of a feature after it has been discarded.

Plus-L Minus-R Selection (LRS)

Plus-L Minus-R(Somol et al., 1999) is a generalization of SFS and SBS. If L>R, LRS starts from the empty set and repeatedly adds '*L*' features and removes '*R*' features. _If *L<R*, LRS starts from the full set and repeatedly removes '*R*' features followed by '*L*' feature addition.

Algorithm

1. If *L>R* then start with the empty set $Y = \{\phi\}$ else start with the full set *Y=X* Goto step3
2. Repeat *L* times $X^+ = argmax \left[J(Y_k + X) \right]; x \notin Y_k$ and
   $$Y_{k+1} = Y_k + X^+; k = k+1$$
3. Repeat *R* times $X^- = argmax \left[J(Y_k - X) \right]; x \notin Y_k$ and
   $$Y_{k+1} = Y_k - X^-; k = k+1$$
4. Goto 2

LRS attempts to compensate for the weaknesses of SFS and SBS with some backtracking capabilities(Ladha and Deepa, 2011). Its main limitation is the lack of a theory to help predict the optimal values of *L* and *R*.

Beam Search and Smart Beam Search

Although the spread factors of features yield useful information about their goodness, it is possible that features with low values of *I* be important for classification, as in the case of multi-modal or non-Gaussian feature distributions. Therefore, a more generic feature selection scheme called the beam search has been used. (Gupta, Doermann, and DeMenthon, 2002)

The beam search algorithm proceeds as follows:

1. Compute the classifier performance using each of the *n* features individually (*n I*-tuples).
2. Select the best *K* (beam-width) features based on a pre-defined selection criterion among these *I*-tuples.
3. Add a new feature to each of these *K* features, forming *K(n-1)* 2-tuples of features. The tuple-size *t* is equal to 2 at this stage.
4. Evaluate the performance of each of these *t*-tuples. Of these, select the best *K*, based on classification performance.

5. Form all possible $(t + 1)$ tuples by appending these K r-tuples with other features (not already in that tuple).
6. Repeat steps 4 to 5 until the stopping criterion is met; the tuple size at this stage is m.
7. The best K m-tuples are the result of beam search.

Randomized Hill-Climbing

Hill-climbing(Yang and Honavar, 1998) is probably the most known algorithm of local search. The idea of hill-climbing is:

1. Start at randomly generated state.
2. Move to the neighbor with the best evaluation value.
3. If a strict local-minimum is reached then restart at other randomly generated state.

This procedure repeats till the solution is found. In the algorithm, that we present here, the parameter Max_Flips is used to limit the maximal number of moves between restarts which helps to leave non-strict local-minimum.

Algorithm Hill-Climbing

1. Procedure hill-climbing(Max_Flips).
2. restart: s <- random valuation of variables.
3. for j:=1 to Max_Flips do.
4. if eval(s)=0 then return s endif.
5. if s is a strict local minimum then.
6. goto restart.
7. else.
8. s <- neighborhood with smallest evaluation value.
9. endif.
10. endfor.
11. goto restart.
12. end hill-climbing.

The hill-climbing algorithm has to explore all neighbors of the current state before choosing the move. This can take lot of time.

Genetic Algorithm

The Genetic Algorithms (GA)(Yang and Honavar, 1998) are efficient methods for function minimization. In descriptor selection context, the prediction error of the model built upon a set of features is optimized. The genetic algorithm mimics the natural evolution by modeling a dynamic population of solutions. The members of the population, referred to as chromosomes, encode the selected features. The encoding usually takes form of bit strings with bits corresponding to selected features set and others cleared. Each chromosome leads to a model built using the encoded features. By using the training data, the error of the model is quantified and serves as a fitness function.

The success of GA depends on several factors. The parameters steering the crossover, mutation and survival of chromosomes should be carefully chosen to allow the population to explore the solution space and to prevent early convergence to homogeneous population occupying a local minimum. The choice of initial population is also important in genetic feature selection. To address this issue, e.g. a method based on Shannon's entropy combined with graph analysis can be used.

Genetic algorithm based on the Darwinian survival of the fittest theory, is an efficient and broadly applicable global optimization algorithm. In contrast to conventional search techniques, genetic algorithm starts from a group of points coded as finite length alphabet strings instead of one real parameter set. The three basic operators of genetic algorithms are: selection, crossover and mutation. It selects some individuals with stronger adaptability from population according to the fitness, and then decides the copy number of individual according to the selection methods such as Backer stochastic universal sampling. It exchanges and recombines a pair of chromosome through crossover. Mutation is done to change certain point state via probability. In general, one needs to choose suitable crossover and mutation probability time and again via real problems.

ReliefF (RF) Algorithm

ReliefF(Robnik-Šikonja and Kononenko, 2003) is simple and efficient procedure to estimate the quality of attributes in problem with strong dependencies between attributes.ReliefF is usually applied in data preprocessing as a feature subset selection method.

The key idea of the ReliefF is to estimate the quality of genes according to how well their values distinguish between instances that are near to each other. Given a randomly selected instance I_{ns} from class c, ReliefF searches for K of its nearest neighbors from the same class called nearest hits H, and also K nearest neighbors from each of the different classes, called nearest misses M. It then updates the quality estimation Q_i for gene i based on their values for I_{ns}, H,M. If instance I_{ns} and those in H have different values in gene i then the quality estimation Q_i is decreased. On the other hand, if instance I_{ns} and those in M have different values on gene i, then Q_i is increased. The whole process is repeated n times which is set by user.

Algorithm

Input: Gene variable and labels
Output: W for the gene rank
    1.   Set all weights $W:=0$.
    2.   for each Iteration n do.
    3.   Randomly select an instance I_{ns}.
    4.   Find K nearest hits H.
    5.   for each class $c \neq$ Label m do.
    6.   from class c find K nearest misses M_c.
    7.   end.
    8.   for each g_i do.
    9.   Update Q.
    10.   end.
    11.   end.

Minimum Redundancy Maximum Relevance Feature Selection

mRmR (Minimum Redundancy Maximum Relevance Feature Selection) (Ding and Peng, 2005) is a multivariate feature selection method which starts with an empty set, uses mutual information to weight features and forward selection technique with sequential search strategy to find the best subset of features. It has a parameter k which enables it to stop when there are k features in the selected feature subset.

Mutual Information(MI) is a symmetrical information theoretic measure that measures the amount of information that can be obtained about one random variable by observing another. The mutual information of feature f_i relative to feature f_j is given by:

$$I(f_i,f_j) = \sum_{x,y} p(x,y) \log \frac{p(x,y)}{p(x)p(y)}$$

where x is all possible values of f_i and y is all possible values of f_j

Principal Component Analysis (PCA)

Principal Component Analysis (Ke and Sukthankar, 2004) is an unsupervised Feature selection method for projection of high dimensional data into a new lower dimensional representation of the data that describe as much of the variance in the data as possible with minimum reconstruction error. Principal Component Analysis is a quantitatively rigorous method for achieving this simplification. The method generates a new set of variables, called principal components. Each principal component is linear combination of the original variables.

Input: Data Matrix
Output: Reduced set of features
1. $X \leftarrow$ Create N x d data matrix with one row vector x_n per data point.
2. X subtract mean x from each row vector x_n in X.
3. $\sum \sum \leftarrow$ covariance matrix of X.
4. Find eigen vectors and eigen values of $\sum$.
5. $PC \leftarrow$ the M eigen vectors with largest eigen values.
6. Output PC.

Fisher Score for Feature Selection

Fisher score (Gu, Li, and Han, 2012) is one of the most widely used supervised feature selection method. It selects each feature independently according to their scores under the Fisher criterion, which leads to a suboptimal subset of features.

In particular, given selected m features the input data matrix $X \in R^{d \times n}$ reduce to $Z \in R^{m \times n}$. Fisher score computed as follow

$$F(z) = tr\{(S\tilde{b})(S\tilde{t} + \gamma I)^{-1}\}$$

where γ is a positive regularization parameter, $S\tilde{b}$ $\widetilde{Sb)}$ is called between-class scatter matrix and $S\tilde{t}$ is called total scatter matrix which are defined as

$$S\tilde{b} = \sum_{k=1}^{c} nk(\mu k - \mu)(\mu k - \mu)^T$$

$$S\tilde{t} = \sum_{i=1}^{n} (zi - \mu)(zi - \mu)^T$$

where μk and n_k are the mean vector and size of the k-th class respectively in the reduced data space Z, $\mu = \sum_{k=1}^{c} n k \mu k$ is the overall mean vector of the reduced data. $\tilde{St}$ is usually singular, we add a perturbation term $\gamma \gamma I$ to make it positive semi definite.

Let μ^j_k and ∂^j_k be the mean and standard deviation of the whole data set corresponding to the j-th feature. The Fisher score of the j-th feature is computed below

$$F(x^j) = \sum_{k=1}^{c} n_k (\mu^j_k - \mu^j)^2 / (\delta^j)^2$$

where $(\delta^i)^2 = \sum_{k=1}^{c} n_k (\delta^j_k)^2$

After computing the Fisher score for each feature it selects the top m ranked features with large scores.

Laplacian Score for Feature Selection

Laplacian score (He, Cai, and Niyogi, 2005) is fundamentally based on Laplacian Eigenmaps and locality preserving projection. The basic idea of LS is to evaluate the features according to their locality preserving power.

Algorithm

Let L_n denote the Laplcian score of the n-th feature. Let f_{ni} denote the i-th sample of the n-th feature, $i = 1,.....,m$.

1. Construct a nearest neighbor graph G with m nodes. The i-th nodes correspond to x_i. We put an edge between nodes i and j if x_i and x_j are "close". x_i is among k nearest neighbors of x_j or x_j is among k nearest neighbors of x_i. When the label information is available, one can put an edge between two nodes sharing the same label.

2. If nodes i and j are connected put $S_{ij} = e^{\frac{\|xi-xj\|^2}{t}}$ where t is suitable constant. Otherwise put $S_{ij} = 0$. The weight matrix S of the graph models the local structure of the data space.

3. For the n-th feature we define:

$$f_n = \left[f_{n1}, f_{n2.....}, f_{nm} \right]^T, D = \; diag \; (S_1), I = \; [1,....,1]^T, L \; = \; D - S$$

where the matrix L is often called graph Laplacian. Let

$$\bar{f}_n = f_n \ (f_n^T D_1 I^T D_1) \ I$$

4. Compute the Laplacian score of the n-th feature as follows:

$$L_n = \ \bar{f}_n^T \ L \bar{f}_n \ / \bar{f}_n^T \ D \bar{f}_n$$

The assortment of various feature selection algorithms is shown in Table 6.

Table 6. Assortment of feature selection algorithm

	Model Search	Advantages	Disadvantages	Examples
Filter	Univariate	Fast, Scalable, Independent of classifier	Ignore feature Dependencies, Ignore interaction with the classifier	CHI(X^2) Statistic, Euclidian Distance, t-test, Information gain, Fisher Score, Bhattacharya Distance, Entropy based, Laplacian Score
Filter	Multivariate	Models feature dependencies, independent of classifier, Better Computational Complexity than wrapper methods	Slower than Univariate techniques, Less scalable than Univariate techniques, Ignore interaction with classifier	Corelation based feature selection(CBF), Fast Correlation-based feature selection(FCBF), Relief F, mRmR, SVM-RFE, PCA
Wrapper	Deterministic	Simple, Interact with the classifier, Models feature dependencies, Less computationally intensive than randomized method	Risk of over fitting, More prone than Randomized algorithm to getting stuck in a local optimum(Greedy Search), Classifier dependent Selection	Sequential forward selection(SFS), Sequential backward elimination(SBE), Plus L Minus R, Beam Search
Wrapper	Randomized	Less prone to local optima, Interact with the classifier, Model feature dependencies	Computationally Intensive, classifier dependent selection, High risk of over fitting than deterministic algorithms	Simulated annealing, Randomized hill climbing, Genetic algorithms
Embedded		Interact with the classifier, better computational complexity than wrapper methods, Models feature dependencies	Classifier dependent selection	Decision tress, Weighted naïve Bayes, feature selection using the weight vector of SVM

CONCLUSION

This chapter presented an empirical comparison of feature selection methods and its algorithm. In view of the substantial number of existing feature selection algorithms, the need arises to count on criteria that enable to adequately decide which algorithm to use in certain situation. This chapter also reviewed several fundamental algorithms found in the literature and assess their performance in a controlled scenario.

REFERENCES

Almuallim, H., & Dietterich, T. G. (1991, July). Learning with Many Irrelevant Features. In *AAAI*.

Athanasakis, D., Shawe-Taylor, J., & Fernandez-Reyes, D. (2013). *Principled Non-Linear Feature Selection.* arXiv preprint arXiv:1312.5869

Belanche, L. A., & González, F. F. (2011). *Review and evaluation of feature selection algorithms in synthetic problems.* arXiv preprint arXiv:1101.2320

Bell, D. A., & Wang, H. (2000). A formalism for relevance and its application in feature subset selection. *Machine Learning, 41*(2), 175–195. doi:10.1023/A:1007612503587

Caruana, R., & Freitag, D. (1994, July). Greedy Attribute Selection. In ICML (pp. 28-36). doi:10.1016/B978-1-55860-335-6.50012-X

Craven, M., DiPasquo, D., Freitag, D., McCallum, A., Mitchell, T., Nigam, K., & Slattery, S. (2000). Learning to construct knowledge bases from the World Wide Web. *Artificial Intelligence, 118*(1), 69–113. doi:10.1016/S0004-3702(00)00004-7

Dash, M., & Liu, H. (1997). Feature selection for classification. *Intelligent Data Analysis, 1*(3), 131–156. doi:10.1016/S1088-467X(97)00008-5

Ding, C., & Peng, H. (2005). Minimum redundancy feature selection from microarray gene expression data. *Journal of Bioinformatics and Computational Biology, 3*(02), 185–205. doi:10.1142/S0219720005001004 PMID:15852500

Duda, R. O., Hart, P. E., & Stork, D. G. (2001). *Pattern classification* (2nd ed.). New York: Academic Press.

Furey, T. S., Cristianini, N., Duffy, N., Bednarski, D. W., Schummer, M., & Haussler, D. (2000). Support vector machine classification and validation of cancer tissue samples using microarray expression data. *Bioinformatics (Oxford, England), 16*(10), 906–914. doi:10.1093/bioinformatics/16.10.906 PMID:11120680

Gu, Q., Li, Z., & Han, J. (2012). *Generalized fisher score for feature selection.* arXiv preprint arXiv:1202.3725

Gupta, P., Doermann, D., & DeMenthon, D. (2002). Beam search for feature selection in automatic SVM defect classification. In *Pattern Recognition, 2002. Proceedings. 16th International Conference on* (Vol. 2, pp. 212-215). IEEE. doi:10.1109/ICPR.2002.1048275

Guyon, I., & Elisseeff, A. (2003). An introduction to variable and feature selection. *Journal of Machine Learning Research, 3*, 1157–1182.

Hall, M. A. (1999). *Correlation-based feature selection for machine learning* (Doctoral dissertation). The University of Waikato.

Jain, A., & Zongker, D. (1997). Feature selection: Evaluation, application, and small sample performance. *Pattern Analysis and Machine Intelligence. IEEE Transactions on, 19*(2), 153–158.

Joachims, T. (1998). *Text categorization with support vector machines: Learning with many relevant features.* Springer Berlin Heidelberg.

Kohavi, R., Sommerfield, D., & Dougherty, J. (1996, November). Data mining using 𝓂 𝓁 𝒸++ a machine learning library in c++. In *Tools with Artificial Intelligence, 1996.,Proceedings Eighth IEEE International Conference on* (pp. 234-245). IEEE.

Ladha, L., & Deepa, T. (2011). Feature selection methods and algorithms. *International Journal on Computer Science and Engineering, 3*(5).

Lee, K., Joo, J., Yang, J., & Honavar, V. (2006). Experimental comparison of feature subset selection using GA and ACO algorithm. In *Advanced Data Mining and Applications* (pp. 465–472). Springer Berlin Heidelberg. doi:10.1007/11811305_51

Lee, M. S., & Moore, A. W. (2014, June). Efficient algorithms for minimizing cross validation error. In *Machine Learning Proceedings 1994:Proceedings of the Eighth International Conference* (p. 190). Morgan Kaufmann.

Liu, H., & Motoda, H. (Eds.). (2007). *Computational methods of feature selection.* CRC Press.

Liu, H., & Setiono, R. (1996, July). A probabilistic approach to feature selection-a filter solution. In ICML (Vol. 96, pp. 319-327).

Mao, K. Z. (2004). Orthogonal forward selection and backward elimination algorithms for feature subset selection. *Systems, Man, and Cybernetics, Part B: Cybernetics. IEEE Transactions on, 34*(1), 629–634.

Masaeli, M., Dy, J. G., & Fung, G. M. (2010). From transformation-based dimensionality reduction to feature selection. In *Proceedings of the 27th International Conference on Machine Learning (ICML-10)* (pp. 751-758).

Molina, L. C., Belanche, L., & Nebot, À. (2002). Feature selection algorithms: A survey and experimental evaluation. In *Data Mining, 2002. ICDM 2003. Proceedings. 2002 IEEE International Conference on* (pp. 306-313). IEEE. doi:10.1109/ICDM.2002.1183917

Peng, H., Long, F., & Ding, C. (2005). Feature selection based on mutual information criteria of max-dependency, max-relevance, and min-redundancy. *Pattern Analysis and Machine Intelligence. IEEE Transactions on, 27*(8), 1226–1238.

Reinartz, T. (1999). *Focusing solutions for data mining: analytical studies and experimental results in real-world domains.* Springer-Verlag. doi:10.1007/3-540-48316-0

Robnik-Šikonja, M., & Kononenko, I. (2003). Theoretical and empirical analysis of ReliefF and RReliefF. *Machine Learning, 53*(1-2), 23–69. doi:10.1023/A:1025667309714

Saeys, Y., Inza, I., & Larrañaga, P. (2007). A review of feature selection techniques in bioinformatics. *Bioinformatics, 23*(19), 2507-2517.

Sewell, M. (2007). *Feature selection.* Retrieved from http://machine-learning. martinsewell. com/feature-selection

Somol, P., Pudil, P., Novovičová, J., & Paclık, P. (1999). Adaptive floating search methods in feature selection. *Pattern Recognition Letters, 20*(11), 1157–1163. doi:10.1016/S0167-8655(99)00083-5

Srivastava, Sharma, & Singh. (2014). Empirical Analysis of Supervised and Unsupervised Filter Based Feature Selection Methods for Breast Cancer Classification from Digital Mammograms. *International Journal of Computers and Applications, 88*(8).

Tao, Y., Xia, Y., Xu, T., & Chi, X. (2010). Research Progress of the Scale Invariant Feature Transform (SIFT) Descriptors. *Journal of Convergence Information Technology, 5*(1), 116–121. doi:10.4156/jcit.vol5.issue1.13

Yu, L., & Liu, H. (2003, August). Feature selection for high-dimensional data: A fast correlation-based filter solution. In ICML (Vol. 3, pp. 856-863).

Chapter 8

Application of Optimization Techniques for Gene Expression Data Analysis

Suresh Dara
DIT University, India

Arvind Kumar Tiwari
DIT University, India

ABSTRACT

The feature selection from gene expression data is the NP hard problem, few of evolutionary techniques give optimal solutions to find feature subsets. In this chapter, authors introduce some evolutionary optimization techniques and proposed a Binary Particle Swarm Optimization (BPSO) based algorithm for feature subset selection. The Feature selection is one of the important and challenging tasks for gene expression data where many traditional methods failed and evolutionary based methods were succeeded. In this study, the initial datasets are preprocessed using a quartile based fast heuristic technique to reduce the crude domain features which are less relevant in categorizing the samples of either group. The experimental results on three bench-mark datasets vis-a-vis colon cancer, defused B-cell lymphoma and leukemia data are evaluated by means of classification accuracies. Detailed comparative studies with some of popular existing algorithms like Genetic Algorithm (GA), Multi Objective GA are also made to show the superiority and effectiveness of the proposed method.

DOI: 10.4018/978-1-5225-2545-5.ch008

1. INTRODUCTION

The feature selection problem is a high-dimensional optimization problem in the nature and thus needs a solver with high exploration power. On the other hand, if alternative optimal solutions could be provided for a problem, the implementation phase may become more selective depending on the cost and limitations of domain of the problem. The high exploration power and solution conservation capability of optimization methods make them able to find multiple suitable solutions in a single run. Therefore, optimization methods can be considered as a powerful tool of finding suitable feature subsets for feature selection problem. Figure 1 shows that, various optimization techniques in hierarchal format. Here, few of traditional approaches and nontraditional approaches i.e., heuristic approaches are presented.

Feature Selection (FS) is the process of selecting optimal feature subset from a given dataset that can interpret the target concept. Any feature selection algorithm completes in four steps viz. subset generation, subset evaluation, stopping criterion and result validation. Subset generation is the process of searching subsets from the given feature space and then selected subset is evaluated to determine the goodness of feature subset under consideration. The termination of the algorithm is decided by stopping criterion. Finally, validation is performed to identify legitimate feature subsets (Tou & Gonz'alez, 1994). Feature selection has been explored extensively by researchers of data mining and machine learning since 1970s. It has exploited many domains like machine learning, data mining, pattern recognition and other related domains such as software engineering, text categorization, bioinformatics, image retrieval, intrusion detection, information and music retrieval (Mitra & Acharya, 2003).

The microarray experiments produce gene expression patterns that provide dynamic information about cell function. In a single experiment, the DNA microarray technologies can simultaneously monitor and analysis of thousands of different genes in histological or cytological specimens which helps to find diseased samples according to the different levels of expression profiles. Gene expression profiles usually contain a large number of genes but a small number of samples. An important need to analyze and interpret the huge amount of data, involving the decoding of around 24000-30000 human genes (Special Issue on Bioinformatics, 2002) is found to be an NP-Hard problem (Skowron & Rauszer, 1992).

High dimensional feature selection technique may help us to identify important features by applying certain selection criteria which reduces the computation cost and increases the classification accuracy. DNA microarray technologies have been

Figure 1. Different type of optimization techniques

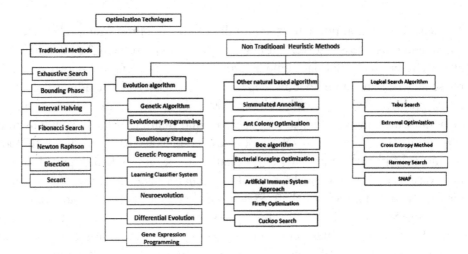

utilized to handle classification (Maji & Das, 2012. Ghorai et al., 2011), clustering (Mitra & Ghosh, 2012) and feature selection (Song, Ni, & Wang, 2013) problems.

The objective of this chapter is to provide some investigation, both theoretical and experimental, addressing some of optimizing techniques for feature selection from high dimensional data. These include evolutionary computations for feature selection and validation through classification in high-dimensional gene expression data. Various methodologies have been developed by using soft computing approaches (i.e., rough sets and evolutionary computing). The emphasis of the developed methodologies is given on (a) Handling datasets which are large (both in dimension and size) and (b) demonstrating the significance of granular computing for selecting important features (viz a viz reduct) from gene expression data.

2. BACKGROUND

In this section, few of well popular evolutionary techniques like GA and MOGA presented to understand the work.

Genetic Algorithms (GA)

GA was introduced in 1970s by John Holland (Glodberg, 1989). GA is a stochastic population based search strategy, works on biological mechanism of natural selection, crossover and mutation. GAs are executed iteratively on a set of coded solutions, called population, with the three basic operators: selection, crossover and mutation.

For solving a problem, GA starts with a set of encoded random solutions (i.e., chromosomes) and evolves better set of solutions over generations by applying the basic GA operators. Better solutions are determined from objective values (i.e. fitness function) that determine the suitability and goodness of the solutions.

The basic concepts and operations in standard GA are as follows. Each encoded (real or binary) string is called chromosome (individual) that is initially generated randomly. The real value can be encoded as a binary string. Each bit in this string is called a gene and the entire string is called a chromosome. A group of chromosomes/individuals constitutes a population. A population thus forms a set of solutions for the problem. Each individual xi corresponds to a fitness value f (xi). GAs use probabilistic rules to evolve a population from one generation to the next. The generations of the new solutions are developed by following operators:

- **Selection:** The objective of selection is to choose good individuals from the population in order to mimic the Darwinian "survival of the fittest" strategy.
- **Crossover:** Crossover combines the "fittest" chromosomes and passes superior genes to the next generation. If no crossover is performed, offspring is exact replica of the parent.
- **Mutation:** Mutation introduces perturbation in the search space and leads the population out of local optima (minima or maxima).
- **Fitness Function:** It is defined as solution of a given problem. It is different from problem to problem.

Algorithm 1: Standard Genetic Algorithm

Step 1: Generate random population of chromosomes (i.e., x suitable solutions for the problem).

Step 2: Evaluate the fitness $f(x)$ for each chromosome x in the population.

Step 3: Perform selection, crossover and mutation operations to generate the new child population.

Step 4: Consider the child population as parent and iterate Steps (2-3) until convergence.

The algorithm 1 is said to be the converge if any of the following conditions are satisfied: (1) When the desired result is found, or (2) when it completes the maximum number of iterations, or (3) when all the solutions become homogeneous.

The standard GA is shown in Algorithm 1. From the optimization point of view, GA is highly parallel, robust and adaptive search processes which generally lead to approximately global optimal solutions even in multidimensional and multi modal surfaces. It considers many points in the search space simultaneously and hence has less chance of converging to local optima. Various attempts have been made on the application of GA's to different fields like classification, segmentation, image enhancement, primitive extraction, membership function selection and many more.

- **Multi Objective Genetic Algorithm (MOGA):** Multi objective evolutionary computations (MOEAs) have been gaining an increasing attention over recent years. If there are a number of objectives, MOGA plays an important role to optimize these objectives simultaneously and separately. These are mainly focused on solutions that can be suitably applied to find multiple Pareto-optimal solutions in one single simulation run. The goal of MOEA is to, first, find a set of well distributed solutions close to the true Pareto-optimal front. In the next phase, using that solutions, some higher level problem information can be used to select one solution. Over the fast few decade, different MOEAs have been developed such as NSGA-II (Deb et al., n.d.), PAES (Knowles & Corne, 2000), PESA (David et al., 2000), etc.

In this chapter, the NSGA-II has been explored for feature selection, using the concept of MOGA along with the proposed BPSO in multi-objective framework. NSGA-II uses non-dominated solutions, crowding distance operator and crowding tournament selection operator. The concept of optimality, behind the multi objective optimization (Deb, 2001), deals with a set of solutions. The conditions for a solution to be dominated with respect to the other solutions are given as below. If there are M objective functions, a solution *s1* is said to dominate another solution *s2*, if both conditions 1 and 2 are true.

1.   The solution *s1* is no worse than *s2* in all the M objective functions.
2.   The solution *s1* is strictly better than *s2* in at least one of the M objective functions.

Otherwise, the two solutions are non-dominating to each other.

When a solution *i* dominates a solution *j*, then rank *ri < rj*. The major steps for finding the non-dominated set in a population *P* of size |*P*| are outlined as follows in Algorithm 2.

Algorithm 2: Nondominated Sorting Algorithm

Step 1: Set solution counter *i = 1* and create an empty non-dominated set **P'**.
Step 2: For a solution *j* **belongs to** *P* (*j ≠ i*)**,** check if the solution *j* dominates the solution *i*. If yes then go to Step 4.

Step 3: If more solutions are left in *P*. increment *j* by one and go to Step 2. Else set *P'= P U {i}.*

Step 4: Increment *i* by one. If *i* ≤ |*P*| then go to Step 2. Else declare *P'* as the non-dominated set.

Crowding Distance: It is used to maintain diversity in the population. To estimate the density of solutions surrounding a particular solution i in the population, take the crowding distance of ith solution in its front is the average distance of two boundary solutions *((i+1)th and (i-1)th).*

The following algorithm computes the crowding distance di of each point in the front *F*.

- Let the number of solutions in *F* be l = |F| and assign *di = 0 for i = 1, 2.....l.*
- For each objective function f_k; *k = 1,2...M,* sort the set in its worse order.
- Set $d_i = d_l = \infty.$
- For *j = 2 to (l - 1)* increment $f_{kj+1} - f_{kj-1}.$

Crowded tournament selection:

A solution *i* wins tournament with another solution *j* if any one of the following is true:

- Solution i has better rank, i.e., $r_i < r_j,$
- Both the solutions are in the same front, i.e., $r_i = r_j,$ but solution i is less densely located in the search space, i.e., $d_i > d_j.$

The NSGA-II algorithm is summarized in Algorithm 3.

Algorithm 3: NSGA-II Algorithm

Step 1: Initialize the population randomly.
Step 2: Calculate the multi-objective fitness functions.
Step 3: Rank the population using dominance criteria.
Step 4: Calculate the crowding distance.
Step 5: Do selection using crowding selection operator.
Step 6: Do crossover and mutation to generate child population.
Step 7: Combine parent and children population.
Step 8: Replace the parent population by the best members of the combined population.

Initially, members of lower fronts replace the parent population. When it is not possible to accommodate all the members of a particular front, then next lower front is considered and last solutions are selected according to the crowding distance. The number selected makes the new parent population of the same size as the size of the old one.

3. BINARY PSO-BASED APPROACH FOR FEATURE SELECTION

PSO is a multi-agent optimization evolutionary technique developed by Kennedy and Eberhart in 1995. The PSO has been found to be the robust solving problem featuring non linearity and non - differentiability, multiple optima and high dimensionality through adaptation which is derived from social-psychological theory (Kennedy, 1997). The original intent was to graphically simulate the graceful yet unpredictable movements of a flock of birds. Initial simulations were modified to form the original version of PSO (Kennedy & Eberhart, 1995). Later, inertia weight (w) introduced into the particle swarm optimizer to produce the standard PSO (Shi & Eberhart, 1998).

At first, the population of solutions (also called particles) are initialized randomly. Each particle is treated as a point in an n-dimensional search space. The ith particle is represented *as $X_i = (x_{i1}, x_{i2}, x_{i3}, ...x_{in})$*, also denoted the position of the particle *i* $=(1,2,...n)$ of the swarm and $p_i = (p_{i1}, p_{i2}, ... p_{in})$ denoted the best position pbest it has ever visited. The index of the best particle among all the particles in the population is represented by the symbol p_g (global best). Each time step t in the simulation the velocity of the ith particle is represented as $V_i = (v_{i1}, v_{i2}, ...v_{in})$. The particles are adjusted according to the following equation:

$$V_{ij}(t+1) = w * V_{ij}(t) + c1 * R1 * (p_{ij}(t) + X_{ij}(t)) + c2 * R2 * (p_{gj}(t) * X_{ij}(t)) \quad (1)$$

$$X_{ij}(t+1) = X_{ij}(t) + V_{ij}(t+1) \quad (2)$$

here $j = 1, 2, 3,... n$ (i.e. dimension of each particle), w is inertia weight which provides balance between global and local exploration and results in fewer iterations on an average to find a sufficiently optimal solution. c1 and c2 are the same positive constants used in flock's simulations and are respectively called the cognitive and social acceleration coefficients. These constants represent the weighting of the stochastic acceleration terms that pull each particle toward **pbest** and **gbest** positions. R1 and R2 are two random numbers in the range of (0, 1).

In equation (1), the first part provides the flying particles with a degree of memory capability allowing the exploration of new search space and the second part is the cognition part, which represents the private thinking of the particle itself. The third part is the social part, which represents the collaboration among the particles. This is used for calculating the particle's new velocity according to its previous velocity, the distances of its current position from its own best experience (position) and the group's best experience.

The particle flies toward a new position according to (2). The velocity V_{t+1} and position X_{t+1} update. The performance of each particle is measured according to a pre-defined fitness function.

The PSO was extended to Binary Particle Swarm Optimization, the position and velocities are restricted to either 0 or 1. In BPSO, the updated positions using (3) and velocities using (1) are updated As

$$\text{If } X_{id} = 1 \text{ if } rand() < S_{id}, \text{ otherwise } X_{id} = 0 \tag{3}$$

where

$$S(V_{id}) = 1/(1 + e^{-Vid}) $$

and rand() is a function, to generate a uniform distributed random number in (0,1). The particle flies toward a new position according to equation (2), velocity updating is based on equation (3). The performance of each particle is measured according to a predefined fitness function.

4. PREPROCESSING OF GENE EXPRESSION DATA

The normalization is performed on each attribute of the input data matrix so that all the features get equal weightage or priority. In this study, authors used quartile normalization, after that convert all features to binary based on idea of literature (Banka et al., n.d.). Finally all values converted into distinction table.

When the preprocessing is over, the reduced features are still high dimensional. A distinction table is generated. The feature selection can be done by the proposed BPSO using the following objective function.

Fitness Function: In this study a fitness function is used, which includes two sub functions (F1 and F2).

F1 finds number of features (i.e number of 1's), F2 decides the extent to which the feature can recognize among the object's pairs. The fitness function is maximized and defined as:

$$F(v) = \alpha_1 F_1(v) + \alpha_2 F_2(v) \tag{4}$$

where the two sub functions

$$F_1(v) = N / (O_v - N) \qquad (4.1)$$

and

$$F_2(v) = Cv /(m * n) \qquad (4.2)$$

under the condition $\alpha_{1+}\ \alpha_2 = 1$.

Here, v is the chosen feature subsets, O_v represents the number of 1's in v, m and n are the number of objects in two classes and C_v is the number of object pairs (rows) in the distinction table v can discern between. The fitness function F_1 gives the candidate credit for containing less number of features or attributes in v and F_2 determines the extent to which the candidates can discern among object pairs in the distinction table.

Implementation: Parameter selection may influence the quality of computational results. Two accelerator coefficients parameters (c1 & c2) were set to 2, the minimum and maximum of velocities were set to -4 and 4, respectively as from literature (Han Huang, Hu Qin, Zhifeng Hao (2012)) related to this problem. The inertia weight (w) is one of the most important parameter in BPSO which can improve performance by properly balancing its local and global search (203). The inertia weight (w) was set to 0.9 after several experiment. The varied population size was taken, to check feature subsets and the swarm size was set equal to population. Also tested different population sizes like 10, 20, 30, 50, 100, 150 and 200. Maximum runs set as 50 and it is observed that when the number of iterations exceeds 50, there is no further improvement.

5. RESULTS

The proposed BPSO algorithm have implemented to find minimal feature subsets on high dimensional cancer datasets; i.e. Colon, Lymphoma and Leukemia. This book chapter focused on two-class problem (i.e normal and diseased samples), as summarized as follows. In this study, three benchmark datasets have been used for training and test purposes as described below.

1. **Colon Cancer:** It is a set of 62 gene expressions, containing 2000 genes (features).
2. Lymphoma dataset2 is a set of 96 gene expressions, having 4026 genes.
3. Leukemia dataset 3 is a set of 38 gene expressions, having 7129 genes.

The experimental results reported here is based on their classification accuracy using different well known classifiers. It may be noted that the results improved to some extent (in some cases) after proper tuning of the parameters. All the results reported here are based on three two-class gene expression datasets with different population sizes (10, 20, 30 and 50). It is observed that, as the number of generation proceed, there are consideration reductions in feature subsets. It was also observed that after 50 generation, there is no further improvement in the solutions.

Different metrics (such as precision= TP /(TP+FP), recall= TP/(TP+FN) etc.) were available in literature for results. Whereas TP=True Positive (the number of items correctly labeled as belonging to the positive class), TN=True Negative (the number of items correctly labeled as belonging to the negative class), FP=False Positive and FN=False Negative (which items are incorrectly labeled as belonging to the class). Nevertheless, reported the results with correct classification accuracy over the selected features using the confusion matrix.

Comparisons: A Binary PSO based feature selection algorithm was proposed by Mohamad et al. (2009), the authors used ratio technique in order to select top ranked genes and LOOCV is employed for cross validation of classification, leukemia data achieved 100% accuracy in subsets with 2 genes, 3 genes and 4 genes, and 96.77% accuracy for colon data. Whereas proposed Hybrid Binary PSO provides 100% accuracy for benchmark data taken for study.

A probabilistic model for feature selection with correlation based on class distinction was proposed by Huang (2004). Classification accuracy for leukemia data is 100% on set of ten genes, whereas colon data, a set of ten genes got 79.0% accuracy. Our proposed method giving 92.11%, 97.91% accuracy on k-NN classifier and 100% accuracy using other classifiers on those datasets.

Figure 2 shows the comparative results of proposed with GA and NSGA-II (Banerjee, Mitra, & Banka, 2007) for benchmark datasets. GA yields classification accuracy of 77:42% with 15 gene set for colon data, 93.76% with 18 gene subset for lymphoma and 73.53% with 19 gene subset for leukemia. The proposed Binary PSO produced 93.76% accuracy. Multiple objective (NSGAII) based method, produced 90.3% with a set of 9 genes on colon data, 95.8% for 2 gene subset lymphoma, and 91.2% on 3 gene subset for leukemia using k -NN classifier. Proposed Binary PSO obtained 100% classification accuracy.

6. FUTURE RESEARCH DIRECTIONS

Many evolutionary algorithms available in literature to solve the feature selection problem. Different approaches with different algorithms can develop like Ant Colony Optimization, Bee Colony Optimization, Firefly algorithm, etc.

Figure 2. k-NN classification results for proposed approach, NSGA-II and GA for colon, lymphoma, and leukemia

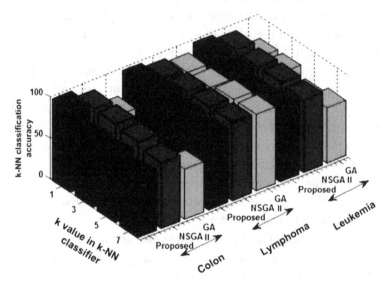

7. CONCLUSION

In this chapter, the Binary PSO algorithm finds minimal feature subsets of high dimensional cancer datasets. Preprocessing is done using heuristic based approach to create binary distinction table, further it identifies the discerning and expressive genes. To improve the results, we have studied with different population sizes. The two sub fitness functions helps in feature selection to find the paradoxical conditions, there by minimal feature subsets can be selected.

The performance of Binary PSO algorithm and some of the existing algorithms are compared by using the predictive accuracy. The results for three benchmark data sets viz. Colon, Lymphoma and Leukemia. The proposed algorithm shows the superiority over the existing algorithms in most of the cases. However, the relevance of the selected genes are to be validated in biological perspective.

REFERENCES

Banerjee, M., Mitra, S., & Banka, H. (2007). Evolutionary rough feature selection in gene expression data. *Systems, Man, and Cybernetics, Part C: Applications and Reviews, IEEE Transactions on, 37*, 622–632.

Corne, Knowles, & Oates. (2000). The pareto envelope-based selection algorithm for multi objective optimization. In Parallel Problem Solving from Nature PPSN VI, (pp. 839–848). Springer.

Deb, K. (2001). *Multi-objective optimization using evolutionary algorithms* (Vol. 16). John Wiley & Sons.

Deb, K., Pratap, A., Agarwal, S., & Meyarivan, T. A. M. T. (2002). A fast and elitist multiobjective genetic algorithm: Nsga-ii. *IEEE Transactions on Evolutionary Computation, 6*(2), 182–197. doi:10.1109/4235.996017

Ghorai, Mukherjee, Sengupta, & Dutta. (2011). Cancer classification from gene expression data by nppc ensemble. *Computational Biology and Bioinformatics, IEEE/ACM Transactions on, 8*(3), 659–671.

Glodberg. (1989). Genetic algorithms in search, optimization, and machine learning. Addison Wesley.

Huang, C. J. (2004). class prediction of cancer using probabilistic neural networks and relatice correlation metric. *Applied Artificial Intelligence: An Internaltional Journal, 18*(2), 117–128. doi:10.1080/08839510490278916

Huang, H., Qin, H., Hao, Z., & Lim, A. (2012). Example-based learning particle swarm optimization for continuous optimization. *Information Sciences, 182*(1), 125–138. doi:10.1016/j.ins.2010.10.018

Kennedy, J. (1997). The particle swarm: social adaptation of knowledge. In *IEEE International Conference on Evolutionary Computation*, (pp. 303–308). doi:10.1109/ICEC.1997.592326

Kennedy, J., & Eberhart, R. (1995). Particle swarm optimization. In *Proc IEEE Int. Conf. On Neural Networks*, (pp. 1942–1948). doi:10.1109/ICNN.1995.488968

Knowles, J. D., & Corne, D. W. (2000). Approximating the nondominated front using the pareto archived evolution strategy. *Evolutionary Computation, 8*(2), 149–172. doi:10.1162/106365600568167 PMID:10843519

Laumanns, Zitzler, & Thiele (2001). *Spea2: Improving the strength pareto evolutionary algorithm*. Academic Press.

Maji, P., & Das, C. (2012). Relevant and significant supervised gene clusters for microarray cancer classification. *NanoBioscience. IEEE Transactions on, 11*(2), 161–168.

Mitra, S., & Ghosh, S. (2012). Feature selection and clustering of gene expression profiles using biological knowledge. *Systems, Man, and Cybernetics, Part C: Applications and Reviews. IEEE Transactions on, 42*(6), 1590–1599.

Mitra & Acharya. (2003). *Data Mining: Multimedia, Soft Computing and Bioinformatics*. New York: John Wiley & Sons.

Mohamad, M. S., Omatu, S., Deris, S., & Yoshioka, M. (2009). Particle swarm optimization for gene selection in classifying cancer classes. *Artificial Life and Robotics, 14*(1), 16–19. doi:10.1007/s10015-009-0712-z

Shi, Y., & Eberhart, R. (1998). A modified particle swarm optimizer.*Proc. IEEE Int. Conf. On Evolutionary Computation*, 69–73.

Skowron & Rauszer. (1992). The discernibility matrices and functions in information systems. In I. D. Support (Ed.), *Theory and Decision Library* (Vol. 11, pp. 331–362). Springer Netherlands.

Song, Q., Ni, J., & Wang, G. (2013). A fast clustering-based feature subset selection algorithm for high-dimensional data. *Knowledge and Data Engineering. IEEE Transactions on, 25*(1), 1–14.

Tou & Gonz'alez. (1994). *Pattern recognition principles*. Addison Wesley.

Zitzler, E., & Thiele, L. (1999). Multiobjective evolutionary algorithms: A comparative case study and the strength pareto approach. *Evolutionary Computation. IEEE Transactions on, 3*(4), 257–271.

Chapter 9

Machine–Learning–Based Approach for Face Recognition

Arvind Kumar Tiwari
DIT University, India

ABSTRACT

Face recognition has been one of the most interesting and important research areas for real time applications. There is a need and necessity to design efficient machine leaning based approach for automatic recognitions and surveillance systems. Face recognition also used the knowledge from other disciplines such as neuroscience, psychology, computer vision, pattern recognition, image processing, and machine learning, etc. This chapter provides a review of machine learning based techniques for the face recognition. First, it presents an overview of face recognition and its challenges then, a literature review of machine learning based approaches for face detection and recognition is presented.

1. INTRODUCTION

In recent years there has been a growing interest in improving all aspects of the interaction between humans and computers with the clear goal of achieving a natural interaction, similar to the way human-human interaction takes place. The most expressive way humans display emotions is through facial expressions. Humans detect and interpret faces and facial expressions in a scene with little or no effort. Still, development of an automated system that accomplishes this task is rather difficult. There are several related problems: detection of an image segment as a face, extraction of the facial expression information, and classification of the expression. A system that performs these operations accurately and in real time

DOI: 10.4018/978-1-5225-2545-5.ch009

would be a major step forward in achieving a human-like interaction between the man and machine. In this chapter, we present several machine learning algorithms applied to face analysis.

Face recognition is one of the most challenging areas in the field of computer vision. Face detection is the first step for face recognition in order to localize and to extract the face region from the background. For face detection, active contour models are used to detect the edges and for locating the face boundary. For face recognition, facial feature extraction algorithm is widely used. The distinguishing features found by the algorithm are used to compare images. There exist several algorithms to extract features such as Principal Component Analysis (PCA) (Wold, S. *et. al.* (1987); Jolliffe, I. (2002)), Linear Discriminate Analysis (LDA) (Chien, et al., 2005; Martínez, et al., 2001), Principal Component Analysis (PCA) (Wold, et al., 1987; Jolliffe, 2002; Holand, 2008). This type of feature extraction algorithms needs manual interaction and do not consider prominent local features of a face, i.e., extracts the various facial features globally. Automatic recognition is a vast and modern research area of computer vision, reaching from recognition of faces, facial expressions and gestures over related topics such as automatically detecting, locating and tracking faces, as well as extraction of face orientation and facial features. Facial recognition system is a computer application for automatically identifying or verifying a person from a digital image or a video frame from a video source (see Figure 1).

The development of face recognition over the past years allows an organization into three types of recognition algorithms, namely frontal, profile, and view-tolerant recognition, depending on both the facial views available, and according to the recognition algorithms. While frontal recognition certainly is the classical approach to tackle the problem at hand, view-tolerant algorithms usually treat it in a more sophisticated fashion by taking into consideration some of the underlying physics, geometry, and statistics.

There are several challenges in face detection and recognition these include:

1. **Illumination Challenged:** Although the performance of face recognition systems in indoor platforms has reached a certain level, face recognition in outdoor platforms still remains as a challenging topic the effect of variation in the illumination conditions, which causes dramatic changes in the face appearance, is one of the most challenging problems that a practical face recognition system needs to achieve.

2. **Face Pose:** In an automatic face recognition system, the camera is mostly mounted to a location where the people cannot reach to the camera. Mounting a camera a high location, the faces are viewed by some angle degree. This is the simplest case in city surveillance applications. The next and the most difficult case is that people naturally pass through the camera view. They do

Figure 1. Face recognition system

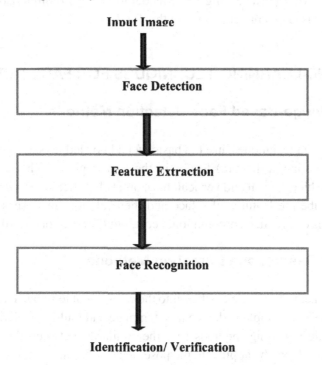

not even look at the camera lens. Authorities cannot restrict people behaviors in public places. Recognition in such cases must be done in an accurate way. However, even state-of-the-art-techniques have 10 or 15 degree angle limitation to recognize a face. Recognizing faces from more angles is another challenge.

3. **Face Expression:** Face expression is less significant issue compare with angle and illumination but it affects the face.

4. **Appearances:** Although a close eye or smiling face does affect the recognition rate by 1% to 10 percent, a face with large laugh has an influence as more as 30% since a laughing face changes the face appearance and distorts the correlation of eyes, mouth and nose.

5. **Face Aging:** Face recognition algorithms are using either geometrical techniques or feature-based approaches or holistic methods. All of them do not solve the aging problem. Almost all of them give an age tolerance as long as 20 years after the training. Faces between 1 year and 15 years cannot be recognized since face appearance changes fast. Face appearance becomes stable after teenage years. A recognition algorithm that can recognize faces for all ages does not exist.

6. **Dynamic Background:** It is easier to recognize a face when the background is stable or single but problems arises when the background is moving or

dynamic. Multiple face-Single face recognition easy in comparison to multiple face so it is also a big challenge in this field.

2. MACHINE-LEARNING TECHNIQUES FOR FACE DETECTION

2.1. Knowledge-Based Face Detection Methods

Knowledge based techniques, use the basic facial knowledge (such as the elliptical shape and the triangle feature) to obtain the final region of the face. It can be classified into hierarchical and vertical/ horizontal classifications. They use simple rules to describe the features of a face and their relationships. These knowledge based methods can reduce computational cost, but they are rotation-dependent.

2.2. Model-Based Face Detection Methods

Model based method can be classified into the category of template matching. They use both predefined template, deformable template and multi-correlation template. These template matching methods find the similarity between the original and training images. It can be applied to the pose, scale and shape of the images. These predefined template image methods are easy to implement, but they are scale-dependent, rotation-dependent, and computationally complex. The major curb of this approach is that it is not effective. The deformable templates are specified by a set of parameters which enables a priori knowledge about the expected shape of the features to guide the detection process.

2.3. Feature-Based Face Detection Methods

Feature based methods are divided into three main categories, viz., Low level analysis, Feature analysis and Active shape analysis techniques. Further, the low level analysis is based on the spatial distribution. It is classified into edge, gray level, texture, motion and generalized methods. It can be divided into Skin colour and Hair based methods. The human skin colour is the fundamental cue that can be used in face detection, from complex images. Human skin colour segmentation strongly relies on the selected colour space because the skin colour distribution depends on the specific colour subspace. Skin colour detection rate is also significantly affected by illumination conditions consequently; large variations of luminance need to be eliminated. These techniques classify the colour models into three group's viz., Device-oriented colour spaces, User-oriented colour spaces and Colorimetric colour spaces. Recent feature analysis uses feature searching and constellation.

These active shape analyses can be divided into snakes, deformable active shape and point distribution models.

2.4. Appearance-Based Face Detection Methods

The appearances of facial features may be captured by different cameras of two-dimensional views of the object-of-interest. The appearance based algorithms mostly rely on extensive training and powerful classification techniques.

3. MACHINE-LEARNING TECHNIQUES FOR FACE RECOGNITION

Face recognition systems architecture broadly consists of the three steps. The first step in any automatic face recognition systems is the detection of faces in images. After a face has been detected, the task of feature extraction is to obtain features that are fed into a face classification system. Depending on the type of classification system, features can be local features such as lines or fiducial points, or facial features such as eyes, nose, and mouth. Face detection may also employ features, in which case features are extracted simultaneously with face detection. Feature extraction is also a key to animation and recognition of facial expressions.

There are various machine learning based approaches are used for the face recognition system. Some important approaches are:

1. Artificial Neural Network (NN).
2. Support Vector Machine (SVM).
3. Hidden Markov Model (HMM).
4. Principal Component Analysis (PCA).
5. Linear Discriminate Analysis (LDA).

3.1. Artificial Neural Network (ANN)

An artificial neural networks Hagan *et al.* (1996), Schalkoff (1997) is inspired by the concept of biological nervous system. ANNs are the collection of computing elements (neurons) that may be connected in various ways. In ANNs the effect of the synapses is represented by the connection weight, which modulates the input signal. The architecture of artificial neural networks is a fully connected, three layered (input layer, hidden layer and output layer) structure of nodes in which information flows from the input layer to the output layer through the hidden layer. ANNs are capable of linear and nonlinear classification. An ANN learns by adjusting the weights in accordance with the learning algorithms. It is capable to process and analyze large complex datasets, containing non-linear relationships. There are various types of artificial neural network architecture that are used in protein function prediction such as perceptron, multi-layer perceptron (MLP), radial basis function networks and kohonen self-organizing maps. In literature various authors have been used Hopfield Neural Networks (HNN), Self-Organizing Map (SOM), Back-Propagation (BP) for face recognition (Yoon, et al., 1998; Wen, et al., 1999; Rowley, et al., 1998; Peng, et al., 1998; Gu, et al., 2000; Terrillon, et al., 2000; Feraund, et al., 2001).

Recently Jindal *et al*. (2013) have been proposed a face recognition system in the combination of artificial neural network and principal component analysis. Principal component analysis was used to retain the majority of the variations present in the data set. The proposed system achieved accuracy and provides better success rates even for noisy face images, but the local features extraction methods is not work well in this approach. Chelali, F. Z. *et. al*. (2014) have proposed a hybrid method with the combination of Gabor wavelets Gabor wavelet faces combined with extended neural net feature space for the face recognition. Farfade, S. S. *e.t al*. (2015) has proposed deep convolution neural network method for the face detection. Roy Chowdhury, et. al. (2015) have been proposed Bilinear Convolution Neural Networks method for face identification and achieved a better performance gains on certain fine-grained recognition problems. The proposed method bridges the gap between the texture models and part-based convolution neural networks methods. Lu, Y., Zeng, et al. (2015) have been proposed a hybrid approach with the combination of Particle Swarm Optimization and Wavelet Neural Network for the face recognition. The proposed method used the concepts of Switching Particle Swarm Optimization (SPSO) algorithm to optimize the parameters of weights, scale factors, translation factors and threshold in Wavelet Neural Network (WNN). The proposed method has fast convergences peed and higher learning ability than conventional WNNs. Especially, a mode dependent velocity updating equation with Markovian switching parameters is introduced in SPSO to overcome the contradiction between the local search and the global search, which makes it easy to jump the local minimum. The proposed method performs better in comparison with other optimization techniques such as Genetic Algorithm Wavelet Neural Network (GA–WNN) and wavelet neural network.

3.2. Support Vector Machine (SVM)

Support vector machine Cortes and Vapnik (1995) is based on the statistical learning theory. The SVM is capable of resolving linear and non-linear classification problems. The principal idea of classification by support vector is to separate examples with a linear decision surface and maximize the margin of separation between the classes to be classified. SVM works by mapping data with a high-dimensional feature space so that data points can be categorized, even when the data are not otherwise linearly separable. A separator between the categories is found, and then the data are transformed in such a way that the separator could be drawn as a hyperplane. Following this, characteristics of new data can be used to predict the group to which a new record should belong. After the transformation, the boundary between the two categories can be defined by a hyperplane. The mathematical function used for the transformation is known as the kernel function. SVM supports the linear, polynomial, radial basis function (RBF) and sigmoid kernel types. When there is a straightforward linear separation then linear function is used otherwise we used polynomial, radial basis function (RBF) and sigmoid kernel function. Besides the separating line between the categories, a SVM also finds marginal lines that define the space between the two categories. The data points that lie on the margins are known as the support vectors.

Phillips, P. J. (1998) has proposed the support vector based approach for the face recognition. In the proposed method the face recognition problem is formulated as a problem in difference space, which models dissimilarities between two facial images. In different space they formulate face recognition as a two class problem. The cases are: (i) Dissimilarities between faces of the same person, and (ii) Dissimilarities between faces of different people. By modifying the interpretation of the decision surface generated a similarity metric between faces that are learned from examples of differences between faces. The SVM-based algorithm is compared with a principal component analysis (PCA) based algorithm on a difficult set of images and the authors of the paper found the SVM performed better in comparison to Principal component analysis. Kim, K. *et. al.* (2002) has been proposed face recognition method, which combines several SVM classifiers and a neural network arbitrator. The proposed method does not use any explicit feature extraction scheme. Instead the SVMs receive the gray level values of raw pixels as the input pattern. The rationale for this configuration is that a SVM has the capability of learning in high dimensional space, such as gray-level face-image space. Furthermore, the SVMs were used with a local correlation provided an effective combination of feature extraction and classification to recognize the face. Huang, J. *et. al.* (1998) proposed a Support vector machine based approach for the face pose discrimination.

3.3. Hidden Markov Model

A Hidden Markov Model (HMM) is developed by L. E. Baum and coworkers. It is a statistical Markov model in which the system being modeled is assumed to be a Markov chain with hidden states. An HMM can be presented as the simplest dynamic Bayesian network. In a simple Markov models the state is directly visible to the observer, and therefore the state transition probabilities are the only parameters. In a hidden Markov model, the state is not directly visible, but the output, dependent on the state, is visible. Each state has a probability distribution over the possible output tokens. Therefore, the sequence of tokens generated by an HMM gives some information about the sequence of states. Hidden Markov models are useful in the temporal pattern recognition such as speech, handwriting, gesture recognition, part-of-speech tagging, musical score following, partial discharges and bioinformatics.

In literature various authors have been used hidden Markov model for the face detection and recognition. Samaria, F. *et. al.* (1994) has been proposed a hidden Morkov model based face recognition and detection method. In this method a frontal face including the significant facial regions such as hair, forehead, eyes, nose and mouth occur in a natural order from top to bottom. So, each of these facial regions is assigned to a state in a left-to right one dimensional continuous hidden Markov model. Nefian, A. V. *et. al.* (1998) have been used hidden Markov model for the face recognition and detection. Bicego, M. *et. al.* (2003) has been proposed a hybrid approach with the combination of Hidden Markov Models and wavelets for the face recognition.

3.4. Principal Component Analysis (PCA)

PCA is based on the information theory approach. It is a statistical dimensionality reduction method, which produces the optimal linear least squares decomposition of a training set. It extracts the pertinent information from the face image and encodes the features efficiently. It identifies the subspace of the image space spanned by the training face image data and de-correlates each pixel values. The classical representation of a face image is obtained by projecting it to the coordinate system, defined by the principal components. The projection of face images into the principal component subspace achieves information compression, de-correlation and dimensionality reduction to facilitate decision making. In mathematical terms, the principal components of the distribution of faces or the eigenvectors of the covariance matrix of the set of face images, is sought by treating an image as a vector in a very high dimensional face space. The PCA based face recognition methods are not very effective, under the conditions of varying pose and illumination, since it considers the global information of each face image and represents them with a set of weights. Under these conditions the weight vectors will vary considerably from the weight vectors of the images with normal pose and illumination, hence it is difficult to identify them correctly.

Toygar, O. *et.al.* (2003) has used PCA to reduce the dimension of filtered feature vectors and then LDA is used for feature extraction. The performances of appearance based statistical methods such as PCA, LDA and ICA are tested and compared for the recognition of colored faces images. Shermina, *et. al.* (2010) proposed a hybrid approach with the combination of two appearance based techniques such as Modified PCA (MPCA) and Locality Preserving Projections (LPP) to give a high face recognition rate. Jadhav, *et. al.* (2011) and Walia, E. (2008) used principal component analysis as a feature extraction technique. Sakthivel, *et. al.* (2010) has proposed a PCA based approach that provided considerable improvements in the case of illumination variations. The authors also found that in this case the PCA and kernel PCA were perform better. Sahoolizadeh *et. al.* (2008) have proposed a hybrid method with the combination of PCA, LDA and neural network for the face recognition. the proposed method consists of four steps: Preprocessing, Dimension reduction using PCA, feature extraction using LDA and classification using neural network. Combination of PCA and LDA were used for improving the capability of LDA when a few samples of images were available and neural classifier was used to reduce number misclassification caused by not-linearly separable classes.

3.5. Linear Discriminate Analysis (LDA)

The PCA based face recognition methods are not very effective, under the conditions of varying pose and illumination, since it considers the global information of each face image and represents them with a set of weights. Under these conditions the weight vectors will vary considerably from the weight vectors of the images with normal pose and illumination, hence it is difficult to identify them correctly. Fisher faces method overcomes the limitations of Eigen faces method by applying the Fisher's linear discriminate criterion This criterion tries to maximize the ratio of the determinant of the between-class scatter matrix of the projected samples to the determinant of the within-class scatter matrix of the projected samples. Fisher discriminates the group images of the same class, which help to separate images of different classes. There has been a tendency in the computer vision community to prefer LDA over PCA. Because LDA deals directly with discrimination between classes. The main drawback of PCA does not pay attention to the underlying class structure. When the training set is small, PCA can outperform LDA. When the number of samples is large and representative for each class, LDA outperforms PCA. LDA represent the face vector space by exploiting the class information. It differentiates individual faces, but recognizes the faces of same individual with the training set of corresponding classes.

Huang et.al. (2010) has proposed a subspace analysis method for face recognition based on the analysis of Linear Discriminate Analysis (LDA), Locality preserving projections (LPP) and kernel function. Liu et. al. (2010) has proposed illumination adaptive linear discriminant analysis (IALDA) to solve illumination variation problems in face recognition. Lu, J.et.al. (2003) has proposed linear discriminate analysis based feature extraction method for face recognition. The Pang Y.et. al. (2004) has proposed a hybrid method based on Gabor-wavelet and linear discriminant analysis for face recognition where training face images, discriminant vectors are computed using LDA. The function of the discriminant vectors is two-fold. First, discriminant vectors are used as a transform matrix, and LDA features are extracted by projecting original intensity images onto discriminant vectors. Second, discriminant vectors are used to select discriminant pixels, the number of which is much less than that of a whole image. Gabor features are extracted only on these discriminant pixels. Then, applying LDA on the Gabor features, one can obtain the Gabor-LDA features. Finally, a combined classifier is formed based on these two types of LDA features for face recognition. The proposed method performs better than traditional approaches in terms of both efficiency and accuracy.

4. CONCLUSION

Face recognition has been one of the most interesting and important research areas for real time applications. Face recognition also used the knowledge from other disciplines such as neuroscience, psychology, computer vision, pattern recognition, image processing, and machine learning, etc. This chapter provided a review of machine learning based techniques for the face recognition. First, it presented an overview of face recognition and its challenges then, a literature review of machine learning based approaches for face detection and recognition is presented.

REFERENCES

Bicego, M., Castellani, U., & Murino, V. (2003, September). Using Hidden Markov Models and wavelets for face recognition. In *Image Analysis and Processing, 2003. Proceedings. 12th International Conference on* (pp. 52-56). IEEE. doi:10.1109/ICIAP.2003.1234024

Blunsom, P. (2004). Hidden Markov models. *Lecture Notes, 15*, 18-19.

Chelali, F. Z., & Djeradi, A. (2014, August). Face recognition system using neural network with Gabor and discrete wavelet transform parameterization. In *Soft Computing and Pattern Recognition (SoCPaR), 2014 6th International Conference of* (pp. 17-24). IEEE. doi:10.1109/SOCPAR.2014.7007975

Chien, J. T., & Wu, C. C. (2005). *Linear Discriminant Analysis*. LDA.

Cortes, C., & Vapnik, V. (1995). Support-vector networks. *Machine Learning, 20*(3), 273–297. doi:10.1007/BF00994018

Eddy, S. R. (1996). Hidden Markov models. *Current Opinion in Structural Biology, 6*(3), 361–365. doi:10.1016/S0959-440X(96)80056-X PMID:8804822

Farfade, S. S., Saberian, M. J., & Li, L. J. (2015, June). Multi-view face detection using deep convolutional neural networks. In *Proceedings of the 5th ACM on International Conference on Multimedia Retrieval* (pp. 643-650). ACM. doi:10.1145/2671188.2749408

Feraund, R., Bernier, O. J., Viallet, J. E., & Collobert, M. (2001). A fast and accurate face detector based on neural networks. *IEEE Transactions on Pattern Analysis and Machine Intelligence, 23*(1), 42–53. doi:10.1109/34.899945

Gu, Q., & Li, S. Z. (2000). Combining feature optimization into neural network based face detection. In *Pattern Recognition, 2000. Proceedings. 15th International Conference on* (Vol. 2, pp. 814-817). IEEE.

Hagan, M. T., Demuth, H. B., Beale, M. H., & De Jesús, O. (1996). *Neural network design* (Vol. 20). Boston: PWS Publishing Company.

Holand, S. M. (2008). *Principal components analysis (PCA)*. Athens, GA: Department of Geology, University of Georgia.

Huang, J., Shao, X., & Wechsler, H. (1998, August). Face pose discrimination using support vector machines (SVM). In *Pattern Recognition, 1998. Proceedings. Fourteenth International Conference on* (Vol. 1, pp. 154-156). IEEE.

Huang, R., Su, C., Lang, F., & Du, M. (2010). Kernel Discriminant Locality Preserving Projections for Human Face Recognition. *Journal of Information & Computational Science, 7*(4), 925–931.

Jadhav, I. S., Gaikwad, V. T., & Patil, G. U. (2011). *Human Identification using Face and Voice Recognition 1*. Academic Press.

Jindal, N., & Kumar, V. (2013). Enhanced face recognition algorithm using pca with artificial neural networks. *International Journal of Advanced Research in Computer Science and Software Engineering, 3*(6).

Jolliffe, I. (2002). *Principal component analysis.* John Wiley & Sons, Ltd.

Kass, G. V. (1980). An exploratory technique for investigating large quantities of categorical data. *Applied Statistics, 29*(2), 119–127. doi:10.2307/2986296

Kim, K. I., Kim, J. H., & Jung, K. (2002). Face recognition using support vector machines with local correlation kernels. *International Journal of Pattern Recognition and Artificial Intelligence, 16*(01), 97–111. doi:10.1142/S0218001402001575

Liu, Z., Zhou, J., & Jin, Z. (2010, August). Face recognition based on illumination adaptive LDA. In *Pattern Recognition (ICPR), 2010 20th International Conference on* (pp. 894-897). IEEE. doi:10.1109/ICPR.2010.225

Lu, J., Plataniotis, K. N., & Venetsanopoulos, A. N. (2003). Face recognition using LDA-based algorithms. *IEEE Transactions on Neural Networks, 14*(1), 195–200. doi:10.1109/TNN.2002.806647 PMID:18238001

Lu, Y., Zeng, N., Liu, Y., & Zhang, N. (2015). A hybrid Wavelet Neural Network and Switching Particle Swarm Optimization algorithm for face direction recognition. *Neurocomputing, 155*, 219–224. doi:10.1016/j.neucom.2014.12.026

Martínez, A. M., & Kak, A. C. (2001). Pca versus lda. *IEEE Transactions on Pattern Analysis and Machine Intelligence, 23*(2), 228–233. doi:10.1109/34.908974

Nefian, A., & Hayes, M. (1999, March). Face recognition using an embedded HMM. In *IEEE Conference on Audio and Video-based Biometric Person Authentication* (pp. 19-24). IEEE.

Nefian, A. V., & Hayes III, M. H. (1998). Hidden Markov models for face recognition. *Choice, 1*, 6.

Nefian, A. V., & Hayes, M. H. (1998, October). Face detection and recognition using hidden Markov models. In *Image Processing, 1998. ICIP 98. Proceedings. 1998 International Conference on* (Vol. 1, pp. 141-145). IEEE. doi:10.1109/ICIP.1998.723445

Pang, Y., Zhang, L., Li, M., Liu, Z., & Ma, W. (2004, November). A novel Gabor-LDA based face recognition method. In *Pacific-Rim Conference on Multimedia* (pp. 352-358). Springer Berlin Heidelberg. doi:10.1007/978-3-540-30541-5_44

Peng, H., Zhang, C., & Bian, Z. (1998, August). A fully automated face recognition system under different conditions. In *Pattern Recognition, 1998. Proceedings. Fourteenth International Conference on* (Vol. 2, pp. 1223-1225). IEEE.

Phillips, P. J. (1998). *Support vector machines applied to face recognition* (Vol. 285). US Department of Commerce, Technology Administration, National Institute of Standards and Technology.

Rowley, H. A., Baluja, S., & Kanade, T. (1998). Neural network-based face detection. *IEEE Transactions on Pattern Analysis and Machine Intelligence, 20*(1), 23–38. doi:10.1109/34.655647

Rowley, H. A., Baluja, S., & Kanade, T. (1998, June). Rotation invariant neural network-based face detection. In *Computer Vision and Pattern Recognition, 1998. Proceedings. 1998 IEEE Computer Society Conference on* (pp. 38-44). IEEE.

RoyChowdhury, A., Lin, T. Y., Maji, S., & Learned-Miller, E. (2015). *Face Identification with Bilinear CNNs*. arXiv preprint arXiv:1506.01342

Sahoolizadeh, A. H., Heidari, B. Z., & Dehghani, C. H. (2008). A new face recognition method using PCA, LDA and neural network. *International Journal on Computer Science and Engineering, 2*(4), 218–223.

Sakthivel, S., & Lakshmipathi, R. (2010). Enhancing face recognition using improved dimensionality reduction and feature extraction algorithms—an evaluation with ORL database. *International Journal of Engineering Science and Technology, 2*(6), 2288–2295.

Samaria, F., & Young, S. (1994). HMM-based architecture for face identification. *Image and Vision Computing, 12*(8), 537–543. doi:10.1016/0262-8856(94)90007-8

Schalkoff, R. J. (1997). *Artificial neural networks*. McGraw-Hill Higher Education.

Shermina, J., & Vasudevan, V. (2010). An Efficient Face recognition System Based on Fusion of MPCA and LPP. *American Journal of Scientific Research*, 6-19.

Terrillon, J. C., McReynolds, D., Sadek, M., Sheng, Y., & Akamatsu, S. (2000). Invariant neural-network based face detection with orthogonal Fourier-Mellin moments. In *Pattern Recognition, 2000. Proceedings. 15th International Conference on* (Vol. 2, pp. 993-1000). IEEE. doi:10.1109/ICPR.2000.906242

Toygar, O., & Acan, A. (2003). Face recognition using PCA, LDA and ICA approaches on colored images. *Journal of Electrical & Electronics Engineering, 3*(1), 735-743.

Walia, E. (2008, May). Face recognition using improved fast PCA algorithm. In Image and Signal Processing, 2008. CISP'08. Congress on (Vol. 1, pp. 554-558). IEEE.

Wen, F., Zhou, J., & Zhang, C. (1999). LLM neural networks and compensation for light condition based color face detection. *Journal-Tsinghua University*, *39*, 37–40.

Wold, S., Esbensen, K., & Geladi, P. (1987). Principal component analysis. *Chemometrics and Intelligent Laboratory Systems*, *2*(1-3), 37–52. doi:10.1016/0169-7439(87)80084-9

Yoon, K. S., Ham, Y. K., & Park, R. H. (1998). Hybrid approaches to frontal view face recognition using the Hidden Markov Model and Neural Network. *Pattern Recognition*, *31*(3), 283–293. doi:10.1016/S0031-3203(97)00052-6

Chapter 10
How Games Improve Language in People With Language Dysfunctions

Robert Wahlstedt
Independent Researcher, USA

ABSTRACT

Many people as they age face a greater challenge of muscular dexterity around their facial muscles. This results in difficulty producing certain sounds, and sometimes the problem is so severe that they are unintelligible. People who could benefit from the methods in this chapter are those who are hard of hearing and do not have feedback readily accessible and people with ALS. This chapter describes a method that uses a computer learning algorithm that predicts what people are about to say based on earlier content and learns what the natural sound of their voice sounds like. This chapter illustrates speech trajectory and voice shaping. Clear Audio is a biologically inspired framework for studying natural language. Like the story behind Jurassic Park, Clear Audio attempts to make predictions about data from existing data, inspired by biological processes. Its main goal is to give feedback for speech pathology purposes.

INTRODUCTION

In order to comprehend meaning in a sentence the software must recognize a bit of language sound or phoneme meaning the software must then predict sentence trajectory of what is to come. In a word with more digital data than ever before, each word is a trap door to another set of meanings. Words are fossils of another time

DOI: 10.4018/978-1-5225-2545-5.ch010

and another place brought back to evoke sentiment including thoughts or feelings of previous experiences. For example, in a paragraph that mentions "snow" denotes that the paragraph is about snow. Lieberman argues that the brain is always in the mode of social communications and that it does not turn off. Lieberman argues that although a person is not born with social mechanisms in place he or she quickly develops social capacity as the brain adapts to its environment. The human needs 10,000 hours' practice to become an expert in a specialty. The brain achieves this social learning by age ten (Lieberman, 2011). The Second Machine Age argues that while computers are not capable of doing anything other than what a human tells them to do, if they have an exact enough feature set, they are better than humans at determining how the proper order of events. One process is modeled by the Zachman framework of asking who, what, when, and why. For example, the Google Chafer project, a project to designed a computer to drive a car. The feature set was as good as of 2014 the car had only two accidents, one of which was rear ended at a stop light. Should the Zachman framework be used in natural sentence processors such as our Clear Audio Project can predict as some critics of natural language processing say, predict the surprising punch line of Grandpa's unpredictable jokes. Filters become more essential with the growing field of data mining and big data. Recently Google and Apple (Siri) released new versions of speech recognition in Google Now and IOS 6. These represent the best of today's big data. Traditionally data scientists compare the concept of big data to a big hard drive full of stuff that the scientists process. However, as this big pile of data grows the only people who are able to sort it have many hundreds of processor cores. Jeff Stibel points out that large internet-based companies have their servers based in cheap places to get electricity (Stibel, 2014). Cnet, in their review of IOS Maverick, claims that the catch or the storage of internet files on the macs is overbearing. Worse is the concern that having even anonymous data can have legal implications because people with unique conversations would stand out in a crowd. Aiden explains how almost in a decade worth of Google searches some queries stand out (Aiden, 2013). Particular phrases such as idioms from cultural minorities can distinguish a person's conversation. This predicament reveals a required feature set. Data without a feature set is useless. Mathematics is defined by The Oxford Dictionary as "the abstract science of number, measure, and space." Language and mathematics share the definition as being omnipresent, constant, without regards to feelings or sentiments. People argue that language is more chaotic.

Fortunately, mathematics offers fractals such as the Mandelbrot Fractal shown above to help people understand complexity and chaos in simple terms. Computers can find similarities in pictures without knowing what they are. Recently Peter Norvig of Google gave a talk to Brown University about memorization or a way that the computer can know what an image consists of although it may not know

Figure 1. Shows a computer rendering of the Mandelbrot fractal (credits go to Wikimedia)

the name of these items the computer found similar. In Surfaces and Essences, compares an object being placed in a box and then taken out of the box to words being conceptualized and formatted. Consider all the meanings of the word band. This can connote everything from a marching band to a wedding band to a Band-Aid that filters air to a wound so it is not infected. Which one of these is a metaphor? We can never tell which usage of the phrase is the original as opposed to the ones are comparable to the original fossil of the metaphor. With the Zachman framework, we come close to determining the usage of phrases. While metaphors are an important aspect of word origins, writers of newspapers write articles so people with a ten-year-old child's vocabulary and intellect can understand them. We cannot assume that many ten-year old children can understand metaphors such as a broken record or see an activist as something that acts upon an agenda. This network of vernacular fossils composes much of our language today. Therefore, something else is happening. Iacoboni asks why is it that a person gestures when they are talking on a phone and it the other person cannot see these gestures. It is because we use words as a vehicle to transport the other person to a thought or feeling we wish to convey (Iacobon, 2008). Using this method, I will refer to as capture and transport method, in chapter two of this paper, we discuss how educational games and by letting people have experiences using augmented reality to reinforce Hebbian learning of experiences. What we need to find out is how spelling constructs etymological concepts. If we were strictly, follow a formula for the English of yesterday of pragmatically tagging parts of speech (P.O.S.) we would never be able to keep up with new words as the as people use these words new to our corpus. In the later part of the last century, stock traders worked on algorithms to decide in which direction stocks will go. A key advantage was that stocks exist in numerical form. However, this does not relinquish the marvel of predicting what would happen next. Natural language processing researchers can take lessons from stock market predictions and apply them to both word and concept formation. Humans tend to repeat language behaviors if they were effective or energy-efficient or economical. The researcher's goal is to use the Maven Markup Modeling Language (MMML) based on predictive modeling markup language (PMML) to find ways of correlating words to integrate new words faster into the corpus. Text mining projects at Universitat Politecnica de Catalunya depend on lexical categories for their lexical analysis tagging. Yagoda suggests "According to grammarians, adjectives, nouns, verbs, and injunctions are 'open' parts of speech because they shift functions... and because new words are continually added to their ranks. This proves that classification of words is not always necessary." (Yagoda, 2006). To make matters worse, a gerund is using a verb in its – ing form as a noun such as living. Although the English language has synoptically, there are two types of words, content words and structure words. The natural language processing engine can remove structure words such as "hope that" "clearly" "strangely"" indeed" "conceivably" "seriously" "ultimately" "theoretically" "naturally" "ironically" "fortunately" incidentally" do not containing meaning in themselves however they send signals to listeners about words that are coming later. The word "like" is overused because it is often used as filler words while the person thinks of something else to say. The National Science Foundation did a study that demonstrated when a storyteller used the word "this" instead of "a" or "an" the person demonstrated better retention. Another concern is that these systems do not account for pragmatically that is the study of context is it situational.

BACKGROUND

There are two classes of people with speech challenges; the first class consists of those who had trouble speaking since birth. They are aware of the fact they are more challenging to understand. One hypothesis on speaking challenges is the disorder is more prevalent in children because the work of both conceptualizing and the formatting tasks of language overwhelms them. Bell Labs engineer Robert Lucky estimated the cortex cannot take more than 50 bits per second. Mihaly Csikszentmihalyi estimated one apperception to take 1/15th of a second or 105 bits per second. Regardless of the figure a person has limited bandwidth or computing power. Because it takes a lot of concentration to come up with metaphors and categorize ideas with words, the quality of speech declines. Along with this speech has limited prosody referred to in this paper as words per minute, pitch variance, and stress of syllables. With the knowledge that they are unintelligible, they compensate using repetition or choose words that do not contain the element that they have trouble with. They may do these substitutions or repetitions unconsciously. People with speech aphasia often have trouble with pronouns. A goal of Clear Audio is to find the use of pronouns and the repetition by using summarizing tools. Section 2 explains these methods. Section 3 describes other people who have difficulty speaking later in life due to a stroke are confident that their pronunciation is the same as it was before their decline and may not utilize either repetition or choice of words.

WHAT DO COCHLEAR IMPLANTS SUGGEST ABOUT SOUND?

Helping Those Who Repeat to Be Understood

In order for a contextual agent of software that recognizes speech, it must develop a cohesive hypothesis about what a speaker is saying. Denworth discusses the requirements of language for cochlear implant patients. She suggests that processing sound is a multifaceted event including both contextual clues for perception and the stemming. Denworth introduces David Pisoni's work on "visual speech" that Denworth describes as the act of a person to see objects without cognition of what they are. Densworth gave this as a reason her son has an implant starting at age three (Densworth, 2014). While experimenting with Audacity, we realize how redundant speech is as opposed to music. A more sporadic sampling of voice is enough for voice while for music every sound we must accommodate for. Summary generation for detecting repetitions A piece of literature is similar to a piece of music in that both contain repeated themes throughout the piece. While the BBC has a recording of Tchaikovsky's 1812 overture that lasts 17 minutes, most people remember only the theme. In this paper, we discuss the methods how literature themes stand out from the rest of the piece through both exact repetition and supporting variations of the theme. Some scientists who study the brain call this grouping "chunking." Many textbooks of text mining hold the author's beliefs that word categories or parts of speech are important. These papers create summaries by deleting irrelevant words until only the nuclear core remains. However, these authors overlook context. A new approach seeks to use structural knowledge of pragmatic through latent semantic analysis. For example, to get to the best diagnosis of patients, it is important to take into account their entire medical histories and not just a few quotes. This method does analysis on the entire document before concluding so metaphors and words with multiple meanings are not confused. This paper proposes if using metadata, or data about the data, to distinguish repetition of the theme from supporting variations, also known as satellites. This is achievable by finding the roots of words through their origins, translating the word prefix, root, and suffix into metadata. The brain constantly encounters more information than it can digest. Oliver Sacks discusses how Chinese speakers represent a higher than average percentage of people who have pure tone. Of these, the greatest were musicians who started learning their instrument before age six. This is because the tonal system of the Chinese language is a very important element and is necessary to distinguish words from each other. The brain of the Chinese speakers adapts so it is accustomed to listening to other Chinese speakers (Sacks, 2007). At the time of birth, a person is born they can absorb much information from their senses including hearing. Around 80 percent of the energy they get from food goes to developing their brain. Swaab discusses one theory that a person uses the equivalent of $1500 for their entire life or 15 watts per hour (Swaab, 2014). In order to come up with a computational model we need to ask the right questions. As they start building heuristics and finding out what is important and what is not then less energy goes to fuel for the brain. Dean Buonomano commented on how musicians dedicate larger than average part of their brain to muscular memory in their fingertips through reallocation. He goes on to say the brain does not consciously govern the real estate in the nervous system so this was a subconscious process. Why do English speakers who are not musicians have such a seeming disadvantage? One dominant theory is that of the Hebbian Synapse that neurons that fire together wire together. In other words, if two events are not linked by the human brain as related, the brain acts like a filter and events are never associated or learned with one another (Buonomano, 2011). Stanislas Dehaene takes this notion further and discusses the history of the mind and body model. In the ancient world, philosophers like Descartes often thought that the heart was the headquarters of human thought (Dehaene, 2014). The soul or spirit was a detachable element from the physical body. This is similar to today's notion between the difference between computer software and computer hardware. Later scientists developed interfaces for working with the injured brain to capture electrical signals. These in addition to fMRI have introduced new material under review as far as what a person can understand. Through the new methods, we can detect electrical signals of which the brain encodes information into neurons. We now have empirical evidence that people see other people through filters and this becomes imprinted on their brain based on prior experiences. For example, we know that when person has had a negative experience with big dogs, certain elements the perception system exaggerate such as teeth, when the person encountering future dogs. This conceptualization is utilized in visual speech.

In designing a program, it is necessary to understand what one has to work with. Imagine a machine with two cameras perceiving words. When a person reads a word like "unbuttoning" the human brain strips off the "un" and the "ing" and it is left with two morphemes, "but" and "ton." There is a priming effect where a person is more inclined to think about a certain flow of words. For example, after casa, there sometimes is the word Blanca like the movie. This is why we understand differing homograph meaning. A grapheme is a letter or a series of letters that map a phoneme in the target language. Imagine a web of words that links all words in existence. Pulverm introduces a word-related functional web. It is a synchronous firing chain or synfire chain (Pulverm 2002). At first glance, automata might be similar to this web. However, a computer differs from a brain because even computers with multiple processing cores are asynchronous in the sense that the computer can only process a few threads unified by a central process. The human brain is a democracy having processes happening simultaneously and the strongest impulse, usually by a collective number of neurons fire that is what the human brain thinks. Miguel Nicolelis argues there is not a separate part of the brain language support.

However, a certain sequence of neurons that light up when a person reads about an object because it invokes an emotion (Nicolelis, 2011). Kenneally describes how non-humans animals could use simple language. Instances of non-humans are territorial warning signs and primitive inner species communication (Kenneally, 2007). The article "How Dolphins Say Hello" says that dolphins only whistle when they are in a group of dolphins and find themselves through echolocation. Grammar is a set of rules in a language that allows people to communicate and understand. There is a debate between B.F. Skinner and Noam Chomsky. Skinner believes that a person learns language through association, the sight of things along with the sound of the word. There conformity of this association matching constructs a dialect. Chomsky believes that a Martian scientist observing children in a single-language community would see that language is very similar regardless of the culture and therefore innate. Although reading is unnatural, our brain wants to see patterns and group objects together. We recognize lines and shapes that we read as characters. We then group these characters into morphemes. We then put these morphemes into phrases, idioms, words, and sentences. These sentences form a paragraph. Similar to computers recognition is easy, recalling meaning is difficult. Henry Hitchings discusses how it is possible to use stemming while the human language evolves. He says it is amazing that people spell words uniformly. Before computers, he points out that even dictionaries were inconsistent (Hitchings, 2011). There was a survey where a computer used phonetics to spell out words and 50 percent of the words did not agree with the phonetic spelling. Steven Pinker tells us that 84 percent of the words have a spelling that conforms to patterns we can notice. As shown by these statistics, the ability to conform is possible (Pickner, 2007).

It is necessary to study of metadata to correlate etymology with words. Etymology is the study of finding word roots and morphology is the study of word making. Today advances in bioinformatics tools have yielded a complex study of the human genome and have made great strides in finding out mutations that can create a higher chance of cancer. We should do so because we can learn about the human race as well as expand our knowledge of words. Here are some examples: nickname originally came from nekename containing the compound eke and name. Eke came from ēac that means also. It means an extra name. The word "hobby" comes from the word hob and yn. Hob or hŏb means a threaded and fluted hardened steel cutter, resembling a tap, used in a lathe for forming the teeth of screw chasers, worm wheels (Webster's Revised Unabridged Dictionary) and yn means "to be." It means to spin time. The word "omelet" comes from the French word omelette. Omelette comes from alemette that comes from alemelle that as comes from la lemelle that means a thin plate like structure. We should know how to find the prefix, root, and suffix because we are able to understand why someone in history responded to situations. The written word often transcends a person's lifespan and the culture changes. A written manuscript is similar to a fossil. For example, rabbit comes from the words robète that means to steal. This explains why Mr. MacGregor thinks Peter Rabbit as such a nuisance. If you are a person that is a Christian, it might please you to know that Nicodemus comes from the word nincompoop. This comes from the Latin phrase non-compos mentis meaning not of sound mind. People regard him as a hero of the Christian faith because he walked by faith and not by knowledge. What does a computer have to do with this? Computers are able to carry out arithmetic or logical operations such as regular expressions or pattern matching. Given some rules and a lexicon file, they are able to study morphology. "A" as in rag or Prague is big and "I" as in pin am small, "e" is somewhere in between. There has been some big vowel shifting in England between 1350 and 1500 known as the big vowel change so words like big and small have the wrong letters. Little and large are right. Pimpf means "a little boy," pimple means a little swelling, and pampers means a lot. Servant is in between. Quick Summary uses Maven Metadata Markup Language or MMML. It has a structure similar to the one shown below.

It may seem everything the software needs are stemming or taking apart words to find their meaning. The book Found in Translation: How Language Shapes our Lives and Transforms the World, talks about how words are associated with different metaphors in different cultures. One example they give is intaxicato solar. This means food poisoning. It looks as though it means intoxicated as though someone had too much to drink. This is an example of what linguists call a "false friend" also known as a false cognate meaning that it looks as though they come from the same linguistic root but have different meaning. Another example is the word okoru in Japanese. Although (Truss, 2004). The word leaves can also be from a plant or it can mean

Figure 2. Shows the XML layout of the word "daisy" in Maven markup modeling language (MMML)

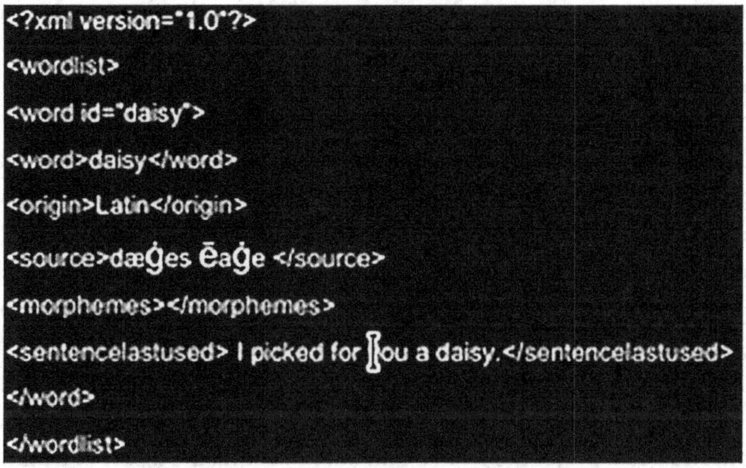

```xml
<?xml version="1.0"?>
<wordlist>
<word id="daisy">
<word>daisy</word>
<origin>Latin</origin>
<source>dæǧes ēaǧe </source>
<morphemes></morphemes>
<sentencelastused> I picked for ǁou a daisy.</sentencelastused>
</word>
</wordlist>
```

to abandon an area. These point out in addition to stemming the software needs to run on a distributed blackboard approach to artificial intelligence. A blackboard is a comprehensive method that has several expert knowledge agents, they feed an aggregate stream with what the agent knows based on a limited perspective, and each agent fills in insufficiency of different agents. In our software, the stemming is one agent and context of the previously spoken topic are another. In addition, features should consist of tone or pitch, the tempo of words were spoken or speed, and vibrancy or liveliness. Pentland introduces a social-o meter that has a microphone for determining pitch and speaking duration. However, this microphone is unable to decide the real words (Pentland, 2014). A key distinguishing reason of the research presented from other software that can recognize speech such as Dragon Speaking Naturally Dictate has pride itself with how many sample voices have trained it. These speech recognition engines do not consider how important tonality is in making speech palatable. The brain needs some difference, dissonance, and variance to stay focused. When a robotic voice speaks, it often takes greater amounts of concentration to listen. In today's high-paced world, people might not always have energy enough to listen. Sounds constantly bombard with data and as we discussed before in this paper under the section A Human's Big Data Filtering Method, the brain does a good job of filtering out what are signals as opposed to noise it looks as though it may resemble the word to occur, it means to get angry. The book Found in Translation goes on to say that, certain brands like Mitsubishi have to rename their Pajero module and Honda Fitta module in particular countries. The countries have different connotations of the words. The word gift means poison in German. The Online Etymology

Dictionary says that it was often associated with prescribed medicine. People used the word gift as in a potion by a doctor and it came to mean something of tangible from a knowing person. Found in Translation tells how jokes in some languages are missed such as in the Harry Potter Series Lord Voldemort is "Tom Marvolo Riddle" is an anagram for I am Lord Voldemort. The Bulgarian translation is Mersvoluko whose anagram translates to "And here I am, Lord Voldemort". The word in Hebrew originally was tohu meant formless and vohu meant empty. In French today toha bohu meant chaos and confusion. These words became associated with chaos later in Hebrew (Kelly, 2012). Sometimes the environment makes it necessary to invent words to present the concepts behind them. For example, to explain to the Hmong people about cancer at UC Davis, they compiled English to Hmong dictionary for medical terms. Martin Luther when translating the scriptures invented words so he can explain to people Latin concepts such as Machtwort (authoritative guidance). Truss indicates this problem by having multiple definitions for the word shoots meaning to fire a fast projectile from a gun or shoots that are a part of a plant (Truss, 2004). The word leaves can also be from a plant or it can mean to abandon an area. These point out in addition to stemming the software needs to run on a distributed blackboard approach to artificial intelligence. A blackboard is comprehensive method that has several expert knowledge agents, they feed an aggregate stream with what the agent knows based on a limited perspective, and each agent fills in insufficiency of different agents. In our software the stemming is one agent and context of the previous spoken topic are another. In addition, features should consist of tone or pitch, tempo of words spoken or speed, and vibrancy or liveliness. Pentland introduces a social-o meter that has a microphone for determining pitch and speaking duration. However, this microphone is unable to decide the real words (Pentland, 2014). A key distinguishing reason of my research is that other software that can recognize speech such as Dragon Speaking Naturally Dictate has pride itself with how many sample voices have trained it. These speech recognition engines do not consider how important tonality is in making speech palatable. The brain needs some difference, dissonance, and variance to stay focused. When a robotic voice speaks, it is often takes greater amounts of concentration to listen. In today's high-paced world, people might not always have energy enough to listen. Sounds constantly bombard with data and as we discussed before in this paper under the section A Human's Big Data Filtering Method the brain does a good job at filtering out what are signals as opposed to noise. to noise. Those who hear a 60-hertz drone of a light fixture will likely ignore the drone because the brain has trained itself to ignore some sounds. Next, I hope I am able to find a feature set to annotate and make computer voices easier for people to listen.

In the Story of English in 100 Words, David Crystal discusses the origin of words. He gives the history of the word jail borrows from the French originating in the about the time of the Norman invasion of 1066 study we can tell because the word gaol is Latin. Crystal explains that languages borrowed this word twice, being what Crystal refers to as double borrowed. We can tell this because the word did not get its origin meaning. This is also true for the word convey originality coming from the French word convoy. Our approach is to take this research and combine with what is known about UML, I* and the Zachman framework to discuss the questions of what, where, when, why, who and how. With this data, it is possible to verify that our summary correctly reflects the emphasis of the paper. In Empires of the World: A Language History of the Word, Nicholas Ostler demonstrates beginning with ancient Babylonians carrying off the Hebrew slaves and forcing them to melt into the culture of the Babylonians how language can melt together. John McWhorter writes this is what happened during the Norman invasion. There was not a bloody war instead slowly, over time the Normans introduced French. English, Crystal says, is like a Our approach is to take this research and combine with what is known about UML, I* and the Zachman framework to discuss the questions of what, where, when, why, who and how. With this data, it is possible to verify that our summary correctly reflects the emphasis of the paper. In Empires of the World: A Language History of the Word, Nicholas Ostler demonstrates beginning with ancient Babylonians carrying off the Hebrew slaves and forcing them to melt into the culture of the Babylonians how language can melt together. John McWhorter writes this is what happened during the Norman invasion. This field of anthropology is transcultural transfusion (McCrum, 2010). This is an example of diffusion by choice. By studying hyperdiffusionism under the belief that man originated in one place, we can learn through cultural similarities. For instance, most civilized cultures today teach us that it is wrong to kill or commit adultery. Noam Chomsky writes about a universal grammar being indistinguishable by a Martian linguist. McWhorter claims that through DNA evidence anthropologists discovered the village where the anthropologists discovered the village where the Germanic dialect began. In tracing word etymologies, it is important to ask ourselves where features of a language began. Guy Deutscher makes the following observation: "Often, it is only the estrangement of foreign tongues, which their many exotic and outlandish features, that brings home the wonder of language's design." By incorporating origin into a NLP translator, we can see by parapraxis, images that speaker has in mind. Through a more careful of word choice, we have the advantage of seeing the speaker's words and come closer to making up for the disadvantage of not seeing him communicate those words to us. We can see how a language would transform and predict new words that might occur. By understanding how the introduction of new words and in what context it helps us predict what the likelihood that a speaker is, uttering these new words and this can greatly help the software that recognizes speech, sucking up words around it. McWhorter likens it to summer camp, where an exchange of ideas takes place. Robert McCrum writes that non-native speakers to surpass the limitations of English by borrowing from other languages use Globish (McCrum, 2010). This field of anthropology is transcultural transfusion. This is an example of diffusion by choice. By studying hyperdiffusionism under the belief that man originated in one place, we can learn through cultural similarities. For instance, most civilized cultures today teach us that it is wrong to kill or commit adultery. Noam Chomsky writes about a universal grammar being indistinguishable by a Martian linguist. McWhorter claims that through DNA evidence anthropologists discovered the village where the Germanic dialect began. In tracing word etymologies, it is important to ask ourselves where features of a language began. Guy Deutscher makes the following observation: "Often, it is only the estrangement of foreign tongues, which their many exotic and outlandish features, that brings home the wonder of language's design" (Deutscher, 2011). By incorporating origin into a NLP translator, we can see by parapraxis, images that speaker has in mind. Through a more careful of word choice, we have the advantage of seeing the speaker's words and come closer to making up for the disadvantage of not seeing him communicate those words to us. We can see how a language would transform and predict new words that might occur. By understanding formation of new words and in what context it helps us predict what the likelihood that a speaker is, uttering these new words and this can greatly help the software that recognizes speech.

How to Assist Those With Speech Issues That Do Not Overcompensate

In people with speech issues who obtained them later in life due to a stroke it is important to utilize elements of traditional speech recognition. These include language based game theory and eliminating what is not the topic. This paper proposes imitation of a biological system.

Language Based Game Theory

A project in the Netherlands led by Jan Dietz seeks to map words as they relate to events in the world. Their premise is that we are like parrots repeating ideas that come to us through movies and books. In a game of broken telephone, a group of people sits in a circle and whisper a message to the person next to them. The message tends to vary as the first person conveys the message to the next person. These researchers claim through recursion we repeat these events demonstrated to us in a particular order. They believe they can forecast behaviors based on the past. The DEMO research group claims that BPMN, UML-AD, EPC, IDEF-3 are method independent. They do not take into account the redundant nature of business. It captures the conversations between actors. Jan Dietz explains that the subject chose to share one of their thoughts called the locutor. It appears as <locutor>: <illocution>: <addressee>: <fact>: <time> For example, let us consider checking a book out from a library. Certain circumstances must satisfy the checkout conditions. First, to check out books the subject must be a member at the library. Then he must not have any pending fees. Essence, the attributes that make the subject what he or she is. He is a candidate who can pick books out of the library. Should there be problems, he cannot check out books from the library. The production act of picking books out of the library is the executioner. It is a repeatable act. David Bellos tells an account of how his father was able to check into a hotel in a non-English speaking community because both he and the hotel staff were familiar with the process (Bellos, 2011).

Another tool that can help with the speech is to find the topics not discussed. As the speaker is generating a narrative the chance of the speaker continuing to speak of a topic becomes greater. This directs the trajectory a certain way. Throughout the conversation, we use the Zachman framework to generate a possible persona of who the speaker is. If the speaker is a 16-year-old, we know there is a greater chance of them looking into colleges as opposed to retirement homes. While in certain situations, this can happen. The computer takes the conversation as a puzzle which has certain elements and can affirm or discredit the personas generated by the computer of who is speaking. To confirm accuracy, information can be gathered through abnormal changes in sediment. There is an emerging field of looking for statements and determining whether they are joking or using sarcasm. This technique is similar to those in visual saliency to help us deduct clues. Barash speaks of language like a stream of water (Barash, 2003). An adversary comes from the Latin word adversus meaning turned towards the flow. Language consists of hundreds or thousands of transactions and our program can learn what to expect. Language is much like the social behavior of ants. Can computers learn enough by watching transaction to find what stands out among the ordinary. The article Ant-Inspired Visual Saliency Detection, gives the image of ant behavior when they take the way that requires the least amount of effort to get towards their food. Saliency provides a method of processing of images for anything that stands out including edges. There is software for finding salience such as the Saliency Toolbox and the Neuromorphic Vision Toolbox. Consider the test for color blindness where a hidden object in an image or CAPTYA in figure one and two below.

Consider the book, Where's Waldo. In the Where's Waldo example the stimulus is when we Consider the book, Where's Waldo. In the Where's Waldo example the stimulus is when we see something that resembles Waldo. For example, the viewer considers the color red with Waldo. Then on to the next level, they consider red stripes. Then they associate glasses. The template starts to form that confirmed by people of different cultures is a grammar. It is possible by using a grammar to spot

Figure 3. Two hidden objects one in a CAPTYA and the other in a color blind test

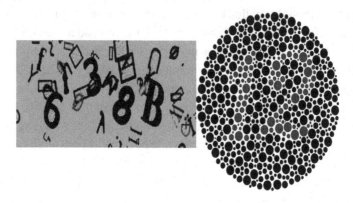

what the topic is not, much like a Bayesian spam filter. This monitors the flow of the conversation and when an unexpected sound appears in the recording it the software can quickly process the sound by assessing it and managing it. Artificial Neural Networks

As discussed before in this section automata are not an adequate algorithm for defining morpheme parsing. A neural network is a statistical algorithm used in machine learning. It is simple yet effective. Biological neural networks inspire artificial neural networks. Neural networks are adaptable and can self-organize in real-time. They also give fault tolerance. The brain forms the basis of an artificial neural network. Consider the images shown in Figure 4. These are both images of a flying object.

The one on the right inspires the one on the left. They both have two wings and a tail and are both of the same air stream figures. When the inventors like Leonardo De Vinci was constructing a flying machine it very much resembled a bird. Similarly, a neural network is a natural model of a brain (Abu-Mostafa, 2012). It is self-organizing, fault tolerant, and adaptable. We need to build a software design that resembles this working model. Looking at the PyBrain code it looks as though we can and should adopt something like this for our sentence processing sequence. In How the Mind

Figure 4. A human invention (the airplane that is to the left) compared with a bird

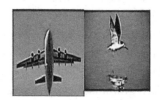

Works, Steven Pinker discusses the benefits of using a neural network; however, linguists need to improve multiple instances of the same object.

The one on the right inspires the one on the left. They both have two wings and a tail and are both of the same air stream figures. When the inventors like Leonardo De Vinci was constructing a flying machine it very much resembled a bird. Similarly, a neural network is a natural model of a brain (Abu-Mostafa, 2012). It is self-organizing, fault tolerant, and adaptable. We need to build a software design that resembles this working model. Looking at the PyBrain code it looks as though we can and should adopt something like this for our sentence processing sequence. In How the Mind Works, Steven Pinker discusses the benefits of using a neural network; however, linguists need to improve multiple instances of the same object.

FUTURE RESEARCH DIRECTIONS

I hope to find a feature set to annotate and make computer's speech easier for people to understand. I am working on looking at integrating the Neuromorphic Vision C++ Toolkit, a vision toolkit, with GBBOpen, an open source blackboard system, and Pybrain, an open source artificial neural network framework. I hope I am able to understand the algorithms well enough to port them all to python and so it can run on an Android. Kivy is an open source virtual machine containing libraries on how to write crossplatform python applications. GBBOpen uses lisp and the Neuromorphic Vision C++ Toolkit uses C++. The requirements are an algorithm that processes events in parallel and learns from reinforced learning. A brain can be thought of as a multi-core or quantum computers that resemble neurons. Change blindness as described in the book The Invisible Gorilla, talks about how we long for continuity (Chabris, 2010). However, in this paper I argue that this pattern matching classification is done to overlook elements in sound. Naturally we each have a certain range of activities that go unnoticed. Sometimes this varies from person to person, a common example being tinnitus. Like light, sound is often measured in how it is different from one element to the next such as pitch. Sound appears unified until broken apart by a prism called a spectrometer. This helps us figure out what the light emitting object is constructed and composed of. We are unable to tell boundaries are twofold. First the mind likes unifying patterns into things it can understand and find patterns between two "corresponding" events. This is so we can communicate what it is we saw. This is despite the entropy and separations posed by natural limitations such as quantum mechanics in harmonic wave functions The second reason is pink noise also known as Brownian motion or noise that we disregard as background noise. This is what audiologists call masking and can dampen boundaries between two events in sound. However, I am uncertain that most pink noise is extraneous. It could provide useful clues as to the context of the speech by harmonic analysis and studying representational theory. This can be explored in the study of continuous-time Markov chain. This uses the analogy of how elements combined in a certain way makes a chemical reaction. Grammar is different and cannot be measured by finite states but rather provide a framework of rules for processing. Rather it can be seen as a horde of ants interacting and otherwise affecting their evolutionary walks. Noam Chomsky talked about how rules do not necessarily guarantee a sentence. For example the notion that "Green colorless ideas sleep furiously" is a sentence is simply unsound. David Ben-Zvi uses a concept he describes as the x-games to describe infinitesimal generator matrix by using differentials to study the elements in an evolution of sounds. In my papers I've discussed the benefits of starting to play musical instruments as a younger person (some would argue ideally preschool aged). This is because it raises the awareness and attention of the threshold between two different events musically.

The blackboard algorithm combined with a neural network is a good approach to the complexity of sound. To fully appreciate the significance of each node, we not only need what is preceding it but what is going on simultaneously that give clues about what might happen in the future. In my paper I suggest that one reason people have difficulty speaking is that their mind is not able to function and keep up with everything. In this area I believe computers can excel because as computers become more powerful, they can surpass human's attention spans. The ants marching in a row is a nice picture but seldom happens because of the simultaneous complex world we live in. I am confident that with the emerging field of multiprocessor concurrency and abandoning the idea of having a master core and adopting a system more like the brain of adopting many neurons firing electrical signals would bear success in the years to come. There is a consensus and each core is aware of what is going on.

CONCLUSION

Much work is necessary to give a feature set to describe the spoken natural language. This paper intends to give a framework of how to think of big data as a filter analogous to a prism that a person can see more clearly through and to ask right questions. The paper discusses why examining why people talk the way they do is important. The paper proposes that the Zachman framework and through deducting what a topic is not aid the process. This paper also examines how a human understands language and sound.

SOLUTIONS AND RECOMMENDATIONS

Having a stroke is difficult because part of the brain may stop functioning. This affects the part of the brain that produces language. To counter this, engaging games that target the mind using neuro-gaming which may include augmented reality should be developed. It has been shown that video games and television can change people's perspectives about what words mean. This can be both used positively and negatively and some of the pioneers in the field include advertisers. Some examples of media which helps people learn words include Sesame Street while those who use this power negatively do so for selling products to enhance how people view their body. What I am proposing differs from competitors because does more immersive experiences similar to those played on PlayStation or GameCube. In order for a person to truly exercise they need to be caught up in the passion of the event and forget that they are exercising. It's like the book "See Spot Run" as compared to "Jurassic Park". You can base a movie on Jurassic Park but I think I'd save my money on the spot video. Athletes can get caught up in a sport such as tennis and forget they are working out The people who could benefit from this the most, the people with early signs of memory loss and mentally illness, are the ones who cost is a barrier to using other platforms. Learning should be based on applicable games based on learning. This differs from conventional mind games because feedback is given and expounded not only showing possible solutions but they take the user's attempts and building upon them so they are guided to a solution. The audio clarifier for the phone works during the assessment phase and does not give feedback. MIT Professor Eric Klopfer says a game that much like a spelling bee gives feedback on whether the answer is correct or not but frustrates the participant by making them feel incompetent. To feel competent the participant must be guided towards a solution. The game's purpose is functionality and how it works to assess whether the person knows about the concept and situation which the clear audio needs to be activated to shape the words. The goal is to become more comfortable taking risks.

The part of the brain lost caused by strokes make it necessary for other parts of the brain to compensate. The parts which compensate may be dormant but they still exist. Language is a foundation about how we communicate with others and often is a way of conveying thoughts that are within us. Studies demonstrate that find that people who have somniloquy or are sleep talkers. WebMD finds that 10% of children make utterances in their sleep or when they are in the process of waking up (Talking in Your Sleep). When a person is asleep in the past they often thought that the brain activity waves would shut down, however recent studies in sleep found that a person uses the brain as much during the night as they do during the day. Eagleman tells of how a patient had hemispherectomy or part of their brain removed to prevent epileptic episodes. As a side effect, they were unable to create new memories but the memories that they had remained. Sometimes memories are activated during the night, however the part of the brain that determines whether the implications of the dream is not functional. As a result of some dreams perceptions change and sometimes people wake up irritated with another person because of an altered inaccurate perception. However, language can come up with ideas. During the reign of the communist leader Nicolae Ceaușescu of Romania and the results of the way he ran his state-run orphanages made clear our dependency on language to communicate ideas. He wanted to increase the number of workers in Romania to increase revenue into the country. Not only were abortions illegal but each family that did not produce at least five offspring were taxed heavy taxes. As the economy collapsed, the shortage of money caused many families to abandon their children in orphanages. In these state operated orphanages, when there should be three care takers for every 15 kids, there was only one. After the fall of the communists in 1989 the children that were in the care of the state grew from 47,405 orphans in the care of 25,870 orphanages in 1990 to 62,000 in the care of 19,000 orphanages. The caretakers were told not to pick up or show any affection to the kids that were in their cribs because of the fear that should the caretaker show affection to one, they all would want attention and draw the energy out of their limited number of caretakers. In 2009 BBC journalist Chris Rodgers was appalled by conditions and found that the orphans spoke a coarse language they made up themselves with the purpose of communicating among themselves to survive.

What does this have to do with patients who had a stroke? The answer is that human language is a foremost tool in comprehension and our survival. Suskind argues that language is the foremost building block of our education system (Suskind, 2015). Noam Chomsky argues that language is itself innate because people from other cultures communicate in much the same way universally. The book, American English compendium: a portable guide to the idiosyncrasies, subtleties, technical lingo, and nooks and crannies of American English by Marv Rubinstein makes the point that there once was a gap between people of different countries, even American English and British English were distinct while Canadian English were a blend between the two. Because of media this gap has somewhat closed, however many phrases are still based on historic culture. Dana Suskind cites Hart and Risley's study showing people who are more successful later in lives have more interaction with their parents that are memorable because they are positive. The people who did not do so well in life according to their study suppressed negative memories of interaction with their parents which were fewer (Suskind, 2015). Questions arise such as who has memories that are dormant that could benefit most from my study into games.

Games are beneficial because they involve multiple inputs of sensory information and can help people become acquainted with Hebbian learning that is that neurons which fire together wire together. Like many professional golfers who learn through muscle memory, because of the intense thought process behind processing language in both mechanically speaking as well as comprehending the conversation the brain often differs from a computer in that once a pattern is found, the brain goes into autopilot. This is why experts sometimes find it difficult to explain their decisions in a series of rules. While people may think that programmers are unequipped to know what an expert knows in topics on medicine, since they are outside the field they have the advantage of a recently acquired understanding of what they had to go through to get knowledgeable about the skill. Music provides a good example. To a person who began taking music lessons early in life, they are unable to, without some practice; describe to someone how to start making music. When the stroke occurs and kicks the stroke person out of autopilot mode acquired during Hebbian learning. Many of the tasks which seem so familiar must now have renewed thought and concentration to each event as though they are relearning how to become acquainted with human life at infancy. The goals are to take what motivates each gender and age group and helps them become motivated towards their goals. We are fortunate to live in an era of simulation games such as Opensimulator or Second Life. These are like Tamagotchi pets, which limit the input, and makes what is expected easier. For example, the Tamagotchi pet shown in figure 5 only has three buttons and from the context we can simulate the entire lifestyle of a dog or a cat.

Computer programmers are used to the concept of intelli-sense which hints given the context about what the person is about to say. However, it is imperative to make sure that it does not frustrate the person with the stroke.

Figure 5. Shows a Tamagotchi pet (credits go to Wikimedia)

REFERENCES

Abu-Mostafa, Y. (2012). *Lecture 10 - Neural Networks*. California Institute of Technology.

Adversus. (2011). *Wiktionary*.

Aiden, E., & Michel, J. (2013). Uncharted: big data as a lens on human culture. New York: Riverhead Books, a member of Penguin Group (USA).

Bellos, D. (2011). *Is that a fish in your ear? Translation and the meaning of everything*. New York: Faber and Faber.

Brynjolfsson, E., & McAfee, A. (2014). *The second machine age: Work, progress, and prosperity in a time of brilliant technologies*. Academic Press.

Buonomano, D. (2011). *Brain bugs: How the brain's flaws shape our lives*. New York: W.W. Norton.

Chabris, C. F., & Simons, D. J. (2010). *The invisible gorilla: And other ways our intuitions deceive us*. New York: Crown.

Crystal, D. (2012). *The Story of English in 100 Words*. New York: St. Martin's.

Dehaene, S. (2014). *Consciousness and the brain: Deciphering how the brain codes our thoughts*. Academic Press.

Denworth, L. (2014). *I can hear you whisper: An intimate journey through the science of sound and language*. Academic Press.

Deutscher, G. (2005). *The unfolding of language: An evolutionary tour of mankind's greatest invention*. New York: Metropolitan Books.

Deutscher, G. (2010). *Through the language glass: Why the world looks different in other languages*. New York: Metropolitan Books/Henry Holt and Co.

Eagleman, D. (2015). *The Brain: The Story of You*. Academic Press.

Hitchings, H. (2011). *The language wars: A history of proper English*. New York: Farrar, Straus and Giroux.

Hofstadter, D., & Sander, E. (2010). *Surfaces and essences*. Perseus Books Group.

Iacoboni, M. (2008). *Mirroring people: The new science of how we connect with others*. New York: Farrar, Straus and Giroux.

Kelly, N., & Zetzsche, J. O. (2012). *Found in translation: How language shapes our lives and transforms the world*. New York: Perigee.

Kenneally, C. (2007). *The first word: the search for the origins of language*. New York: Viking.

Kenneally, Kessler, & Topher. (2013). *Troubleshooting Enhanced Dictation in OS X Mavericks - CNET*. CNET.

Levitin, D. J. (2014). *The organized mind: Thinking straight in the age of information overload*. Academic Press.

Lieberman, M. D. (2013). *Social: Why our brains are wired to connect*. Academic Press.

Nicolelis, M. A. (2011). *Beyond boundaries: the new neuroscience of connecting brains with machines--and how it will change our lives*. New York: Times Books/Henry Holt and Co.

Norgvig, P. (2013, October 25). *2013 Family Weekend Keynote: "Live and Learn: How Big Data and Machine Learning Power the Internet"*. Retrieved January 07, 2017, from https://www.youtube.com/watch?v=vVprmVsCV_k

Sacks, O. (2007). *Musicophilia: Tales of music and the brain*. New York: Alfred A. Knopf.

Sleep Talking Causes and Treatments. (n.d.). Retrieved January 07, 2017, from http://www.webmd.com/sleep-disorders/talking-in-your-sleep#1

Stibel, J. M. (2013). *Breakpoint: Why the web will implode, search will be obsolete, and everything else you need to know about technology is in your brain*. Academic Press.

Suskind, D., Suskind, B., & Lewinter-Suskind, L. (2015). *Thirty million words: Building a child's brain: tune in, talk more, take turns*. Academic Press.

Swaab, D. F. (2014). *We are our brains: A neurobiography of the brain, from the womb, Talking in Your Sleep*. Academic Press.

Truss, L. (2004). *Eats, shoots & leaves: The zero tolerance approach to punctuation*. New York: Gotham Books.

Yagoda, B. (2006). *When you catch an adjective, kill it: The parts of speech for better and/or worse*. New York: Broadway Books.

KEY TERMS AND DEFINITIONS

Artificial Neural Networks: A data processing method in which a representation of the information processing of the brain is mimicked.

Natural Language Processing: A branch subject of artificial intelligence dealing with words as they are spoken and gathering linguistic qualities for a computerized system.

Neural-Gaming: A branch of augmented and simulated reality using a computerized platform meant to benefit the advancement of a human's brain.

Verbal Apraxia: A speech impediment caused by a motor disorder resulting from possible damage in the brain.

Verbal Dyspraxia: A speech impediment caused by a developmental delay.

Voice Recognition: A branch of artificial intelligence and natural language processing interpreting human speech into structured data usable by the computer.

Chapter 11
Conclusion

Pradeep Kumar
Maulana Azad National Urdu University, India

ABSTRACT

This chapter summarize and concludes the issues and challenges elaborated in different chapters using machine learning approaches presented by various authors. It identifies the importance of supervised and unsupervised learning algorithms establishing classification, prediction, clustering, security policies along with object recognition and pattern matching structures. A systematic position for future research and practice is also described in detail. This book presents the capabilities of machine learning methods and ideas on how these methods could be used to solve real-world problems related to health, social and engineering applications.

INTRODUCTION

With ever increasing amounts of data becoming available there is enough reason to believe that smart data analysis will become even more pervasive as a necessary ingredient for technological progress. Over the past two decades Machine Learning has become one of the main-stays of information technology rather part of our life. The purpose of this book is to provide the reader with some specific applications of machine learning over the vast range of applications which have at their heart a machine learning problem.

This book is composed of eleven chapters assessing current state of the art of machine learning, from symbolic concept learning and conceptual clustering to case-based reasoning, neural networks, deep learning, and genetic algorithms. Edited chapters introduces the reader to innovative applications of machine learning techniques in the fields of biometric system, urban sciences, heart disease prognosis,

DOI: 10.4018/978-1-5225-2545-5.ch011

software reliability prediction, data mining, knowledge discovery, computational intelligence, human language technology, user modeling data analysis & discovery sciences.

Over the past few years machine learning has made its way into various areas of administration, commerce, and industry, in an impressive way. Data mining is the most popular widely known demonstration of this phenomenon, complemented by less publicized applications of machine learning, such as adaptive systems in various industrial settings, financial prediction, medical diagnosis, and the construction of user profiles for WWW-browsers. This transfer of machine learning approach from the research labs to the "real world" has caused increased interest in learning techniques, dictating further effort in informing people from other disciplines about the state of the art in machine learning and its uses. The objective of this book is to provide the reader with sufficient information about the research oriented capabilities of machine learning methods, as well as ideas about how the user could make use of these methods to solve real-world problems.

The research issues addressed in book chapters include the relationship of machine learning to knowledge discovery in databases, software reliability prediction, the handling of noisy data, and the modification of the learning problem through feature selection algorithms for classification and clustering.

The first chapter of the book introduces the reader to innovative applications of machine learning and explore wide range of applications, from data mining in finance, marketing, and economics to learning in human language technology and user modeling. Some basic terminology of machine learning used in this chapter described as below:

More recently, in 1997, Tom Mitchell gave a well-posed definition that has proven more useful to engineering types:

A computer program is said to learn from experience E with respect to some task T and some performance measure P, if its performance on T, as measured by P, improves with experience E.

For example if you want your program to predict, for example, traffic patterns at a busy intersection (task T), you can run it through a machine learning algorithm with data about past traffic patterns (experience E) and, if it has successfully "learned", it will then do better at predicting future traffic patterns (performance measure P).

Arthur Samuel in 1959:

Machine Learning is the] field of study that gives computers the ability to learn without being explicitly programmed.

The highly complex nature of many real-world problems, though, often means that inventing specialized algorithms that will solve them perfectly every time is impractical, if not impossible. Some specific examples of machine learning can be related to classification and prediction, market basket analysis, likelihood of a pattern, object recognition, sequence matching etc. All of these problems are excellent targets for a Machine Learning (ML) project, and in fact ML has been applied to each of them with great success.

The process of feature selection in selecting a best subset of features, among all the features that are useful for the learning algorithms may be summarized as:

- To provide faster and more cost effective models by reducing the size of the problem and hence reducing computational time and space required to run classifiers.
- To improve the performance of the classifiers, firstly by removing noisy or irrelevant features secondly by reducing the likelihood of over fitting to noisy data. So the basic objective of feature selection algorithms to improve the performance of the classifier, i.e. prediction performance in the case of classification and better cluster detection in the case of clustering.

Two broad category of ML is supervised and unsupervised learning:

- **Supervised Machine Learning:** The program is "trained" on a pre-defined set of "training examples", which then facilitate its ability to reach an accurate conclusion when given new data.
- **Unsupervised Machine Learning:** The program is given a bunch of data and must find patterns and relationships therein.

In this chapter the basic concepts related to feature selection techniques such as filter, wrapper and hybrid methods and various machine learning techniques such as artificial neural network, Naive Bayes classifier, support vector machine, k-nearest-neighbor, decision trees, bagging, boosting, random subspace method, random forests, k-means clustering and deep learning also presented. In the last the performance measure of the classifier was presented in detail.

In chapter 2, the author explains how does in human's life plant plays an important part to balance the nature and supply food-&-medicine. The traditional manual plant species identification method is tedious and time-consuming process and requires expert knowledge. The rapid developments of mobile and ubiquitous computing make automated plant biometric system really feasible and accessible for anyone-anywhere-anytime. More and more research are ongoing to make it a more realistic tool for common man to access the agro-information by just a click. Based on this, the chapter highlights the significant growth of plant identification and leaf disease recognition over past few years.

At the beginning of this century, there was a tremendous technological revolution in the field of wireless communication and mobile technology. Mobile and ubiquitous computers are increasing their magnitude in every small, portable, wireless computing and communication fields. The technological omnipresence of ubiquitous devices invisibly activates the world by providing accessibility *anywhere-anytime* computing. However, this revolution is still slow in the agricultural sphere, despite the advancements in technologies making it possible to build and deploy wireless sensor networks (WSN) in fields that would radically improves the farming efficiencies. This is because the current wireless technologies are too expensive and complicated for farmers to use especially in the developing countries like India. Two-way radios have long been used by farmers in many such developed countries with large farmlands to contact their employees, farm suppliers, equipment dealers, agents, buyers and farm awareness. Today, world-wide availability of smartphones and cellular networks, the use of mobile phones in agricultural sector is popularly, replacing the use of two-way radios (Wang et al. 2016). The advantage of using two-way radios and mobile phones is that these wireless tools are relatively cheap and very simple to use. Additionally, smartphones have several important advantages such as all the brands of mobile phones are generally compatible for running various types of application software, and are equipped with Wi-Fi, Bluetooth, camera(s) and GPS capabilities.

In this chapter, a brief survey of automated plant biometric systems since decades is presented highlighting the current state-of-the-art. According to several authors, plant leaf patterns are represented mathematically using various transforms including both spatial and frequency domain. More than fifty feature spaces for ten different plant datasets are discussed using different classifiers. Based on this survey, the author find out the pros and cons of different feature spaces and classifiers. The future scopes and applications of such systems in agro-communities also motivate researchers to work in this field. A wide range of research analysis is shown in this chapter in this context. Finally, the chapter showed the future scope and applications of AaaS and similar systems in agro-field.

In chapter 3, author presents some popularly known Deep Learning (DL) algorithms and applications, including Natural Language Processing (NLP), image and video processing, risk assessment, forecasting, control and robotics, gaming and finance. A philosophical orientation and debates about the applications of Deep learning. The author examines some challenges in ethical management of information technology resources. The overall aim of the chapter is to consider moral issues pertaining to machine learning and articulate methods of thinking through various concerns.

DL is the cornerstone technology behind products for image recognition and video annotation, voice recognition, personal assistants, automated translation and autonomous vehicles. DNN works similarly to the brain by extracting high-level, complex abstractions from data in a hierarchical and discriminative or generative way. A key feature of DL algorithms is their capability to learn from large amounts of data with minimal supervision – contrary to shallow models that normally require less data, but with labels and easily reach an accuracy plateau. DL however, comes with a cost: there is no theory to guide the learning algorithms and architecture optimization and hyper-parameters selection rely on complex and time-consuming heuristics – training a single model can take weeks on well-equipped PCs.

Deep Learning is moving to open source and the Cloud. Google, Facebook, IBM, Amazon and Microsoft are trying to establish ecosystems around AI services provided in the cloud. Deep Learning is having a tremendous impact in Natural Language Processing (NLP). Language understanding is one of the oldest, and probably the hardest problem for machines. However, as large corpus of data become available on the Internet, DL is a natural option to solve innumerous problems related to understanding human language. Parsing is a central problem for NLP. It consists in decomposing a sentence in its components (nouns, verbs, adverbs, etc) and built the syntactic relation between them – the parsing tree. It is a very complex problem due the ambiguity in possible decompositions.

The author identifies and explain several potential research areas of deep learning focusing on:

- Deep Generative Adversarial Neural Networks (GANs).
- Recurrent Neural Networks.
- Multimodal learning models.

GANs are a powerful approach to explore unsupervised and semi-supervised learning where the goal is to discover the hidden structure within data without relying on external labels. One of the most interesting models is Generative Adversial Networks (GANs) where a generative networks is trying to confuse a discriminative one in distinguish real data from faked (generated) one. The Deep generative models have widespread applications including probability density estimation, image denoising and inpainting, data compression, scene understanding, representation learning, 3D scene construction, semi-supervised classification, and hierarchical control. New methods to train Recurrent Neural Networks and Multimodal Learning (learning from different data types – video, image, voice, text) are presently very active areas of research and very promising in solving problems related with control and object manipulation, image and video caption and text processing.

In chapter 4 the author explains an urban system, a complex system considering multiple factors which significantly influences the different aspects of it. The influencing factors possess different characteristics as they may be environmental, economical, socio-political or cognitive factors. It is not feasible to characterize an urban system with deterministic approach. Therefore there is a need of study on computational frameworks that can investigate cities from a system's perspective. This kind of study may help in devising different ways that can handle uncertainty and randomness of an urban system efficiently and effectively. Therefore the primary objective of this chapter is to highlight the significance of affective sciences in urban studies. In addition, how machine intelligence techniques can enable a system to control and monitor the randomness of a city is explained. Finally the utility of machine intelligence technique in deciphering the complexity of way finding is conceptually demonstrated.

The author provides a detailed description on the significance of machine intelligence techniques, and their utility in understanding a complex system; a research problem on way finding using a machine intelligent technique and decision tree is demonstrated. This chapter ends with concluding remarks, and suggestions that can be incorporated to strengthen the further study in future.

The author summarized the underlying complexities of an urban system in detail. It further explains the numerous reasons which are responsible for breeding or escalating complexity in functioning of a city. It is highlighted that an event which surfaces on the circumference of a city is a consequence of many factors. Furthermore it is not just the combination of influencing factors which is responsible for its eruption. Instead the magnitude of their participation should also be considered. Moreover the natures of the significant factors that can influence an urban system have strikingly different characteristics. Therefore it is not an easy task to include them in their raw form in the same framework. Instead they need to be normalized on a same scale and then needs to be processed. However incompatible frameworks would fail to process the data accurately and precisely. That means the selection of computational frameworks have huge significance in studying these data sets. In fact, it needs to be understood that absence of models that are flexible enough to accommodate non-linear influencing factors can produce erroneous results. Therefore computational systems that can input and process factors of varying characteristics should be developed. The proposed chapter thus explains the significance of the concept of affective sciences in urban studies. It outlines the basic characteristics of affective sciences. It further highlights the significance of affective sciences. Especially how the principles of affective sciences can be utilized and applied in investigations pertaining to urban systems is explained.

The chapter moves on to describe the utility of machine intelligence techniques in deciphering the complexity of an urban system. Different learning algorithms are briefed in this chapter to provide an idea for selecting appropriate learning algorithm to train a particular set of data. Furthermore principles of different machine learning techniques is provided in the proposed chapter aiming that it would help in selecting the appropriate method for different research investigations. The importance of machine learning in the context of affective computing and urban studies is also highlighted in this chapter. This work ends with a conceptual demonstration of understanding a way finding problem using the principles of affective science and machine learning. This demonstration is aimed to describe the influence of different factors in a way finding problem. The factors can be direct or indirect in their influences. However the significance of many factors in affecting an event is sometimes overshadowed by the presence of factors which are easily perceivable. That creates an erroneous perception regarding the working mechanism of an urban system. There is always a likelihood of presence of those factors that don't have direct presence, but affect the behavior of the system significantly. Therefore the way finding problem was chosen for the conceptual demonstration to insist on the fact that each and every factor has a significant role in an urban event. In addition, how the basic principle of affective science and machine learning can be used to aid decision making regarding way finding is explained.

In chapter 5, the author investigates thoroughly health issues and proposes a new prognostic approach of CHD for T2D patients based on a Holter dataset. This approach, based on machine learning methods, supports the applicability of using the Holter dataset, to efficiently predict T2D patients that are likely to develop CHD. The author highlighted the importance of using feature selection algorithms for the construction of our predictive model. A drawback of this study is the low number of patients that evolve to CHD, therefore the use of bootstrapping technique. The result is a prognostic tool that allows the identification of high-risk subjects in the diabetic population. The entire data set captures 8 years (2006-2014) of clinical visits, and a CHD prognosis can be made with intervals for time windows of 3 and 4 years, with AUC values of 68,06% and 74,33%, respectively using a Naïve Bayes classifier.

It is also shown that proposed predictive model outperforms the Framingham study (D'Agostino, 2000) for this population. Author presented a solution with a higher number of features than the Framingham, but with a higher precision on the prognostic of the CHD. This chapter presented a novel work that provides a risk indicator of CHD in T2D patients just by performing a Holter exam in order to improve clinical decision making, and, ultimately patient clinical outcomes. This chapter is focused on a new proposed approach for CHD prognostic prediction on T2D patients, given a Holter dataset. FS was applied given the high number of available features. Bootstrapping was used to provide a more balanced training data. Cross validation is applied 5x10-fold CV on the training set for different classifiers and selected the classifier that presented the best metrics: AUC, sensitivity and specificity.

As a subsequence of this study, a drawback of this study is the low number of patients that will evolve to CHD. As a future work, the author aim to include a temporal analysis, to add new features to the classification that will represent their evolution over time, and could therefore improve predictive model. This is a data enrichment which is used to investigate possible improvements on classification. The author also suggested to test other machine learning packages such as Theano - it will allow to attain speeds rivalling hand-crafted C implementations for problems involving large amounts of data in order to make a comparative performance analysis before making generalization.

In chapter 6, author reviews the machine learning techniques applied for predicting software reliability. Reliability is increasingly becoming more important during the design of software systems, as our daily lives and schedules are more dependent than ever before on the satisfactory functioning of these systems. The common examples of such systems are computers, critical safety system, automobiles, aircraft, and space satellites. Some of the specific factors that are playing a key role in increasing the importance of reliability in designed systems include system complexity and sophistication, global market competition, increasing reliability and quality-related issues, high acquisition cost, the past well-publicized system failures, and loss of prestige. On the other hand, the importance of quality in business and industry is increasing rapidly due to market competition, growing demand from customers for better quality, increasing various quality-related lawsuits, and the global economy.

Chapter six is focused on software reliability prediction models that play an important role in developing software systems and enhancing computer software. The classical software reliability theory deals with probabilistic methods applied to the analysis of random occurrence of failures in a given software system. In general, software reliability models fall into two categories depending on the operating domain. The most popular category of models depends on time, whose main feature is that probability measures, such as the mean time between failures and the failure intensity function depend on failure time. The second category of software reliability models measures reliability as the ratio of successful runs to the total number of runs.

In a digital world billions of dollars are spent annually to produce new products using modern information and communication technologies. Many of these products are highly sophisticated and contain millions of parts. Therefore, reliability and quality of software systems have become more important than ever before. Moreover, global competition and other factors are forcing software practitioners and industry professionals to produce highly reliable and good quality software. As the cost of software application failures grows tremendously, its impact on business performance and software reliability has become more important. Thus, project managers and industry professionals need to employ effective software reliability prediction techniques to improve the product and process reliability.

In this chapter, author investigated various software reliability prediction techniques focusing on methods, metrics and failure databases, the current trends and existing issues. The applications of machine learning techniques for the prediction of software reliability in place of traditional statistical techniques have shown remarkable improvement in recent years. The goal of this chapter is to help researchers and industrial professionals for relevant expert estimation and prediction of software reliability realistically.

Chapter 7 is focused on feature selection problem is inescapable in inductive machine learning or data mining setting and its significance is beyond doubt. Author illustrate main benefit of a correct selection is the terms of learning speed, speculation capacity or simplicity of the induced model. On the other hand there are the straight benefits related with a smaller number of features: a reduced measurement cost and hopefully a better understanding of the domain. A feature selection algorithm (FSA) is a computational solution that should be guided by a certain definition of subset relevance although in many cases this definition is implicit or followed in a loose sense. This is so because, from the inductive learning perspective, the relevance of a feature may have several definitions depending on precise objective (Caruana and Freitag, 1994).

The feature selection algorithm can be classified according to the kind of output one are giving a (weighed) linear order of features and second are giving a subset of the original features. In this research, several fundamental algorithms found in the literature are studied to assess their performance in a controlled scenario. This measure computes the degree of matching between the output given by a FSA and the known optimal solution. Sample size effect also studied. The result illustrates the strong dependence on the particular conditions of the FSA used and on the amount of irrelevance and redundancies in the data set description, relative to the total number of feature. This should prevent the use of single algorithm even when there is poor knowledge available about the structure of the solution. The basic idea in feature selection is to detect irrelevant and/or redundant features as they harm the learning algorithm performance (Lee and Moore, 2014). There is no unique definition of relevance, however it has to do with the discriminating ability of a feature or a subset to distinguish the different class labels (Dash and Liu, 1997). However, as pointed out in the paper (Guyon and Elisseeff, 2003a), an irrelevant variable may be useful when taken with others and even two irrelevant variables that are useless by themselves can be useful when taken together. In this chapter several fundamental algorithms found in the literature are studied to assess their performance in a controlled scenario

In chapter 8, author addresses the problem of feature selection in the nature and thus needs a solver with high exploration power. On the other hand, if alternative optimal solutions could be provided for a problem, the implementation phase may become more selective depending on the cost and limitations of domain of the problem. The high exploration power and solution conservation capability of optimization methods make them able to find multiple suitable solutions in a single run. Therefore, optimization methods can be considered as a powerful tool of finding suitable feature subsets for feature selection problem.

The author illustrates the process of selecting optimal feature subset from a given dataset that can interpret the target concept. Any feature selection algorithm completes in four steps viz. subset generation, subset evaluation, stopping criterion and result validation. Subset generation is the process of searching subsets from the given feature space and then selected subset is evaluated to determine the goodness of feature subset under consideration. The termination of the algorithm is decided by stopping criterion. Finally, validation is performed to identify legitimate feature subsets [Julius T Tou and Rafael C Gonz'alez (1994)]. Feature selection has been explored extensively by researchers of data mining and machine learning since 1970s. It has exploited many domains like machine learning, data mining, pattern recognition and other related domains such as software engineering, text categorization, bioinformatics, image retrieval, intrusion detection, information and music retrieval.

Many evolutionary algorithms available in literature to solve the feature selection problem. Different approaches with different algorithms can develop like Ant Colony Optimization, Bee Colony Optimization, Firefly algorithm etc. In this chapter, the Binary PSO algorithm finds minimal feature subsets of high dimensional cancer datasets. Preprocessing is done using heuristic based approach to create binary distinction table, further it identifies the discerning and expressive genes. To improve the results, author presented different population sizes. The two sub fitness functions helps in feature selection to find the paradoxical conditions, there by minimal feature subsets can be selected. The performance of Binary PSO algorithm and some of the existing algorithms are compared by using the predictive accuracy. The results for three benchmark data sets viz. Colon, Lymphoma and Leukemia. The proposed algorithm shows the superiority over the existing algorithms in most of the cases. However, the relevance of the selected genes are to be validated in biological perspective.

In chapter 9 author applies the machine learning based approach for face recognition. Face recognition has been one of the most interesting and important research areas for real time applications. There is a need and necessity to design efficient machine leaning based approach for automatic recognitions and surveillance systems. Face recognition also used the knowledge from other disciplines such as neuroscience, psychology, computer vision, pattern recognition, image processing, and machine learning, etc. This chapter provides a review of machine learning based techniques for the face recognition. First, it presents an overview of face recognition and its challenges followed by the detailed literature review of machine learning based approaches for face detection and recognition is presented.

In recent years there has been a growing interest in improving all aspects of the interaction between humans and computers with the clear goal of achieving a natural interaction, similar to the way human-human interaction takes place. The most expressive way humans display emotions is through facial expressions. Humans detect and interpret faces and facial expressions in a scene with little or no effort. Still, development of an automated system that accomplishes this task is rather difficult. There are several related problems: detection of an image segment as a face, extraction of the facial expression information, and classification of the expression. A system that performs these operations accurately and in real time would be a major step forward in achieving a human-like interaction between the man and machine. In this chapter, we present several machine learning algorithms applied to face analysis.

Face recognition is one of the most challenging areas in the field of computer vision. Face detection is the first step for face recognition in order to localize and to extract the face region from the background. For face detection, active contour models are used to detect the edges and for locating the face boundary. For face recognition, facial feature extraction algorithm is widely used. The distinguishing features found by the algorithm are used to compare images. There exist several algorithms to extract features such as Principal Component Analysis (PCA)

In chapter 10 author describes a method with the help of a computer learning algorithm that predicts what people are about to say based on earlier content and learns what the natural sound of their voice sounds like. This chapter illustrates speech trajectory and voice shaping. Clear Audio is a biologically inspired framework for studying natural language. Like the story behind Jurassic Park, Clear Audio attempts to make predictions about data from existing data, inspired by biological processes. Its main goal is to give feedback for speech pathology purposes.

Author illustrated with the help of an example citing brain stroke which affects the part of brain that produces language. To counter this, engaging games that target the mind using neuro-gaming which may include augmented reality should be developed. It has been shown that video games and television can change people's perspectives about what words mean. This can be both used positively and negatively and some of the pioneers in the field include advertisers. Some examples of media which helps people learn words include Sesame Street while those who use this power negatively do so for selling products to enhance how people view their body.

The game's purpose is functionality and how it works to assess whether the person knows about the concept and situation which the clear audio needs to be activated to shape the words. The goal is to become more comfortable taking risks. The part of the brain lost caused by strokes make it necessary for other parts of the brain to compensate. The parts which compensate may be dormant but they still exist. Language is a foundation about how we communicate with others and often is a way of conveying thoughts that are within us. What does this have to do with patients who had a stroke? The answer is that human language is a foremost tool in comprehension and our survival.

The author emphasizes that games are beneficial because they involve multiple inputs of sensory information and can help people become acquainted with Hebbian learning that is that neurons which fire together wire together. Like many professional golfers who learn through muscle memory, because of the intense thought process behind processing language in both mechanically speaking as well as comprehending the conversation the brain often differs from a computer in that once a pattern is found, the brain goes into autopilot. This is why experts sometimes find it difficult to explain their decisions in a series of rules. While people may think that programmers are unequipped to know what an expert knows in topics on medicine, since they are outside the field they have the advantage of a recently acquired understanding of what they had to go through to get knowledgeable about the skill. Music provides a good example. To a person who began taking music lessons early in life, they are unable to, without some practice; describe to someone how to start making music.

REFERENCES

Aggarwal, K. K., Singh, Y., Kaur, A., & Malhotra, R. (2008). Empirical analysis for investigating the effect of object-oriented metrics on fault proneness: A replicated case study. *Software Process Improvement and Practice*, *14*(1), 39–62. doi:10.1002/spip.389

Breiman, L. (2001). Random Forests. *Machine Learning*, *35*(1), 5–32. doi:10.1023/A:1010933404324

Funatsu. (2011). *Knowledge-Oriented Applications in Data Mining*. In Tech.

Han, J., & Kamber, M. (2006). *Data Mining: Concepts and Techniques*. Morgan Kaufmann Publishers.

Hastie, T., Tibshirani, R., & Friedman, J. (2001). *The Elements of Statistical Learning: Data Mining, Inference, and Prediction*. New York: Springer. doi:10.1007/978-0-387-21606-5

Kohavi, R. (1995). The power of decision tables. *The Eighth European Conference on Machine Learning (ECML-95)*, 174-189.

Lyu, M. R. (1999). *Handbook of Software Reliability Engineering*. McGraw Hill.

Malhotra, R., Singh, Y., & Kaur, A. (2009). Comparative analysis of regression and machine learning methods for predicting fault proneness models. *International Journal of Computer Applications in Technology, 35*(2), 183–193.

Mueller, J., & Lemke, F. (1999). Self-Organizing Data Mining: An Intelligent Approach to Extract Knowledge from Data. Academic Press.

Musa, D. (2009). *Software Reliability Engineering: More Reliable Software Faster and Cheaper* (2nd ed.). McGraw-Hill.

Ross, Q. (1993). *C4.5: Programs for Machine Learning*. San Mateo, CA: Morgan Kaufman Publishers.

Scott, E., & Christian, L. (1991). *The Cascade-Correlation Learning Architecture. CMU-CS-90-100*. School of Computer Science Carnegie Mellon University Pittsburgh.

Singh & Kumar. (2010). Application of feed-forward networks for software reliability prediction. *ACM SIGSOFT Software Engineering Notes, 35*(5), 1-6. DOI: 10.1145/1838687.1838709

Singh, Y., Kaur, A., & Malhotra, R. (2009). Application of support vector machine to predict fault prone classes. *ACM SIGSOFT Software Engineering Notes, 34*(1). http://doi.acm.org/10.1145/1457516.1457529, 2009.

Singh, Y., & Kumar, P. (2010). A software reliability growth model for three-tier client-server system. *International Journal of Computers and Applications, 1*(13), 9–16. doi:10.5120/289-451

Singh, Y., & Kumar, P. (2010). Determination of software release instant of three-tier client server software system. *International Journal of Software Engineering, 1*(3), 51–62.

Singh, Y., & Kumar, P. (2010). Prediction of Software Reliability using Feed Forward Neural Networks. *Proceedings of Computational Intelligence and Software Engineering (CiSE), 2010 International Conference*. doi:10.1109/CISE.2010.5677251

Witten, I., & Frank, E. (2011). Data Mining: Practical Machine Learning Tools and Techniques with Java Implementations (3rd ed.). Morgan Kaufman.

Compilation of References

Abu-Mostafa, Y. (2012). *Lecture 10 - Neural Networks*. California Institute of Technology.

Adamek, T., & Connor, N. E. O. (2004). A Multiscale Representation Method for Nonrigid Shapes with a Single Closed Contour. *IEEE Transactions on Circuits and Systems for Video Technology*, *14*(5), 742–753. doi:10.1109/TCSVT.2004.826776

Adversus. (2011). *Wiktionary*.

Aggarwal, K. K., Singh, Y., Kaur, A., & Malhotra, R. (2008). Empirical analysis for investigating the effect of object-oriented metrics on fault proneness: A replicated case study. *Software Process Improvement and Practice*, *14*(1), 39–62. doi:10.1002/spip.389

Aha, D. W., Kibler, D., & Albert, M. K. (1991). Instance-based learning algorithms. *Machine Learning*, *6*(1), 37–66. doi:10.1007/BF00153759

Aiden, E., & Michel, J. (2013). Uncharted: big data as a lens on human culture. New York: Riverhead Books, a member of Penguin Group (USA).

Alajlan, N., El, I., Kamel, M. S., & Freeman, G. (2007). Shape retrieval using triangle-area representation and dynamic space warping. *Pattern Recognition*, *40*(7), 1911–1920. doi:10.1016/j. patcog.2006.12.005

Almuallim, H., & Dietterich, T. G. (1991, July). Learning with Many Irrelevant Features. In *AAAI*.

Amodei, D. (2015). Deep Speech 2: End-to-End Speech Recognition in English and Mandarin. *CoRR*.

Andrade, I. M., Mayo, S. J., Kirkup, D., & Van Den Berg, C. (2008). Comparative morphology of populations of Monstera Adans. (Araceae) from natural forest fragments in Northeast Brazil using elliptic Fourier analysis of leaf outlines. *Kew Bulletin*, *63*(2), 193–211. doi:10.1007/s12225-008-9032-z

Arunpriya, C., & Thanamani, A. S. (2014). A novel leaf recognition technique for plant classification. *Int J Comput Eng Appl*, *4*, 42–55.

Assign Score - Prioritising Prevention of Cardiovascular Disease. (n.d.). Retrieved March 2015 from http://assign-score.com/

Athanasakis, D., Shawe-Taylor, J., & Fernandez-Reyes, D. (2013). *Principled Non-Linear Feature Selection*. arXiv preprint arXiv:1312.5869

Backes, A. R., Gonalves, W. N., Martinez, A. S., & Bruno, O. M. (2010). Texture analysis and classification using deterministic tourist walk. *Pattern Recognition, 43*(3), 685–694. doi:10.1016/j.patcog.2009.07.017

Bakhsh, A., Colvin, T. S., Jaynes, D. B., Kanwar, R. S., & Tim, U. (2000). Using Soil Attributes and GIS for Interpretation of Spatial Variability in Yield. *Transactions of the ASAE. American Society of Agricultural Engineers, 43*(3), 819–828. doi:10.13031/2013.2976

Banerjee, M., Mitra, S., & Banka, H. (2007). Evolutionary rough feature selection in gene expression data. *Systems, Man, and Cybernetics, Part C: Applications and Reviews, IEEE Transactions on, 37*, 622–632.

Basu, Ganguly, Mukhopadhyay, DiBiano, Karki, & Nemani. (2015). DeepSat – A Learning framework for Satellite Imagery. *CoRR*.

Belanche, L. A., & González, F. F. (2011). *Review and evaluation of feature selection algorithms in synthetic problems*. arXiv preprint arXiv:1101.2320

Bell, D. A., & Wang, H. (2000). A formalism for relevance and its application in feature subset selection. *Machine Learning, 41*(2), 175–195. doi:10.1023/A:1007612503587

Bellos, D. (2011). *Is that a fish in your ear? Translation and the meaning of everything*. New York: Faber and Faber.

Bicego, M., Castellani, U., & Murino, V. (2003, September). Using Hidden Markov Models and wavelets for face recognition. In *Image Analysis and Processing, 2003. Proceedings. 12th International Conference on* (pp. 52-56). IEEE. doi:10.1109/ICIAP.2003.1234024

Blunsom, P. (2004). Hidden Markov models. *Lecture Notes, 15*, 18-19.

Bourne, L. S. (1998). *Whither Urban Systems? A commentary on research needs and the marketing of ideas*. The Annual Meeting of the Canadian Regional Science Association, Ottawa, Canada.

Bradley, A. P. (1997). The use of the area under the ROC curve in the evaluation of machine learning algorithms. *Pattern Recognition, 30*(7), 1145–1159. doi:10.1016/S0031-3203(96)00142-2

Breiman, L. (1996). Bagging predictors. *Machine Learning, 24*(2), 123–140. doi:10.1007/BF00058655

Breiman, L. (2001). Random forests. *Machine Learning, 45*(1), 5–32. doi:10.1023/A:1010933404324

Breiman, L., Friedman, J., Stone, C. J., & Olshen, R. A. (1984). *Classification and regression trees*. CRC Press.

Brenden, M. L., Salakhutdinov, R., & Tenenbaum, J. B. (2015). Human-level concept learning through probabilistic program induction. *Science*, 1332. PMID:26659050

Brugger, F. (2011). *Mobile Applications in Agriculture*. Retrieved from http://www. gsma.com/mobilefordevelopment/wpcontent/uploads/2011/12/SyngentaReportonm-Agricultureabridgedwebversion.pdf

Bruno, O. M., deOliveira Plotze, R., Falvo, M., & deCastro, M. (2008). Fractal dimension applied to plant identification. *Inform. Sciences, 178*(12), 2722–2733. doi:10.1016/j.ins.2008.01.023

Bryll, R., Gutierrez-Osuna, R., & Quek, F. (2003). Attribute bagging: Improving accuracy of classifier ensembles by using random feature subsets. *Pattern Recognition, 36*(6), 1291–1302. doi:10.1016/S0031-3203(02)00121-8

Brynjolfsson, E., & McAfee, A. (2014). *The second machine age: Work, progress, and prosperity in a time of brilliant technologies*. Academic Press.

Buonomano, D. (2011). *Brain bugs: How the brain's flaws shape our lives*. New York: W.W. Norton.

Burghard, C. (2012). *Big Data and Analytics Key to Accountable Care Success*. I. H. Insights.

Calvo, R. A. (2010). Affect Detection: An interdisciplinary review of models, methods, and their applications. IEEE Transactions on Affective Computing, 1(1).

Candan, K. S., Kim, J. W., Nagarkar, P., Nagendra, M., & Yu, R. (2011). RanKloud: Scalable multimedia data processing in server clusters. *IEEE MultiMedia, 18*(1), 64–77. doi:10.1109/MMUL.2010.70

Caruana, R., & Freitag, D. (1994, July). Greedy Attribute Selection. In ICML (pp. 28-36). doi:10.1016/B978-1-55860-335-6.50012-X

Casanova, D., de Mesquita Sa Junior, J. J., & Bruno, O. M. (2009). Plant leaf identification using Gabor wavelets. *International Journal of Imaging Systems and Technology, 19*(3), 236–243. doi:10.1002/ima.20201

Chabris, C. F., & Simons, D. J. (2010). *The invisible gorilla: And other ways our intuitions deceive us*. New York: Crown.

Chathura, H. A., & Withanage, D. K. (2015) Computer assisted plant identification system for Android. Moratuwa engineering research conference, 148–153.

Chawla, N. V., Bowyer, K. W., Hall, L. O., & Kegelmeyer, W. P. (2011). SMOTE: Synthetic minority over-sampling technique. *Journal of Artificial Intelligence Research, 16*, 321–357.

Chelali, F. Z., & Djeradi, A. (2014, August). Face recognition system using neural network with Gabor and discrete wavelet transform parameterization. In *Soft Computing and Pattern Recognition (SoCPaR), 2014 6th International Conference of* (pp. 17-24). IEEE. doi:10.1109/SOCPAR.2014.7007975

Chien, J. T., & Wu, C. C. (2005). *Linear Discriminant Analysis*. LDA.

Clark, J. (2004). Identification of botanical specimens using artificial neural networks. *Proc. of the 2004 IEEE Symp. On Computational Intelligence in Bioinformatics and Computational Biology*, 87-94. Retrieved from http://ieeexplore.ieee.org/xpls/abs all.jsp?arnumber=1393938

Clark, J. Y. (2009). Neural networks and cluster analysis for unsupervised classification of cultivated species of Tilia (Malvaceae). *Botanical Journal of the Linnean Society, 159*(2), 300–314. doi:10.1111/j.1095-8339.2008.00891.x

Coffey, W. J. (1998). Urban systems research: An overview. *The Canadian Journal of Regional Science.*

Cook, N. R. (2008). Statistical evaluation of prognostic versus diagnostic models: Beyond the ROC curve. *Clinical Chemistry, 54*(1), 17–23. doi:10.1373/clinchem.2007.096529 PMID:18024533

Cope, J. S., Remagnino, P., Barman, S., & Wilkin, P. (2010). The extraction of venation from leaf images by evolved vein classifiers and ant colony algorithms. In Advanced Concepts for Intelligent Vision Systems (Vol. 6474 LNCS, pp. 135-144). doi:10.1007/978-3-642-17688-3_14

Cope, J. S., Corney, D., Clark, J. Y., Remagnino, P., & Wilkin, P. (2012). Plant species identification using digital morphometrics: A review. *Expert Systems with Applications, 39*(8), 7562–7573. doi:10.1016/j.eswa.2012.01.073

Corne, Knowles, & Oates. (2000). The pareto envelope-based selection algorithm for multi objective optimization. In Parallel Problem Solving from Nature PPSN VI, (pp. 839–848). Springer.

Cortes, C., & Vapnik, V. (1995). Support-vector networks. *Machine Learning, 20*(3), 273–297. doi:10.1007/BF00994018

Cover, T., & Hart, P. (1967). Nearest neighbor pattern classification, Information Theory. *IEEE Transactions on, 13*(1), 21–27.

Craven, M., DiPasquo, D., Freitag, D., McCallum, A., Mitchell, T., Nigam, K., & Slattery, S. (2000). Learning to construct knowledge bases from the World Wide Web. *Artificial Intelligence, 118*(1), 69–113. doi:10.1016/S0004-3702(00)00004-7

Crystal, D. (2012). *The Story of English in 100 Words*. New York: St. Martin's.

DAgostino, R. B., Russell, M. W., Huse, D. M., Ellison, R. C., Silbershatz, H., Wilson, P. W., & Hartz, S. C. (2000). Primary and subsequent coronary risk appraisal: New results from the Framingham study. *American Heart Journal, 139*(2), 272–281. doi:10.1016/S0002-8703(00)90236-9 PMID:10650300

Dash, M., & Liu, H. (1997). Feature selection for classification. *Intelligent Data Analysis, 1*(3), 131–156. doi:10.1016/S1088-467X(97)00008-5

Deb, K. (2001). *Multi-objective optimization using evolutionary algorithms* (Vol. 16). John Wiley & Sons.

Deb, K., Pratap, A., Agarwal, S., & Meyarivan, T. A. M. T. (2002). A fast and elitist multiobjective genetic algorithm: Nsga-ii. *IEEE Transactions on Evolutionary Computation, 6*(2), 182–197. doi:10.1109/4235.996017

Dehaene, S. (2014). *Consciousness and the brain: Deciphering how the brain codes our thoughts.* Academic Press.

Demšar, J. (2006). Statistical comparisons of classifiers over multiple data sets. *Journal of Machine Learning Research, 7*(Jan), 1–30.

Deng, L., & Yu, D. (2014). Deep Learning. *Signal Processing, 7,* 3–4.

Denworth, L. (2014). *I can hear you whisper: An intimate journey through the science of sound and language.* Academic Press.

Deutscher, G. (2005). *The unfolding of language: An evolutionary tour of mankind's greatest invention.* New York: Metropolitan Books.

Deutscher, G. (2010). *Through the language glass: Why the world looks different in other languages.* New York: Metropolitan Books/Henry Holt and Co.

Ding, C., & Peng, H. (2005). Minimum redundancy feature selection from microarray gene expression data. *Journal of Bioinformatics and Computational Biology, 3*(02), 185–205. doi:10.1142/S0219720005001004 PMID:15852500

Domingos, P. (2012). A few useful things to know about machine learning. *Communications of the ACM, 55.*

Duda, R. O., Hart, P. E., & Stork, D. G. (2001). *Pattern classification* (2nd ed.). New York: Academic Press.

Du, J. X., Huang, D. S., Wang, X. F., & Gu, X. (2006). Computer-aided plant species identification (CAPSI) based on leaf shape matching technique. *Transactions of the Institute of Measurement and Control, 28*(3), 275–285. doi:10.1191/0142331206tim176oa

Eagleman, D. (2015). *The Brain: The Story of You.* Academic Press.

Eddy, S. R. (1996). Hidden Markov models. *Current Opinion in Structural Biology, 6*(3), 361–365. doi:10.1016/S0959-440X(96)80056-X PMID:8804822

Empana, J. P., Ducimetiere, P., Arveiler, D., Ferrieres, J., Evans, A., & Ruidavets, J. B. et al.. (2003). Are the Framingham and PROCAM coronary heart disease risk functions applicable to different European populations? *European Heart Journal, 24*(21), 1903–1911. doi:10.1016/j.ehj.2003.09.002 PMID:14585248

Farfade, S. S., Saberian, M. J., & Li, L. J. (2015, June). Multi-view face detection using deep convolutional neural networks. In *Proceedings of the 5th ACM on International Conference on Multimedia Retrieval* (pp. 643-650). ACM. doi:10.1145/2671188.2749408

Fawcett, T. (2006). An introduction to ROC analysis. *Pattern Recognition Letters, 27*(8), 861–874. doi:10.1016/j.patrec.2005.10.010

Feraund, R., Bernier, O. J., Viallet, J. E., & Collobert, M. (2001). A fast and accurate face detector based on neural networks. *IEEE Transactions on Pattern Analysis and Machine Intelligence, 23*(1), 42–53. doi:10.1109/34.899945

Freund, Y., & Mason, L. (1999, June). The alternating decision tree learning algorithm. In ICML (Vol. 99, pp. 124-133). Academic Press.

Fu, H., & Chi, Z. (2006). Combined thresholding and neural network approach for vein pattern extraction from leaf images. *IEE Process-Vision, Image and Signal Process, 153*(6), 881–892. doi:10.1049/ip-vis:20060061

Funatsu. (2011). *Knowledge-Oriented Applications in Data Mining.* In Tech.

Furey, T. S., Cristianini, N., Duffy, N., Bednarski, D. W., Schummer, M., & Haussler, D. (2000). Support vector machine classification and validation of cancer tissue samples using microarray expression data. *Bioinformatics (Oxford, England), 16*(10), 906–914. doi:10.1093/bioinformatics/16.10.906 PMID:11120680

Gage, E., & Wilkin, P. (2008). A morphometric study of species delimitation in Sternbergialutea (Alliaceae, Amaryllidoideae) and its allies S. sicula and S. greuteriana. *Botanical Journal of the Linnean Society, 158*(3), 460–469. doi:10.1111/j.1095-8339.2008.00903.x

Gamon, M., Aue, A., Corston-Oliver, S., & Ringger, E. (n.d.). *Pulse: Mining customer opinions from free text.* Academic Press.

Gardete-Correia, L., Boavida, J. M., Raposo, J. F., Mesquita, A. C., Fona, C., Carvalho, R., & Massano-Cardoso, S. (2010). First diabetes prevalence study in Portugal: PREVADIAB study. *Diabetic Medicine, 27*(8), 879–881. doi:10.1111/j.1464-5491.2010.03017.x PMID:20653744

Ghorai, Mukherjee, Sengupta, & Dutta. (2011). Cancer classification from gene expression data by nppc ensemble. *Computational Biology and Bioinformatics, IEEE/ACM Transactions on, 8*(3), 659–671.

Gill, T. M. (2012). The central role of prognosis in clinical decision making. *Journal of the American Medical Association, 307*(2), 199–200. doi:10.1001/jama.2011.1992 PMID:22235093

Glodberg. (1989). Genetic algorithms in search, optimization, and machine learning. Addison Wesley.

Goatly, A. (2008). Metaphor as Resource for the Conceptualization and Expression of Emotion. *Workshop on Emotion, Metaphor, Ontology, and Terminology (EMOT).*

Goeau, H., Joly, A., & Bonnet, P. (2015). LifeClef plant identification task 2015. CLEF Working Notes 2015.

Goodfellow, I., Bengio, Y., & Courville, A. (2006). *Deep Learning.* Boston: MIT Press.

Gopal, S., Tang, X., Phillips, N., Nomack, M., Pasquaellar, V., & Pitts, J. (2016). Characterizing urban landscapes using fuzzy sets. *Computers, Environment and Urban Systems*, *57*, 212–223. doi:10.1016/j.compenvurbsys.2016.02.002

Gore, K., Lobo, S., & Doke, P. (2012). *GappaGoshti*: Digital inclusion for rural mass. In *2012 4th Int. Conf. on Communication Systems and Networks, COMSNETS 2012* (pp. 1-6). doi:10.1109/COMSNETS.2012.6151383

Grzymala-Busse, J. W., Stefanowski, J., & Wilk, S. (2005). A comparison of two approaches to data mining from imbalanced data. *Journal of Intelligent Manufacturing*, *16*(6), 565–573. doi:10.1007/s10845-005-4362-2

Gu, Q., & Li, S. Z. (2000). Combining feature optimization into neural network based face detection. In *Pattern Recognition, 2000. Proceedings. 15th International Conference on* (Vol. 2, pp. 814-817). IEEE.

Gu, Q., Li, Z., & Han, J. (2012). *Generalized fisher score for feature selection*. arXiv preprint arXiv:1202.3725

Gu, X., Du, J.-X., & Wang, X.-F. (2005). Leaf recognition based on the combination of wavelet transform and Gaussian interpolation. *Advances in Intelligent Computing*, 253-262. doi:2710.1007/11538059

Gupta, P., Doermann, D., & DeMenthon, D. (2002). Beam search for feature selection in automatic SVM defect classification. In *Pattern Recognition, 2002. Proceedings. 16th International Conference on* (Vol. 2, pp. 212-215). IEEE. doi:10.1109/ICPR.2002.1048275

Guyon, I., & Elisseeff, A. (2003). An introduction to variable and feature selection. *Journal of Machine Learning Research*, *3*, 1157–1182.

Hagan, M. T., Demuth, H. B., Beale, M. H., & De Jesús, O. (1996). *Neural network design* (Vol. 20). Boston: PWS Publishing Company.

Hagan, M. T., Demuth, H. B., & Beale, M. H. (1996). *Neural network design*. Boston: Pws Pub.

Hall, M. A. (1999). *Correlation-based feature selection for machine learning* (Doctoral dissertation). The University of Waikato.

Hall, M., Frank, E., Holmes, G., Pfahringer, B., Reutemann, P., & Witten, I. H. (2009). The WEKA data mining software: an update. *ACM SIGKDD Explorations Newsletter*, *11*(1), 10-18.

Han, J., & Kamber, M. (2006). *Data Mining: Concepts and Techniques*. Morgan Kaufmann Publishers.

Han, J., Kamber, M., & Pei, J. (2012). *Data mining concepts and techniques*. Waltham, MA: Morgan Kaufmann Publishers.

Hartigan, J. A., & Wong, M. A. (1979). Algorithm AS 136: A k-means clustering algorithm. *Journal of the Royal Statistical Society. Series C, Applied Statistics*, *28*(1), 100–108.

Hastie, T., Tibshirani, R., & Friedman, J. (2001). *The Elements of Statistical Learning: Data Mining, Inference, and Prediction*. New York: Springer. doi:10.1007/978-0-387-21606-5

He, Zhang, Ren, & Sun. (2015). Deep Residual Learning for Image Recognition. *CoRR.*

Hearn, D. J. (2009). Shape analysis for the automated identification of plants from images of leaves. *Taxon, 58*(3), 934–954.

Heartscore. (n.d.). Retrieved March 2015 from http://www.heartscore.org/Pages/welcome.aspx

Heinze, C., Goss, S., & Pearce, A. (1999). Plant recognition in military simulation: Incorporating machine learning with intelligent agents.*Proc. of IJCAI-99 Workshop on Team Behavior and Plan Recognition*, 53-64.

Hertzmann, A., & Fleet, D. (2010). *Machine Learning and Data Mining Lecture Notes*. Computer Science Department, University of Toronto.

Hinton & Salakhutdinov. (2006). Reducing the dimensionality of data with neural networks. *Science, 313*(5786).

Hinton, G. E., Osindero, S., & Teh, Y. W. (2006). A fast learning algorithm for deep belief nets. *Neural Computation, 18*(7), 1527–1554. doi:10.1162/neco.2006.18.7.1527 PMID:16764513

Hitchings, H. (2011). *The language wars: A history of proper English*. New York: Farrar, Straus and Giroux.

Hofstadter, D., & Sander, E. (2010). *Surfaces and essences*. Perseus Books Group.

Holand, S. M. (2008). *Principal components analysis (PCA)*. Athens, GA: Department of Geology, University of Georgia.

Hong, A., Gang, C., Jun-li, L., Chi, Z., & Zhang, D. (2004). A flower image retrieval method based on ROI feature. *Journal of Zhejiang University. Science, 5*(7), 764–772. doi:10.1631/jzus.2004.0764 PMID:15495304

Ho, S., Xie, M., & Goh, T. (2003). A study of the connectionist models for software reliability prediction. *Computers & Mathematics with Applications (Oxford, England), 46*(7), 1037–1045. doi:10.1016/S0898-1221(03)90117-9

Ho, T. K. (1998). The random subspace method for constructing decision forests, Pattern Analysis and Machine Intelligence. *IEEE Transactions on, 20*(8), 832–844.

Huang, J., Shao, X., & Wechsler, H. (1998, August). Face pose discrimination using support vector machines (SVM). In *Pattern Recognition, 1998. Proceedings. Fourteenth International Conference on* (Vol. 1, pp. 154-156). IEEE.

Huang, Yu, Liu, Sedra, & Weinberger. (2016). Deep Networks with Stochastic Depth. *CoRR.*

Huang, Z., Huang, D.-S., Du, J.-X., Quan, Z., & Gua, S.-B. (2006). Bark Classification Based on Contourlet Filter Features. In Intelligent Computing (pp. 1121-1126). Springer Berlin Heidelberg.

Huang, C. J. (2004). class prediction of cancer using probabilistic neural networks and relatice correlation metric. *Applied Artificial Intelligence: An Internaltional Journal, 18*(2), 117–128. doi:10.1080/08839510490278916

Huang, H., Qin, H., Hao, Z., & Lim, A. (2012). Example-based learning particle swarm optimization for continuous optimization. *Information Sciences, 182*(1), 125–138. doi:10.1016/j.ins.2010.10.018

Huang, Q., Jain, A. K., Stockman, G. C., & Smucker, A. J. M. (1992). Automatic Image Analysis of Plant Root Structures. In *11th IEEE IAPR Int. Conf. on Pattern Recognition* (pp. 569-572). doi:10.1109/ICPR.1992.201842

Huang, R., Su, C., Lang, F., & Du, M. (2010). Kernel Discriminant Locality Preserving Projections for Human Face Recognition. *Journal of Information & Computational Science, 7*(4), 925–931.

Iacoboni, M. (2008). *Mirroring people: The new science of how we connect with others*. New York: Farrar, Straus and Giroux.

INFARMED National Authority of Medicines and Health Products. (n.d.). Retrieved March 2015 from http://www.infarmed.pt/portal/page/portal/INFARMED

Izzat Din Abdul Aziz, M. H. H., Ismail, M. J., Mehat, M., & Haroon, N. S. (2009). Remote monitoring in agricultural greenhouse using wireless. *Int. J. Engg. Techlon, 9*(9), 35–43.

Jadhav, I. S., Gaikwad, V. T., & Patil, G. U. (2011). *Human Identification using Face and Voice Recognition 1*. Academic Press.

Jain, A., & Zongker, D. (1997). Feature selection: Evaluation, application, and small sample performance. *Pattern Analysis and Machine Intelligence. IEEE Transactions on, 19*(2), 153–158.

Jain, D. K., Tim, U., & Jolly, R. W. (1995). A spatial decision support system for livestock production planning and environmental management. *Applied Engineering in Agriculture, 11*(5), 711–719. doi:10.13031/2013.25795

Jassmann, T. J. (2015). *Mobile Leaf Classification Application Utilizing a Convolutional Neural Network* (Doctoral dissertation). Appalachian State University.

Jindal, N., & Kumar, V. (2013). Enhanced face recognition algorithm using pca with artificial neural networks. *International Journal of Advanced Research in Computer Science and Software Engineering, 3*(6).

Joachims, T. (1998). *Text categorization with support vector machines: Learning with many relevant features*. Springer Berlin Heidelberg.

John, G. H., & Langley, P. (1995, August). Estimating continuous distributions in Bayesian classifiers. In *Proceedings of the Eleventh conference on Uncertainty in artificial intelligence* (pp. 338-345). Morgan Kaufmann Publishers Inc.

Jolliffe, I. (2002). *Principal component analysis*. John Wiley & Sons, Ltd.

Jovanov, E., Gelabert, P., Adhami, R., Wheelock, B., & Adams, R. (1999, August). Real time Holter monitoring of biomedical signals. In DSP Technology and Education conference DSPS (Vol. 99, pp. 4-6). Academic Press.

Karunanithi, N., Whitley, D., & Malaiya, Y. (1992). Prediction of software reliability using connectionist models. *IEEE Transactions on Software Engineering, 18*(7), 563–574. doi:10.1109/32.148475

Kass, G. V. (1980). An exploratory technique for investigating large quantities of categorical data. *Applied Statistics, 29*(2), 119–127. doi:10.2307/2986296

Keller, F. (2002). *Naive Bayes Classifiers*. Connectionist and Statistical Language Processing, Course at Universität des Saarlandes.

Kelly, N., & Zetzsche, J. O. (2012). *Found in translation: How language shapes our lives and transforms the world*. New York: Perigee.

Kenneally, Kessler, & Topher. (2013). *Troubleshooting Enhanced Dictation in OS X Mavericks - CNET*. CNET.

Kenneally, C. (2007). *The first word: the search for the origins of language*. New York: Viking.

Kennedy, J. (1997). The particle swarm: social adaptation of knowledge. In *IEEE International Conference on Evolutionary Computation*, (pp. 303–308). doi:10.1109/ICEC.1997.592326

Kennedy, J., & Eberhart, R. (1995). Particle swarm optimization. In *Proc IEEE Int. Conf. On Neural Networks*, (pp. 1942–1948). doi:10.1109/ICNN.1995.488968

Khurshid, A. (2008). Introduction:*Affect Computing and Sentiment Analysis. Workshop on Emotion, Metaphor, Ontology, and Terminology (EMOT)*.

Kim, K. (n.d.). *Emotion modeling and machine learning in affective computing*. Unpublished manuscript.

Kim, S. M. (2011). *Recognizing emotions and sentiments in text* (Thesis). School of Electrical and Information Engineering, The University of Sydney.

Kim, K. I., Kim, J. H., & Jung, K. (2002). Face recognition using support vector machines with local correlation kernels. *International Journal of Pattern Recognition and Artificial Intelligence, 16*(01), 97–111. doi:10.1142/S0218001402001575

Kim, T., Bae, N.-J., Shin, C.-S., Park, J. W., Park, D., & Cho, Y.-Y. (2013). An Approach for a Self-Growing Agricultural Knowledge Cloud in Smart Agriculture. In *Multimedia and Ubiquitous Eng* (pp. 699–706). Springer. doi:10.1007/978-94-007-6738-6_86

Kiros, Zhu, Salakhutdinov, Zemel, Torralba, Urtasun, & Fidler. (2015). Skip-Thought Vectors. *CoRR*.

Knowles, J. D., & Corne, D. W. (2000). Approximating the nondominated front using the pareto archived evolution strategy. *Evolutionary Computation*, *8*(2), 149–172. doi:10.1162/106365600568167 PMID:10843519

Kohavi, R. (1995, August). A study of cross-validation and bootstrap for accuracy estimation and model selection. In IJCAI (Vol. 14, No. 2, pp. 1137-1145). Academic Press.

Kohavi, R., Sommerfield, D., & Dougherty, J. (1996, November). Data mining using 𝓂 𝓁 𝒸++ a machine learning library in c++. In *Tools with Artificial Intelligence, 1996.,Proceedings Eighth IEEE International Conference on* (pp. 234-245). IEEE.

Kohavi, R. (1995). The power of decision tables. *The Eighth European Conference on Machine Learning (ECML-95)*, 174-189.

Kohavi, R., & John, G. H. (1997). Wrappers for feature subset selection. *Artificial Intelligence*, *97*(1), 273–324. doi:10.1016/S0004-3702(97)00043-X

Krizhevsky, A., Sutskever, I., & Hinton, G. (2012). Imagenet classification with deep convolutional neural networks. In Advances in Neural Information Processing Systems. Urran Associates, Inc.

Kruse, O. M. O., Prats-Montalban, J. M., Indahl, U. G., Kvaal, K., Ferrer, A., & Futsaether, C. M. (2014). Pixel classification methods for identifying and quantifying leaf surface injury from digital images. *Computers and Electronics in Agriculture*, *108*, 155–165. doi:10.1016/j.compag.2014.07.010

Kuei, C., Yeu, H., & Tzai, L. (2008). A study of software reliability growth from the perspective of learning effects. *Reliability Engineering & System Safety*, *93*(10), 1410–1421. doi:10.1016/j.ress.2007.11.004

Kumar, N., Belhumeur, P. N., Biswas, A., Jacobs, D. W., Kress, W. J., Lopez, I. C., & Soares, J. V. B. (2012). Leafsnap: A computer vision system for automatic plant species identification. In Comput. Vision - ECCV 2012 (Vol. 7573 LNCS, pp. 502-516). doi: 36 doi:10.1007/978-3-642-33709-3

Kurakin, Goodfellow, & Bengio. (2016). Adversarial Examples in the Physical World. *CoRR*.

Ladha, L., & Deepa, T. (2011). Feature selection methods and algorithms. *International Journal on Computer Science and Engineering*, *3*(5).

Lan, G.-C., Lee, C.-H., Lee, Y.-Y., Tseng, V., Chin, C.-Y., Day, M.-L., & Wu, J.-S. et al. (2012November) Disease risk prediction by mining personalized health trend patterns: A case study on diabetes. In *2012 Conference on Technologies and Applications of Artificial Intelligence* (pp. 27-32). IEEE. doi:10.1109/TAAI.2012.53

Laumanns, Zitzler, & Thiele (2001). *Spea2: Improving the strength pareto evolutionary algorithm.* Academic Press.

LeCun, Y., Bengio, Y., & Hinton, G. (2015). Deep learning. *Nature*, *521*(7553), 436–444. doi:10.1038/nature14539 PMID:26017442

Lee, B. J., & Kim, J. Y. (2016). Identification of Type 2 Diabetes Risk Factors Using Phenotypes Consisting of Anthropometry and Triglycerides based on Machine Learning. *IEEE Journal of Biomedical and Health Informatics, 20*(1), 39-46.

Lee, M. S., & Moore, A. W. (2014, June). Efficient algorithms for minimizing cross validation error. In *Machine Learning Proceedings 1994:Proceedings of the Eighth International Conference* (p. 190). Morgan Kaufmann.

Lee, S. H., Chan, C. S., Wilkin, P., & Remagnino, P. (2015, September). Deep-Plant: Plant Identification with convolutional neural networks. In *Image Processing (ICIP), 2015 IEEE International Conference on* (pp. 452-456). IEEE.

Lee, C., & Chen, S. (2006). Classification of leaf images. *International Journal of Imaging Systems and Technology, 16*(1), 15–23. doi:10.1002/ima.20063

Lee, K., Joo, J., Yang, J., & Honavar, V. (2006). Experimental comparison of feature subset selection using GA and ACO algorithm. In *Advanced Data Mining and Applications* (pp. 465–472). Springer Berlin Heidelberg. doi:10.1007/11811305_51

Levin, R. I., Cohen, D., Frisbie, W., Selwyn, A. P., Barry, J., Deanfield, J. E., & Campbell, D. Q. et al. (1986). Potential for real-time processing of the continuously monitored electrocardiogram in the detection, quantitation, and intervention of silent myocardial ischemia. *Cardiology Clinics, 4*(4), 735–745. PMID:3096569

Levitin, D. J. (2014). *The organized mind: Thinking straight in the age of information overload.* Academic Press.

Lexer, C., Joseph, J., van Loo, M., Prenner, G., Heinze, B., Chase, M. W., & Kirkup, D. (2009). The use of digital image-based morphometrics to study the phenotypic mosaic in taxa with porous genomes. *Taxon*, 349–364.

Lieberman, M. D. (2013). *Social: Why our brains are wired to connect.* Academic Press.

Ling, H., Member, S., & Jacobs, D. W. (2007). Shape Classification Using the Inner-Distance. *IEEE Transactions on Pattern Analysis and Machine Intelligence, 29*(2), 286–299. doi:10.1109/TPAMI.2007.41 PMID:17170481

Liu, H., & Setiono, R. (1996, July). A probabilistic approach to feature selection-a filter solution. In ICML (Vol. 96, pp. 319-327).

Liu, Z., Zhou, J., & Jin, Z. (2010, August). Face recognition based on illumination adaptive LDA. In *Pattern Recognition (ICPR), 2010 20th International Conference on* (pp. 894-897). IEEE. doi:10.1109/ICPR.2010.225

Liu, H., & Motoda, H. (Eds.). (2007). *Computational methods of feature selection.* CRC Press.

Liu, J., Zhang, S., & Deng, S. (2009). A method of plant classification based on wavelet transforms and support vector machines. In *Emerging Intelligent Computing Technology and Applicat* (pp. 253–260). Springer Berlin Heidelberg.

Li, W.-S., Candan, K. S., & Hirata, K. (1997). SEMCOG: An Integration of SEMantics and COGnition- based Approaches for Image Retrieval. In *12th Annual Symp. on Applied Computing (SAC-97)*, (pp. 36-43). doi:10.1145/331697.331727

Li, W.-S., Seluk Candan, K., Hirata, K., & Hara, Y. (1998). Hierarchical image modeling for object-based media retrieval. *Data & Knowledge Engineering, 27*(2), 139–176. doi:10.1016/S0169-023X(97)00058-X

Li, Y., Chi, Z., & Feng, D. D. (2006). Leaf vein extraction using independent component analysis. In *IEEE Int. Conf. on Systems, Man and Cybernetics*, (pp. 3890-3894). doi:10.1109/ICSMC.2006.384738

Long, M., Cao, Y., Wang, J., & Jordan, M. I. (2015). *Learning Transferable Features with Deep Adaptation Networks*. ICML.

Lu, J., Plataniotis, K. N., & Venetsanopoulos, A. N. (2003). Face recognition using LDA-based algorithms. *IEEE Transactions on Neural Networks, 14*(1), 195–200. doi:10.1109/TNN.2002.806647 PMID:18238001

Lu, Y., Zeng, N., Liu, Y., & Zhang, N. (2015). A hybrid Wavelet Neural Network and Switching Particle Swarm Optimization algorithm for face direction recognition. *Neurocomputing, 155*, 219–224. doi:10.1016/j.neucom.2014.12.026

Lyu, M. R. (1999). *Handbook of Software Reliability Engineering*. McGraw Hill.

Ma, W. M. W., Zha, H. Z. H., Liu, J. L. J., Zhang, X. Z. X., & Xiang, B. X. B. (2008). Image-based plant modeling by knowing leaves from their apexes. In *2008 IEEE 19th Int. Conf. on Pattern Recognition*, (pp. 2-5). doi:10.1007/978-3-642-04070-2_29

MacLeod, N., Benfield, M., & Culverhouse, P. (2010). Time to automate identification. *Nature, 467*(7312), 154–155. doi:10.1038/467154a PMID:20829777

Maji, P., & Das, C. (2012). Relevant and significant supervised gene clusters for microarray cancer classification. *NanoBioscience. IEEE Transactions on, 11*(2), 161–168.

Malhotra, R., Singh, Y., & Kaur, A. (2009). Comparative analysis of regression and machine learning methods for predicting fault proneness models. *International Journal of Computer Applications in Technology, 35*(2), 183–193.

Mallah, C., Cope, J., & Orwell, J. (2013). Plant leaf classification using probabilistic integration of shape, texture and margin features. Signal Processing. *Pattern Recognition and Applications, 5*, 1.

Mamoshina, P., Vieira, A., Putin, E., & Zhavoronkov, A. (2016). Applications of deep learning in biomedicine. *Molecular Pharmaceutics, 13*(5), 1445–1454. doi:10.1021/acs.molpharmaceut.5b00982 PMID:27007977

Mao, K. Z. (2004). Orthogonal forward selection and backward elimination algorithms for feature subset selection. *Systems, Man, and Cybernetics, Part B: Cybernetics. IEEE Transactions on, 34*(1), 629–634.

Martínez, A. M., & Kak, A. C. (2001). Pca versus lda. *IEEE Transactions on Pattern Analysis and Machine Intelligence, 23*(2), 228–233. doi:10.1109/34.908974

Masaeli, M., Dy, J. G., & Fung, G. M. (2010). From transformation-based dimensionality reduction to feature selection. In *Proceedings of the 27th International Conference on Machine Learning (ICML-10)* (pp. 751-758).

McLellan, T., & Endler, J. A. (1998). The relative success of some methods for measuring and describing the shape of complex objects. *Systematic Biology, 47*(2), 264–281. doi:10.1080/106351598260914

Meade, C., & Parnell, J. (2003). Multivariate analysis of leaf shape patterns in Asian species of the Uvaria group (Annonaceae). *Botanical Journal of the Linnean Society, 143*(3), 231–242. doi:10.1046/j.1095-8339.2003.00223.x

Melville, R. (1937). The accurate definition of leaf shapes by rectangular coordinates. *Annals of Botany, 1*, 673–679.

Menotti, A., Puddu, P. E., & Lanti, M. (2000). Comparison of the Framingham risk function-based coronary chart with risk function from an Italian population study. *European Heart Journal, 21*(5), 365–370. doi:10.1053/euhj.1999.1864 PMID:10666350

Mikolov & Le. (2014). Distributed Representations of Sentences and Documents. *CoRR*.

Mikolov, T., Chen, K., Corrado, G. S., Dean, J., & Sutskever, I. (2013). Distributed representations of words and phrases and their compositionality. *Proceedings of NIPS*, 3111.

Mitra & Acharya. (2003). *Data Mining: Multimedia, Soft Computing and Bioinformatics*. New York: John Wiley & Sons.

Mitra, S., & Ghosh, S. (2012). Feature selection and clustering of gene expression profiles using biological knowledge. *Systems, Man, and Cybernetics, Part C: Applications and Reviews. IEEE Transactions on, 42*(6), 1590–1599.

Mohamad, M. S., Omatu, S., Deris, S., & Yoshioka, M. (2009). Particle swarm optimization for gene selection in classifying cancer classes. *Artificial Life and Robotics, 14*(1), 16–19. doi:10.1007/s10015-009-0712-z

Molina, L. C., Belanche, L., & Nebot, À. (2002). Feature selection algorithms: A survey and experimental evaluation. In *Data Mining, 2002. ICDM 2003. Proceedings. 2002 IEEE International Conference on* (pp. 306-313). IEEE. doi:10.1109/ICDM.2002.1183917

Morrish, N. J., Wang, S. L., Stevens, L. K., Fuller, J. H., & Keen, H. (2001). Mortality and causes of death in the WHO Multinational Study of Vascular Disease in Diabetes. *Diabetologia, 44*(2), S14–S21. doi:10.1007/PL00002934 PMID:11587045

Mosadeghi, R., Warnken, J., Tomlinson, R., & Mirfenderesk, H. (2015). Comparison of Fuzzy-AHP and AHP in a spatial multi-criteria decision making model for urban land-use planning. *Computers, Environment and Urban Systems, 49*, 54–65. doi:10.1016/j.compenvurbsys.2014.10.001

Mouine, S., Yahiaoui, I., & Verroust-Blondet, A. (2013). A Shape based Approach for Leaf Classification using Multiscale Triangular Representation. In *Process. of the 3rd ACM Conf. on Int. Conf. on multimedia retrieval*, (pp. 127134). ACM.

Mueller, J., & Lemke, F. (1999). Self-Organizing Data Mining: An Intelligent Approach to Extract Knowledge from Data. Academic Press.

Mullen, R. J., Monekosso, D., Barman, S., Remagnino, P., & Wilkin, P. (2008). Artificial ants to extract leaf outlines and primary venation patterns. In Ant Colony Optimization and Swarm Intelligence, (Vol. 5217 LNCS, pp. 251-258). = doi:10.1007/978-3-540-87527-7_24

Murphy, K.P. (n.d.). *Machine learning a probabilistic perspective*. The MIT Press.

Musa, D. (2009). *Software Reliability Engineering: More Reliable Software Faster and Cheaper* (2nd ed.). McGraw-Hill.

Mzoughi, O., Yahiaoui, I., Boujemaa, N., & Zagrouba, E. (2015). Semantic-based automatic structuring of leaf images for advanced plant species identification. *Multimedia Tools and Applicat.*, 1-32. doi:10.1007/s11042-015-2603-8

Nam, Y., Hwang, E., & Kim, D. (2008). A similarity-based leaf image retrieval scheme: Joining shape and venation features. *Computer Vision and Image Understanding*, *110*(2), 245–259. doi:10.1016/j.cviu.2007.08.002

Natho, G. (1959). Variationsbreite und Bastardbildung bei mitteleuropischen Birkensippen. *Repertorium Novarum Specierum Regni Vegetabilis*, *61*(3), 211–273. doi:10.1002/fedr.19590610304

Nefian, A. V., & Hayes III, M. H. (1998). Hidden Markov models for face recognition. *Choice, 1*, 6.

Nefian, A. V., & Hayes, M. H. (1998, October). Face detection and recognition using hidden Markov models. In *Image Processing, 1998. ICIP 98. Proceedings. 1998 International Conference on* (Vol. 1, pp. 141-145). IEEE. doi:10.1109/ICIP.1998.723445

Nefian, A., & Hayes, M. (1999, March). Face recognition using an embedded HMM. In *IEEE Conference on Audio and Video-based Biometric Person Authentication* (pp. 19-24). IEEE.

Neto, J. C., Meyer, G. E., Jones, D. D., & Samal, A. K. (2006). Plant species identification using Elliptic Fourier leaf shape analysis. *Computers and Electronics in Agriculture*, *50*(2), 121–134. doi:10.1016/j.compag.2005.09.004

Nicolelis, M. A. (2011). *Beyond boundaries: the new neuroscience of connecting brains with machines--and how it will change our lives*. New York: Times Books/Henry Holt and Co.

Nilsback, M. E., & Zisserman, A. (2010). Delving deeper into the whorl of flower segmentation. *Image and Vision Computing*, *28*(6), 10491062. doi:10.1016/j.imavis.2009.10.001

Norgvig, P. (2013, October 25). *2013 Family Weekend Keynote: "Live and Learn: How Big Data and Machine Learning Power the Internet".* Retrieved January 07, 2017, from https://www.youtube.com/watch?v=vVprmVsCV_k

Orphanou, K., Stassopoulou, A., & Keravnou, E. (2016). DBN-Extended: A Dynamic Bayesian Network Model Extended With Temporal Abstractions for Coronary Heart Disease Prognosis. *IEEE Journal of Biomedical and Health Informatics, 20*(3), 944-952.

Orr, G., Pettersson-Yeo, W., Marquand, A. F., Sartori, G., & Mechelli, A. (2012). Using Support Vector Machine to identify imaging biomarkers of neurological and psychiatric disease: A critical review. *Neuroscience and Biobehavioral Reviews, 36*(4), 1140–1152. doi:10.1016/j.neubiorev.2012.01.004 PMID:22305994

Pande, A., Jagyasi, B. G., & Choudhuri, R. (2009). Late Blight Forecast Using Mobile Phone Based Agro Advisory System. In Pattern Recognition and Machine Intelligence, (pp. 609-614). Springer Berlin Heidelberg. doi:10.1007/978-3-642-11164-8_99

Pang, Y., Zhang, L., Li, M., Liu, Z., & Ma, W. (2004, November). A novel Gabor-LDA based face recognition method. In *Pacific-Rim Conference on Multimedia* (pp. 352-358). Springer Berlin Heidelberg. doi:10.1007/978-3-540-30541-5_44

Park, J., Hwang, E., & Nam, Y. (2008). Utilizing venation features for efficient leaf image retrieval. *Journal of Systems and Software, 81*(1), 71–82. doi:10.1016/j.jss.2007.05.001

Pauwels, E. J., de Zeeuw, P. M., & Ranguelova, E. B. (2009). Computer-assisted tree taxonomy by automated image recognition. Eng. *Applied Artificial Intelligence, 22*(1), 26–31. doi:10.1016/j.engappai.2008.04.017

Peng, H., Zhang, C., & Bian, Z. (1998, August). A fully automated face recognition system under different conditions. In *Pattern Recognition, 1998. Proceedings. Fourteenth International Conference on* (Vol. 2, pp. 1223-1225). IEEE.

Peng, H., Long, F., & Ding, C. (2005). Feature selection based on mutual information criteria of max-dependency, max-relevance, and min-redundancy. *Pattern Analysis and Machine Intelligence. IEEE Transactions on, 27*(8), 1226–1238.

Phillips, P. J. (1998). *Support vector machines applied to face recognition* (Vol. 285). US Department of Commerce, Technology Administration, National Institute of Standards and Technology.

Pimentel, A., Gomes, R., Olstad, B. H., & Gamboa, H. (2015). A New Tool for the Automatic Detection of Muscular Voluntary Contractions in the Analysis of Electromyographic Signals. *Interacting with Computers, 27*(5), 492–499. doi:10.1093/iwc/iwv008

Plant Glossary. (2009). Retrieved April 12, 2015, from http://www.vplants.org/plants/glossary/index.html

Platt, J. (1998). *Sequential minimal optimization: A fast algorithm for training support vector machines.* Academic Press.

Pogorelc, B., Bosni, Z., & Gams, M. (2012). Automatic recognition of gait-related health problems in the elderly using machine learning. *Multimedia Tools and Applications*, *58*(2), 333–354. doi:10.1007/s11042-011-0786-1

Prasad, S., Kudiri, K. M., & Tripathi, R. C. (2011). Relative sub-image based features for leaf recognition using support vector machine. In *Proceedings of the 2011 Int. Conf. on Commun., Computing & Security*, (pp. 343-346). Retrieved from doi:10.1145/1947940.1948012

Prasad, S., Kumar, P. S., & Ghosh, D. (2013b). Mobile Plant Species Classification: A Low Computational Approach. In *Process. of the 2013 IEEE Second Int. Conf. on Image Inform. Process.*, (pp. 405-409). doi:10.1109/ICIIP.2013.6707624

Prasad, S., Kumar, P. S., & Ghosh, D. (2015). Agriculture-as-a-Service. *IEEE Potentials*.

Prasad, S., Kumar, P., & Tripathi, R. C. (2011). Plant leaf species identification using curvelet transform. In *2011 2nd Int. Conf. on Comput. and Communication Technology (ICCCT)*, (pp. 646-652). IEEE. doi:10.1109/ICCCT.2011.6075212

Prasad, S., Kumar, P. S., & Ghosh, D. (2013a). *AgroMobile*: A Cloud-Based Framework for Agriculturists on Mobile Platform. *Int. J. of Advanced Sci. and Technology*, *59*, 41–52. doi:10.14257/ijast.2013.59.04

Prasad, S., Kumar, P. S., & Ghosh, D. (2016a). An efficient low vision plant leaf shape identification system for smart phones. *Multimedia Tools and Applications*, 1–25.

Prasad, S., Kumar, S. P., & Ghosh, D. (2014). Energy Efficient Mobile Vision System for Plant Leaf Disease Identification. In *IEEE Wireless Commun. and Networking Conf. (WCNC)*, (pp. 3356-3361). doi:10.1109/WCNC.2014.6953083

Prasad, S., Peddoju, S. K., & Ghosh, D. (2016b). Multi-resolution mobile vision system for plant leaf disease diagnosis. Signal. *Image and Video Processing*, *10*(2), 379–388. doi:10.1007/s11760-015-0751-y

QRISK - Cardiovascular Disease Risk Calculator. (n.d.). Retrieved March 2015 from http://www.qrisk.org/

Quinlan, J. R. (1996). Bagging, boosting, and C4. 5. AAAI/IAAI, 1, 725-730.

Quinlan, R. (2004). *Data mining tools See5 and C5*. Academic Press.

Quinlan, J. R. (1996). Learning decision tree classifiers. *ACM Computing Surveys*, *28*(1), 71–72. doi:10.1145/234313.234346

Quinlan, J. R. (2014). *C4. 5: programs for machine learning*. Elsevier.

Raghupathi, W. (2016). Data Mining in Healthcare. *Healthcare Informatics: Improving Efficiency Through Technology, Analytics, and Management*, 353.

Raj, K., & Ravi, V. (2008). Software reliability prediction by using soft computing techniques. *Journal of Systems and Software*, 576–583. doi:10.1016/jss.2007.05.005

Randall, J. E. (1998). *Reflections on Urban Systems Research.* The Annual Meeting of the Canadian Regional Science Association, Ottawa, Canada.

Reinartz, T. (1999). *Focusing solutions for data mining: analytical studies and experimental results in real-world domains.* Springer-Verlag. doi:10.1007/3-540-48316-0

Revenaz, A., Ruggeri, M., & Martelli, M. (2010). Wireless communication protocol for agricultural machines synchronization and fleet management. In *IEEE Int. Symp. on Industrial Electron,* (pp. 3498-3504). doi:10.1109/ISIE.2010.5637476

Reyes, A. K., Caicedo, J. C., & Camargo, J. E. (2015). Fine-tuning deep convolutional networks for plant recognition. Working notes of CLEF 2015 conference.

Ribeiro, B., & Lopes, N. (2011). Deep belief networks for financial prediction. *International Conference on Neural Information Processing.* Springer. doi:10.1007/978-3-642-24965-5_86

Rish, I. (2001, August). An empirical study of the naive Bayes classifier. In IJCAI 2001 Workshop on Empirical Methods in Artificial Intelligence (Vol. 3, No. 22, pp. 41-46). IBM .

Robnik-Šikonja, M., & Kononenko, I. (2003). Theoretical and empirical analysis of ReliefF and RReliefF. *Machine Learning, 53*(1-2), 23–69. doi:10.1023/A:1025667309714

Ross, Q. (1993). *C4.5: Programs for Machine Learning.* San Mateo, CA: Morgan Kaufman Publishers.

Rowley, H. A., Baluja, S., & Kanade, T. (1998, June). Rotation invariant neural network-based face detection. In *Computer Vision and Pattern Recognition, 1998. Proceedings. 1998 IEEE Computer Society Conference on* (pp. 38-44). IEEE.

Rowley, H. A., Baluja, S., & Kanade, T. (1998). Neural network-based face detection. *IEEE Transactions on Pattern Analysis and Machine Intelligence, 20*(1), 23–38. doi:10.1109/34.655647

RoyChowdhury, A., Lin, T. Y., Maji, S., & Learned-Miller, E. (2015). *Face Identification with Bilinear CNNs.* arXiv preprint arXiv:1506.01342

Rumelhart, D. E., Smolensky, P., McClelland, J. L., & Hinton, G. (1986). Parallel distributed models of schemata and sequential thought processes. In *Psychological and Biological Models* (pp. 5–57). Cambridge, MA: MIT Press.

Rumpunen, K., & Bartish, I. V. (2002). Comparison of differentiation estimates based on morphometric and molecular data, exemplified by various leaf shape descriptors and RAPDs in the genus Chaenomeles (Rosaceae). *Taxon, 51*(1), 69–82. doi:10.2307/1554964

Sabourin, J. L., & Lester, J. (2014). Affect and engagement in game-based learning environments. IEEE Transactions on Affective Computing, 5(1).

Sacks, O. (2007). *Musicophilia: Tales of music and the brain.* New York: Alfred A. Knopf.

Saeys, Y., Inza, I., & Larrañaga, P. (2007). A review of feature selection techniques in bioinformatics. *Bioinformatics, 23*(19), 2507-2517.

Sahoolizadeh, A. H., Heidari, B. Z., & Dehghani, C. H. (2008). A new face recognition method using PCA, LDA and neural network. *International Journal on Computer Science and Engineering*, *2*(4), 218–223.

Sakthivel, S., & Lakshmipathi, R. (2010). Enhancing face recognition using improved dimensionality reduction and feature extraction algorithms—an evaluation with ORL database. *International Journal of Engineering Science and Technology*, *2*(6), 2288–2295.

Salford Predictive Modelling System. (n.d.). Retrieved from http//www.salford-systems.com

Samaria, F., & Young, S. (1994). HMM-based architecture for face identification. *Image and Vision Computing*, *12*(8), 537–543. doi:10.1016/0262-8856(94)90007-8

Schalkoff, R. J. (1997). *Artificial neural networks*. New York: McGraw-Hill.

Schmidhuber, J. (2015). Deep learning in neural networks: An overview. *Neural Networks*, *61*, 85–117. doi:10.1016/j.neunet.2014.09.003 PMID:25462637

Schneider, C. K. (1912). *Illustriertes Handbuchder Laubholzkunde*. Ripol Klassik.

Scotland, R. W., & Wortley, A. H. (2003). How many species of seed plants are there? *Taxon*, *52*(1), 101–104. doi:10.2307/3647306

Scott, E., & Christian, L. (1991). *The Cascade-Correlation Learning Architecture. CMU-CS-90-100*. School of Computer Science Carnegie Mellon University Pittsburgh.

Sderkvist, O. J. O. (2001). *Computer Vision Classification of Leaves from Swedish Trees*. Academic Press.

Sewell, M. (2007). *Feature selection*. Retrieved from http://machine-learning. martinsewell. com/feature-selection

Shaw, J. E., Sicree, R. A., & Zimmet, P. Z. (2010). Global estimates of the prevalence of diabetes for 2010 and 2030. *Diabetes Research and Clinical Practice*, *87*(1), 4–14. doi:10.1016/j.diabres.2009.10.007 PMID:19896746

Shermina, J., & Vasudevan, V. (2010). An Efficient Face recognition System Based on Fusion of MPCA and LPP. *American Journal of Scientific Research*, 6-19.

Sherrod, P. H. (2003). *DTReg predictive modeling software*. Available at http://www.dtreg.com

Shinde, S., Piplani, D., Srinivasan, K., Singh, D., Sharma, R., & Mohnaty, P. (2014). *mKRISHI* Simplification Of IVR Based Services For Rural Community. In *Process. of the India HCI2014 Conf. on Human Comput. Interaction* (p. 154). ACM.

Shi, Y., & Eberhart, R. (1998). A modified particle swarm optimizer.*Proc. IEEE Int. Conf. On Evolutionary Computation*, 69–73.

Singh & Kumar. (2010). Application of feed-forward networks for software reliability prediction. *ACM SIGSOFT Software Engineering Notes*, *35*(5), 1-6. DOI: 10.1145/1838687.1838709

Singh, Y., & Kumar, P. (2010). Prediction of Software Reliability using Feed Forward Neural Networks. *Proceedings of Computational Intelligence and Software Engineering (CiSE), 2010International Conference*. doi:10.1109/CISE.2010.5677251

Singh, Y., Kaur, A., & Malhotra, R. (2009). Application of support vector machine to predict fault prone classes. *ACM SIGSOFT Software Engineering Notes, 34*(1). http://doi.acm.org/10.1145/1457516.1457529, 2009.

Singh, Y., & Kumar, P. (2010). A software reliability growth model for three-tier client-server system. *International Journal of Computers and Applications, 1*(13), 9–16. doi:10.5120/289-451

Singh, Y., & Kumar, P. (2010). Determination of software release instant of three-tier client server software system. *International Journal of Software Engineering, 1*(3), 51–62.

Sitte, R. (1999). Comparison of software reliability growth predictions: Neural Networks vs. Parametric Recalibration. *IEEE Transactions on Reliability, 48*(3), 285–291. doi:10.1109/24.799900

Sivanandam, S. N., & Deepa, S. N. (2014). *Principles of soft computing*. New Delhi: Wiley India Pvt. Ltd.

Skowron & Rauszer. (1992). The discernibility matrices and functions in information systems. In I. D. Support (Ed.), *Theory and Decision Library* (Vol. 11, pp. 331–362). Springer Netherlands.

Sleep Talking Causes and Treatments. (n.d.). Retrieved January 07, 2017, from http://www.webmd.com/sleep-disorders/talking-in-your-sleep#1

Software Life Cycle Empirical/Experience Database (SLED). (n.d.). Retrieved from http://www.dacs.org

Somol, P., Pudil, P., Novovičová, J., & Paclık, P. (1999). Adaptive floating search methods in feature selection. *Pattern Recognition Letters, 20*(11), 1157–1163. doi:10.1016/S0167-8655(99)00083-5

Song, Q., Ni, J., & Wang, G. (2013). A fast clustering-based feature subset selection algorithm for high-dimensional data. *Knowledge and Data Engineering. IEEE Transactions on, 25*(1), 1–14.

Srivastava, R. K., Greff, K., & Schmidhuber, J. (2015). *Highway network*. arXiv preprint arXiv:1505.00387

Srivastava, Sharma, & Singh. (2014). Empirical Analysis of Supervised and Unsupervised Filter Based Feature Selection Methods for Breast Cancer Classification from Digital Mammograms. *International Journal of Computers and Applications, 88*(8).

Stibel, J. M. (2013). *Breakpoint: Why the web will implode, search will be obsolete, and everything else you need to know about technology is in your brain*. Academic Press.

Sünderhauf, N., McCool, C., Upcroft, B., & Perez, T. (2014). Fine-Grained Plant Classification Using Convolutional Neural Networks for Feature Extraction. In CLEF (Working Notes) (pp. 756-762).

Suskind, D., Suskind, B., & Lewinter-Suskind, L. (2015). *Thirty million words: Building a child's brain: tune in, talk more, take turns.* Academic Press.

Sutskever, I., Vinyals, O., & Le, Q. (2014). Sequence to sequence learning with neural networks. *Advances in Neural Information Processing Systems.*

Swaab, D. F. (2014). *We are our brains: A neurobiography of the brain, from the womb, Talking in Your Sleep.* Academic Press.

Tao, J., & Tan, T. (2005). Affective computing: A review. LNCS, 3784, 981 – 995.

Tao, Y., Xia, Y., Xu, T., & Chi, X. (2010). Research Progress of the Scale Invariant Feature Transform (SIFT) Descriptors. *Journal of Convergence Information Technology, 5*(1), 116–121. doi:10.4156/jcit.vol5.issue1.13

Teng, C. H., Kuo, Y. T., & Chen, Y. S. (2009). Leaf segmentation, its 3D position estimation and leaf classification from a few images with very close viewpoints. In *Image Analysis and Recognition* (pp. 937–946). Springer Berlin Heidelberg. doi:10.1007/978-3-642-02611-9_92

Terrillon, J. C., McReynolds, D., Sadek, M., Sheng, Y., & Akamatsu, S. (2000). Invariant neural-network based face detection with orthogonal Fourier-Mellin moments. In *Pattern Recognition, 2000. Proceedings. 15th International Conference on* (Vol. 2, pp. 993-1000). IEEE. doi:10.1109/ICPR.2000.906242

Tim, U. S. (1995). The application of GIS in environmental health sciences: Opportunities and limitations. *Environmental Research, 71*(2), 75–88. doi:10.1006/enrs.1995.1069 PMID:8977616

Tou & Gonz'alez. (1994). *Pattern recognition principles.* Addison Wesley.

Toygar, O., & Acan, A. (2003). Face recognition using PCA, LDA and ICA approaches on colored images. *Journal of Electrical & Electronics Engineering, 3*(1), 735-743.

Truss, L. (2004). *Eats, shoots & leaves: The zero tolerance approach to punctuation.* New York: Gotham Books.

Vellidis, G., Garrick, V., Pocknee, S., Perry, C., Kvien, C., & Tucker, M. (2007). How Wireless Will Change Agriculture. *Precision Agriculture, 7,* 57–67.

Venugopalan, Xu, Donahue, Rohrbach, Mooney, & Saenko. (2015). Translating Videos to Natural Language Using Deep Recurrent Neural Networks. *CoRR.*

Vieira, A., & Barradas, N. (2003). A training algorithm for classification of high-dimensional data. *Neurocomputing, 50,* 461–472. doi:10.1016/S0925-2312(02)00635-5

Vinyals & Le. (2015). A Neural Conversational Model. *CoRR.*

Walia, E. (2008, May). Face recognition using improved fast PCA algorithm. In Image and Signal Processing, 2008. CISP'08. Congress on (Vol. 1, pp. 554-558). IEEE.

Wang, B., Brown, D., Gao, Y., & La Salle, J. (2015). MARCH: Multiscale-arch-height description for mobile retrieval of leaf images. *Inform. Sciences*, *302*, 132–148. doi:10.1016/j.ins.2014.07.028

Wang, Z., Chi, Z., & Feng, D. (2003). Shape based leaf image retrieval. IEE Process. -. *Vision, Image, and Signal Process.*, *150*(1), 34. doi:10.1049/ip-vis:20030160

Wang, Z., Li, H., Zhu, Y., & Xu, T. (2016). Review of Plant Identification Based on Image Processing. *Archives of Computational Methods in Engineering*, 1–18.

Warren, D. (1997). Automated leaf shape description for variety testing in chrysanthemums. In *IET 6th Int. Conf. on Image Process. and its Applicat.* (pp. 497 - 501). doi:10.1049/cp:19970943

Wen, F., Zhou, J., & Zhang, C. (1999). LLM neural networks and compensation for light condition based color face detection. *Journal-Tsinghua University*, *39*, 37–40.

White, S. M., Marino, D. M., & Feiner, S. (2006). *LeafView*: A User Interface for Automated Botanical Species Identification and Data Collection. In *ACM UIST 2006 Conf. Companion*, (pp. 1-2). Montreux, Switzerland: ACM.

White, S. M., Marino, D., & Feiner, S. (2007). Designing a mobile user interface for automated species identification. In Human Factors in Computing Systems, CHI'07, (pp. 291-294). doi:10.1145/1240624.1240672

White, S., Feiner, S., & Kopylec, J. (2006). Virtual vouchers: Prototyping a mobile augmented reality user interface for botanical species identification. In *Process* (p. 133). IEEE Virtual Reality. doi:10.1109/VR.2006.145

WHO. (n.d.). Retrieved January 2015 from http://www.who.int/en/

Witten, I., & Frank, E. (2011). Data Mining: Practical Machine Learning Tools and Techniques with Java Implementations (3rd ed.). Morgan Kaufman.

Witten, I. H., Frank, E., & Hall, M. A. (2011). *Data Mining: Practical Machine Learning Tools and Techniques*. Elsevier.

Wold, S., Esbensen, K., & Geladi, P. (1987). Principal component analysis. *Chemometrics and Intelligent Laboratory Systems*, *2*(1-3), 37–52. doi:10.1016/0169-7439(87)80084-9

Worster, A., Fan, J., & Upadhye, S. (2006). Understanding receiver operating characteristic (ROC) curves. *Canadian Journal of Emergency Medical Care*, *8*(1), 19–20. doi:10.1017/S1481803500013336 PMID:17175625

Wu, S. G., Bao, F. S., Xu, E. Y., Wang, Y., Chang, Y., & Xiang, Q. (2007). A Leaf Recognition Algorithm for Plant Classification Using Probabilistic Neural Network. In *Int. Symp. on Signal Process. and Inform. Technology,* (pp. 11-16). doi:10.1109/ISSPIT.2007.4458016

Yagoda, B. (2006). *When you catch an adjective, kill it: The parts of speech for better and/or worse*. New York: Broadway Books.

Yanikoglu, B., Aptoula, E., & Tirkaz, C. (2014). Automatic plant identification from photographs. *Machine Vision and Applications, 25*(6), 1369–1383. doi:10.1007/s00138-014-0612-7

Ye, L., & Keogh, E. (2009). Time series shapelets: a new primitive for data mining. *Process. of the 15th ACM SIGKDD Int.Conf. on Knowledge Discovery and Data Mining*, 947-956. doi:10.1145/1557019.1557122

Yoon, K. S., Ham, Y. K., & Park, R. H. (1998). Hybrid approaches to frontal view face recognition using the Hidden Markov Model and Neural Network. *Pattern Recognition, 31*(3), 283–293. doi:10.1016/S0031-3203(97)00052-6

Yoshioka, Y., Iwata, H., Ohsawa, R., & Ninomiya, S. (2004). Analysis of petal shape variation of Primula sieboldii by elliptic Fourier descriptors and principal component analysis. *Annals of Botany, 94*(5), 657–664. doi:10.1093/aob/mch190 PMID:15374833

Yu, L., & Liu, H. (2003, August). Feature selection for high-dimensional data: A fast correlation-based filter solution. In ICML (Vol. 3, pp. 856-863).

Yu, D., Deng, L., & Yu, D. (2014). *Deep Learning Methods and Applications*. Foundations and Trends in Signal Processing.

Zeng, G., Birchfield, S. T., & Wells, C. E. (2010). Rapid automated detection of roots in minirhizotron images. *Machine Vision and Applications, 21*(3), 309–317. doi:10.1007/s00138-008-0179-2

Zhao, Z.-Q., Ma, L.-H., Cheung, Y., Wu, X., Tang, Y., & Chen, C. L. P. (2015). *ApLeaf*: An efficient android-based plant leaf identification system. *Neurocomputing, 151*, 1112–1119. doi:10.1016/j.neucom.2014.02.077

Zheng, J. (2009). Predicting software reliability with neural network ensembles. *Expert Systems with Applications, 36*(2), 216–222. doi:10.1016/j.eswa.2007.12.029

Zio, E. (2016). Challenges in the vulnerability and risk analysis of critical infrastructures. *Reliability Engineering & System Safety, 152*, 137–150. doi:10.1016/j.ress.2016.02.009

Zitzler, E., & Thiele, L. (1999). Multiobjective evolutionary algorithms: A comparative case study and the strength pareto approach. *Evolutionary Computation. IEEE Transactions on, 3*(4), 257–271.

Zulkifli, Z., Saad, P., & Mohtar, I. A. (2011). Plant leaf identification using moment invariants & General Regression Neural Network. In *2011 11th Int.Conf. on Hybrid Intelligent Systems (HIS)*, (pp. 430-435). doi:10.1109/HIS.2011.6122144

About the Contributors

Pradeep Kumar is Associate Professor in the Department of Computer Science & Information Technology at Maulana Azad National Urdu University, Hyderabad, India. He received his Master's degree in Computer Technology and Applications from Delhi Technological University, formerly Delhi College of Engineering, Delhi University. He completed his Ph.D. from the University School of Information & Communication Technology (USICT), Guru Gobind Singh Indraprastha University (GGSIPU), Delhi. His research interests include software reliability engineering, models for software metrics, machine learning, neural network modeling and soft computing. He has more than 25 publications in journals of international repute including national journals, conferences and proceedings of the international conferences. He is a Member of Association for Computing Machines (ACM), India, Member of Computer Science Teachers Association (CSTA), USA, Senior Member of International Association of Engineers (IAENG), Member of International Association of Computer Science and Information Technology (IACSIT), Singapore and Senior member of Universal Association of Computer and Electronics Engineers (UACEE). He is a member of editorial board for various national and international journals in the field of software engineering and program committee member/reviewer for several international conferences.

* * *

Isa Maria Almeida was born in Vila Viçosa (Alentejo, Portugal). She has lived in Lisbon since 2005. Degree in Cardiopneumology (2005) Masters Degree in Cardiovascular Rehabilitation (2012). She worked for 11 years as a Trainer, Rescue Worker and Volunteer Coordinator.

Hugo Gamboa is an Assistant Professor at the Physics Department of Faculdade de Ciências e Tecnologia of Universidade Nova de Lisboa and a member of LIBPHYS. He founded Plux in 2007 a company devoted to bisignals instrumentation and has grown the company from an individual research project to product medical device company with growing international sales and research seeking second round of financing. He received a PhD in Electrical and Computer Engineering from Instituto Superior Técnico, Technical University of Lisbon. His thesis entitled "Multi-Modal Behavioral Biometrics Based on HCI and Electrophysiology" presents new behavioral biometrics modalities which are an important contribute for the state-of-the-art in the field.). In recognition of his work by the European Biometric Forum, he was among the three finalists of the EBF Biometric Research Award 2007. In 2008 he was the winner of the Portuguese National Award "Futuras Promessas" ISA/Millennium BCP, granted to the best PhD thesis on Physics, Electronics, Informatics or Biomedical Engineering fields.

Akhouri Pramod Krishna, with long working experience in academics and research, is the Professor and Head, Department of Remote Sensing at BIT Mesra, India. His major domain of work includes remote sensing and geoinformatics application areas such as natural resource management, urban system research, disaster management and cryospheric research related to climate change.

Pedro Matos was born in Lisbon, Portugal, in 1955, received his MD degree in 1978 and has been a Cardiologist since 1988.

Alok Bhushan Mukherjee is currently pursuing PhD in Remote Sensing from Birla Institute of Technology, Mesra, Ranchi. He earlier had academic qualifications in Mathematics (Hons.), Information Science (M.Sc), and M-tech (Remote Sensing) respectively. His research interests span across various fields such as uncertainty modelling, sensitivity analysis, urban sciences, and cognitive computing.

Nilanchal Patel is presently Professor in the Department of Remote Sensing at the Birla Institute of Technology Mesra, Ranchi, India. He obtained his Ph.D. in Remote Sensing from Indian Institute of Technology Kanpur in 1992. Subsequently he served as a Senior Lecturer at Indian Institute of Technology Delhi and as a Scientist (Fellow) at National Environmental Engineering Research Institute, Nagpur. He is in the Editorial Board of several international journals including the Arabian Journal of Geosciences (Springer), The International Journal of Sustainable Development & World Ecology (Taylor & Francis), Journal of Forestry Research (Springer) and Journal of Earth Sciences and Climate Change (USA). He has published about 60 papers in various international journals and conferences. He has visited the University of Nova, Lisbon as a Visiting Scholar, Aalborg University, Denmark as a Visiting Professor, University of Aveiro, Portugal as a Visiting Scholar, Institute of Geographical Studies and Natural Resources Research, Chinese Academy of Sciences, Beijing as a Visiting Scientist, University of Poitiers, France as a Visiting

Scholar and the University of Cape Town as a Visiting Professor. His major areas of research comprise Environmental Remote Sensing and GIS, Urbanization, Traffic Congestion and Road Network Analysis, Land Degradation, Desertification, Natural Hazards, Climate Change and Glacier and Snow Dynamics, Landuse and Landcover Change, Pattern Recognition and Image Processing etc. He is a member of the Consortium of the European Landuse Institute (ELI). He is interested in interdisciplinary and collaborative research from across the globe. Besides he is a protagonist of the environmental conservation and human peace and development.

Angela Pimentel came to Lisbon, Portugal in 2007 to join the Faculty of Science and Technology from New University of Lisbon where she fulfilled a bachelor and master degree in Biomedical Engineering. In her master thesis she developed an algorithm for the characterization of behavioural models of Parkinson's disease using a biosensor, which were developed in collaboration with PLUX – Wireless Biosignals, S. A. and with Instituto de Medicina Molecular in Lisbon. She did 2 years of Phd in Biomedical Engineering at the Faculty of Science and Technology in collaboration with APDP - Associação Protectora dos Diabéticos de Portugal. Her main objectives were to use machine learning algorithms in diabetes area. In 2015 she joined BNP Paribas as a Data Scientist where she still continues to work in the machine learning area.

Shitala Prasad joined NTU Singapore as a Research Fellow. He was post-doctoral fellow at GREYC CNRS, France. He completed his Ph.D. from Indian Institute of Technology Roorkee (IITR), Uttarakhand, India in the Computer Science and Engineering department. Earlier, he received his M.Tech. degree from Indian Institute of Information Technology Allahabad (IIITA), in Information Technology in the year 2011 and B.Tech. degree in Computer Science in the year 2009 from IILM, Greater Noida, India. He is specialized in Human Computer Interaction (HCI). His major research work interest is in Image Processing, Biometric Recognition, Gesture Recognition, Virtual and Augmented Reality, Biomedical Imaging and Optical and Handwritten Character Recognition. Along with this he also works on Image Processing in Mobile Computing and Cloud Computing on Android platform.

João Filipe Cancela Santos Raposo was born November 20, 1964 and graduated in Medicine from the Faculty of Medicine of the University of Lisbon (1988) with a doctorate in Medicine - subspecialty Endocrinology, Faculty of Medical Sciences, Universidade Nova de Lisboa (2004). Internship of the Specialty of Endocrinology at the Portuguese Oncology Institute of Lisbon (1991-1997). Assistant Professor of Public Health, Faculty of Medical Sciences, Universidade Nova de Lisboa. Current Clinical Director of Associação Protectora dos Diabéticos de Portugal.

Rogério Tavares Ribeiro has a PhD in Biomedicine, from the Faculty of Medical Sciences of Lisbon. He is a researcher focused on Diabetes, at the Education and Research Centre of APDP – Diabetes Portugal (APDP-ERC) and at the Chronic Diseases Research Centre (CEDOC), NOVA Medical School.

Armando Vieira is a Physicist turned into a data scientist. He started working on machine learning after his PhD in Physics in 1997. From the beginning he is an aficionado of Artificial Neural Networks, and recently he is focused on Deep Neural Networks, especially for unsupervised and semi-supervised learning problems. He has more than 50 publications and writing a book on business applications of Deep Learning. He works as a Data Scientist consultant on several companies and startups. More on Armando.lidinwise.com.

Index

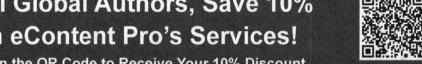

Information Resources Management Association

Become an IRMA Member

Members of the **Information Resources Management Association (IRMA)** understand the importance of community within their field of study. The Information Resources Management Association is an ideal venue through which professionals, students, and academicians can convene and share the latest industry innovations and scholarly research that is changing the field of information science and technology. Become a member today and enjoy the benefits of membership as well as the opportunity to collaborate and network with fellow experts in the field.

IRMA Membership Benefits:

- **One FREE Journal Subscription**
- **30% Off Additional Journal Subscriptions**
- **20% Off Book Purchases**
- Updates on the latest events and research on Information Resources Management through the IRMA-L listserv.
- Updates on new open access and downloadable content added to Research IRM.
- A copy of the Information Technology Management Newsletter twice a year.
- A certificate of membership.

IRMA Membership $195

Scan code or visit **irma-international.org** and begin by selecting your free journal subscription.

Membership is good for one full year.

Printed in the United States
By Bookmasters